LOCK UP

MASCOT
BOOKS
an imprint of Amplify Publishing Group

www.mascotbooks.com

Lock Up: Professional Wrestling in Our World

Although the author and publisher have made every effort to ensure that the information in this book was correct at press time, the author and publisher do not assume and hereby disclaim any liability to any party for any loss, damage, or disruption caused by errors or omissions, whether such errors or omissions result from negligence, accident, or any other cause.

For more information, please contact:
Mascot Books, an imprint of Amplify Publishing Group
620 Herndon Parkway, Suite 220
Herndon, VA 20170
info@amplifypublishing.com

Library of Congress Control Number: 2024911051

CPSIA Code: PRV0824A

ISBN-13: 979-8-89138-316-6

Printed in the United States

To all those who have played a part of creating the wonderous spectacle that is professional wrestling.

To all those who have chronicled professional wrestling history, analyzed the industry, or otherwise thoughtfully commented on the world of professional wrestling.

To my parents for taking me to my first professional wrestling show and never looking back.

To my loving wife for being my best friend, always being in my corner, and tolerating my fandom.

To my son for being my inspiration.

Professional Wrestling in Our World

LOCK UP

Ray Lopez

ILLUSTRATIONS BY **Eduardo Romero**

MASCOT BOOKS

an imprint of Amplify Publishing Group

CONTENTS

INTRODUCTION

There is no offseason. No end of the year trophy celebration or ticker-tape parade to cap everything off. No season finale that will leave fans scrambling to figure out what will we do now? No series finale that will leave you with that—great, now what am I going to watch feeling. It never ends, never stops, and never ceases to entertain us and scratch that primal itch. There's nothing else like it, and for that we are grateful.

Maybe it's the blur that makes it all so good. No other art form comes close to having their audience wonder: Is any of this real? How many times have we thought . . . yeah, it's staged but these two guys they really hate each other, they might really be going at it out there. That promo was off script, it was just way too personal. This guy lives his gimmick so much now that that's just who he is.

We see the seemingly inhuman levels physical violence and wonder, man that had to hurt. Even the most well-informed professional wrestling fan who thinks they know the business inside and out question what's reality and what's storyline. Keeping us all guessing is a part of the fun. It's a wild variety show where we are consistently wondering when the show ends. There's nothing else like it out there.

In performance art we know people are playing characters and when the show ends everyone goes back to reality. Not many people wonder if Johnny Deep is really a pirate or if any of the Broadway performers in *Cats* are into some kind of odd lifestyle. In professional wrestling, characters or gimmicks can be exaggerations of real-life personalities. Storylines can play off of or be born from real-life situations. That's what is so different about professional wrestling: we never really know when the show stops. That exhilarating blur is the secret sauce.

It is the sport of professional wrestling that makes it so inherently based in reality. We know sports are real. You feel it firsthand, and even if you never have been on the field, you can just see it. The atmosphere changes when the competition between the two whistles is underway. We still know the truth though. Professional wrestling is not real competition, it is scripted athletic theater with predetermined outcomes.

We also know another truth: that professional wrestling is a collaborative effort. Multiple people have to agree to follow the script just to have one match, let alone an entire card or continuous storyline. We know that at any given time any one of them could go off script. We also know that if any of them did, the others may try to cover it up or retaliate. When you find moments like these, it's a glorious blur of entertainment and reality.

We might know the real names of our favorite professional wrestlers. We might know their fictitious as well as real-life backstories. We might guess at when a moment is planned and when it's not. We might even think we know when a move legitimately hurts and when it doesn't. But in reality, for the fans, the truth of those things are only known to those on the other side of that ringside rail. For those of us in the stands, it's all an addictive blur. A reliable spectacle that gives us that rush that we can't find anywhere else.

This compelling entertainment has seeped its way into mainstream American culture. From politics to entertainment, professional wrestling's influence can be seen in virtually every facet of our culture. Vice versa, our culture influences the creative product we see in the world of professional wrestling. Everything going on in the world and our current social norms impacts professional wrestling's creative direction. We can learn something about our world by looking at it through professional wrestling's blurry glasses.

From film to politics, professional wrestling's involvement in our world will be discussed. Even if some sophisticated thinkers out there feel that there is nothing substantive to be learned by watching this madness, well it's also a lot of fun. The charismatic personalities, the elite physiques, and the compelling stories bring us joy. The seemingly superhuman physical feats constantly bring a smile to our faces. It's a thrilling world worth diving headfirst into.

Some may be asking what does any non-wrestler know about professional wrestling? I would ask what does any critic know about anything they comment on? Should Siskel and Elbert's opinions on film be disregarded because they have never starred in a feature film? Is society not allowed to critique the President of the United States because 99.99 percent of us have never been President? An unattached voice might be worth hearing, but as in all things wrestling, that's ultimately up to the public to decide.

All of mainstream professional wrestling in America is up for discussion here. This book is a celebration of professional wrestling and its place in our culture. This is not a historical accounting, although professional wrestling history is discussed. It is not a biography, though many well-known wrestling personalities are discussed. It's not a purely "What if?" book, but there is some of that. It's a book that brings it all together. We have included graphs, tables, charts, and illustrations for your amusement.

Shout out to our illustrator Eduardo Romero for contributing his talent to this project.

You do not have to read this book in any particular order. Although it does help for some chapters: for example, the "The Gimmicks of Professional Wrestling" chapter should be read before "The Math and Science of a Wrestler" chapter. Please enjoy our look at the world of American professional wrestling, its history, its characters, its spectacle, and its place in our culture.

CHAPTER 1

THE GIMMICKS OF PROFESSIONAL WRESTLING

At its core professional wrestling is just another mechanism for the oldest form of entertainment: storytelling. Storytelling where overgrown spandex clad warriors throw each other through tables, but storytelling nonetheless. Professional wrestling is an athletic play, one whose brutality and grace are broadcast all over the world. The attention it garners both simultaneously impresses and disgusts any Broadway producer. The seemingly superhuman physical feats get us through the door, but there's something else that keeps us coming back again and again.

It's the personas, the relationships, the drama, or in other words the stories. The cornerstone of any good storytelling is its characters. Compelling characters can invoke love, hate, and every emotion in-between from a captivated audience. Good storytelling, like good professional wrestling, is an art built on solid characters and their dramatic interplay. Some professional wrestlers catch fire instantaneously, some take years of development to find their footing. Either way if you want to put on an acclaimed play or write an epic novel, you'll need to develop a captivating cast of characters.

In the world of professional wrestling, the in-ring performers use their physical prowess and acting ability to bring these characters to life. In exchange, they are showered in riches and admiration, some even immortalized. It's little surprise that every professional wrestling promotion out there tries to out-bid, out-maneuver, out-create, and out-develop these vital characters. They are the essential ingredient in any successful professional wrestling show. In professional wrestling parlance, the core basis for these characters is known as an individual wrestler's gimmick.

In classic professional wrestling, these gimmicks are traditionally separated into two categories: faces or babyfaces (the good guys) and heels (the bad guys). There are also the in-betweeners, those whose moral compass straddles the ever-shifting line between good and evil. But even for these so-called in-betweeners, on any given night one can distinguish whether they are playing a face or a heel. Whether your stories are being told in a sparsely-populated bingo halls or on display in front of a record-breaking crowd at one of the world's major stadiums, you're going to need some solid characters to evoke emotions and keep the people invested in this never-ending story that is professional wrestling.

Character development in any medium is an arduous task. Now developing them in a collaborative creative environment where the promotor, the writers, the wrestlers, and countless others all have input, well, that is an even more laborious task. It's no surprise that a promoter and a professional wrestler can often fight for ownership of a character who is born through this joint process. Capturing the right words, style, music, look, and physical performance needed for a professional wrestler to develop an overall persona that resonates with the fans can feel like catching lightning in a bottle. It's not easy, but when it's done right, it's electric.

Throughout the history of professional wrestling the role of gimmicks has undergone an ever-evolving transformation. In the early days of professional wrestling, gimmicks were virtually nonexistent. A wrestler's personality was who they were in and out of the ring. Not much was done to elevate their personas. These personalities were so matter-of-fact about wrestling in the ring and on the microphone that it served to strengthen the business's claim of sports legitimacy.

In the late 1940s, a pompous professional wrestler emerged onto the national scene and would change the business forever. George Raymond Wagner, aka Gorgeous George, was an arrogant pretty boy heel, the kind who would beg you not to punch him in the face and then poke your eye when you held your arms out in frustration. He was a pioneer in turning straightforward wrestlers into larger-than-life personalities. Many say he was the first outrageous character in professional wrestling, but he would certainly not be the last.

In the 1980s, the World Wrestling Federation's (WWF) rock 'n' wrestling era emphasized the importance of character development. This was a stark contrast to the focus on pure wrestling ability that preceded it. A new thought emerged: if a professional wrestler got his gimmick over, he could put butts in seats. That wrestler's actual wrestling ability became an afterthought. These gimmicks were very straightforward. Without much thought at all, we knew who the bad guy was and why we should hate him. We instantly knew who the good guys were and gladly cheered on their overt heroic personas. A fan who strayed from the formula of cheering the face and booing the heel embedded into our psyches felt like a sin.

As professional wrestling moved into the early 1990s,

gimmicks evolved and, in many cases, seemed to possess even more cartoon buffoonery than its predecessors. That was until 1996, when a victorious Steve Austin vehemently declared that "Austin 3:16 means I just whooped your ass!" Ever since those iconic words were uttered, professional wrestling characters have become deeper and more complex. Today's gimmicks have become more reliant on being exaggerations of real personalities. Yet, despite this evolution, modern professional wrestling still relies on the use of the classic wrestling gimmicks.

Pretty much any professional wrestling gimmick can be played as a heel or a face. In all practicality, most are usually thrown into one category or the other, but there is plenty of room for overlap. As professional wrestling has moved toward more reality-based gimmicks, the determination of who is a heel and who is a face is often left for the fans to determine. The classical gimmicks discussed here are broken down into three categories: dual-threat gimmicks, ones that can be played as either face or heel, gimmicks that are most often portrayed as faces, and those gimmicks that are most often portrayed as heels. Out of these categories several families of gimmicks have emerged.

Heel or face gimmicks are different from the heel or face wrestling tactics that we know. The tactic is a common move that a heel or face wrestler may repeatedly use in the ring. The poke in eye, the low blow, and the planned opponent distraction are all common heel tactics designed to draw the fans' ire. Getting heat, as they say. The throwing of swag into the crowd, the insistence upon fairness in a match, and the embracing of the local sports team are all face tactics designed to elicit cheers. Chasing the hug, as they say. A fan might initially see a wrestler portraying a particular gimmick and wonder whether they are a heel or face, but once these tactics come into play, we all know exactly what we're being sold.

Some gimmicks are so commonplace they have become ingrained into the professional wrestling business. Others are used sparingly but still have left their mark on sports entertainment history. When you are telling a story that spans decades and consists of an ever-rotating troupe of players, you're going to need a playbook to develop these captivating personalities. Here is a layout of the time-tested reliable professional wrestling gimmicks. Find the right blue-chip athlete, give them a gimmick, and push them through the curtain to see if they can become a legend of the squared circle.

DUAL THREAT GIMMICKS

THE FOREIGNER GIMMICK (NON-AMERICAN)

In a smoke-filled room the old-school, droopy eyed promoter on his fifth cup of coffee sees a new wrestler and says, "Oh you're from where? Ok, well let's play off of that!" It is one of the oldest and most reliable gimmicks in the world of professional wrestling. This gimmick relies on one overarching trait to develop an identity: nationality. Sure, oftentimes it's been portrayed in an overly simplistic fashion, but it's always worked.

There is an old adage in professional wrestling: give them something they have never seen before. In some of the crowds on the American professional wrestling tour circuit, being the dude from wherever-stan might be enough to check that box. The exotic foreigner gimmick will be accentuated with their esoteric cultural garb. Their ring music will have strange aspects to it and may incorporate instruments sparsely heard to American audiences, i.e., bagpipes, gongs, accordions, violins, chimes, etc. When a person is from foreign land with a unique history and unfamiliar traditions (or at least are portrayed that way), well, that on its own is different.

Heel Foreigners—This character will aggravate the American audience by obnoxiously proclaiming the many ways their homeland is superior to America. They will act with disdain toward pretty much all revered aspects of American culture. This gimmick is an easy sell if you are from a country with hostile relations toward the US, though that is not a necessary requirement. The Russian or Middle Eastern strongmen have continuously played this villainous foreign menace role. Though as a result of America's competitive nature, really any non-American evil doer can play this role.

The heel foreigner will carry their nation's flag to the ring; for some reason the crowd will see any flag lacking in stars and stripes as objectionable. However, promotors should know that if a significant portion of the audience has some heritage with any particular foreign flag it will most certainly not be treated as objectionable. The heel foreigner will speak in a strange tongue, again unless many in the crowd speak the language, it will be deemed unacceptable. It is very easy to hate what one doesn't understand. Yet even if the wrestler employs a translator, the crowd may still find this undesirable. The message is clear: if you want to be our hero, you better speak our language. After all, being a voice for the people is exceptionally difficult if you don't share the common tongue.

At times, this gimmick will be portrayed as an unrelenting savage who will not succumb to the norms of American sportsmanship. The savage version of the foreign menace will often display uncouth tactics such as biting, eye gouging, and head butting. The foreign savage cannot be reasoned with, and our heroes must face them with pure unbridled brute force.

Occasionally, the foreign wrestler will insist on performing their mother country's national anthem or displaying other cultural rituals (throwing of the sand, saluting of the flag, etc.) before their match. This version of the stall-the-action heel tactic will most assuredly annoy the crowd. The foreigner will obnoxiously sing off key while demanding the crowd's undivided attention. This character may nauseatingly preach about their superiority both physically and culturally toward any American competitor.

NOTABLE EXAMPLES

Iron Sheik, Ivan Koloff, Nikolai Volkoff, The Bolsheviks, Yokozuna, Jinder Mahal, Kamala the Ugandan Giant, Alberto Del Rio, Lord Steven Regal, Muhammad Hassan, La Résistance, The Great Khali, Canadian Strongman Dino Bravo, The Wild Samoans, Haku, The Great Muta, Mr. Fuji, The Fabulous Rougeaus, Sheamus, Rowdy Roddy Piper, Abdullah the Butcher, The Orient Express, Rusev/Miro

Face Foreigners—This gimmick will proudly display their heritage in a very palatable manner for the American audience. Typically, they will reside from an allied or at least nonhostile nation. Instead of constantly proclaiming superiority by virtue of their nationality, the face foreigner will offer a picturesque window into their cultural traditions. They will serve as your tips-appreciated tour guide through their homeland. Their apropos ring music will be upbeat and may incorporate traditional sounds and dances for the crowd's amusement. They will make an effort to speak English, which the American fans will positively interpret as a sign that this person wants to assimilate. Instead of emphasizing the differences between two nationalities, the face will rely on the commonalities that all members of the human race can relate to.

The face foreigner may team up with the All-American hero. If any professional wrestling fans are unsure whether they should cheer or boo the foreigner, the friendly All-American hero will reassure them. The rub from an established face will almost certainly be needed at some point in the face foreigner's climb up the card.

In a reversal of the heel foreigner's reliance on xenophobia, the face foreigner will rebut any heel who blasts them with prejudice by declaring that the fans do not share the same xenophobia as the bad guy does. The face foreigner will embrace America, along with the promotion employing them, as the place where the best professional wrestling competition lives. After all, any face will always pledge to compete against the very best in the world.

NOTABLE EXAMPLES:

Superfly Jimmy Snuka, early Usos, Rey Mysterio, The British Bulldogs, The Bushwhackers, Asuka, the Jamaican version of Kofi Kingston, Último Dragón, Becky Lynch, Drew McIntyre, Hart Foundation

THE HEARTTHROB GIMMICK

Since the dawn of the entertainment industry there has always been one universal truth: sex sells. It is the most intimate of human contact and causes most of us to crave it more than anything else. It's biological. It's natural. It's fun. When pretty much your entire cast of players are chiseled men and women who perform in not much more than their underwear, the audience's lustful appreciation for the human body will almost certainly be banked on.

Heel Heartthrobs—Historically, professional wrestling fans are predominately heterosexual males, thus instinctively the male sex symbol gimmick will most certainly be booed. This character will taunt the male audience, bragging about how their sexual prowess can satisfy the unfulfilled desires of their wives or girlfriends. They will taunt the audience proclaiming how their body is vastly superior to the beer belly full audience. Odds are the words "real man" will be uttered during the heel heartthrob's promo.

The heel heartthrob will boast about the large number of romantic partners they regularly engage with, conjuring up feelings of envy and anger within the audience. The heel may rhythmically gyrate their hips in a sensual, and for many of the audience a detestable, manner. Occasionally, they will show more skin than their face counterparts, finding opportune moments to reveal their buttocks. This will be met with hostility by the alcohol- and adrenaline-infused crowd.

For the "average" heterosexual male, perhaps nothing is more loathed than the good-looking guy who gets all the attention from women. Life seems all too easy for that guy, and that stirs our inner nerd feelings with resentment. The heel heartthrob doesn't work hard to succeed with women—he doesn't even try, and it's abundantly evident by his cocky attitude. The gift of good looks bestowed upon him is taken for granted without any humility. This gimmick is the person we all want to be and the one whom we hate the most when the realization hits that their debaucherously exciting life journey was a path we would not travel.

NOTABLE EXAMPLES

HBK, Rick Rude, Tyler Breeze, Rick 'The Model' Martel, Ric Flair, Val Venus, Los Lotharios, Gorgeous George, Austin Theory, Pretty Deadly

Face Heartthrobs—The rules for being a professional wrestling face heartthrob traditionally have been distinctly different for the two sexes. In the not so distant past a female performer seemingly only needed a swimsuit model physique and a flirtatious attitude to get over with the fans. In the 1990s and 2000s, when *Playboy* cover shoots were customary for top female wrestling talent, the recipe was simply: to get in, show more skin. The more clothes that she shed, the louder the crowd roars.

Since then, women wrestlers have evolved from the simplistic eye candy to athletic performers who demand their place in the business. They are no longer dependent on the applause received during a bikini contest showdown. The current female wrestlers don't solely rely on sex appeal, yet most don't shy away from it. In a business where a significant portion of the business model is built on admiration for the human body, why would they?

The male face heartthrob is more sparingly used despite the character's simple recipe. Take a reformed heel heartthrob, tone down the sex, add some humility, and send him through the curtain. The face heartthrob faces a unique challenge of allowing the crowd to live vicariously through them. They will have to build common ground with the audience. Captivating promos are vital. It also helps if by the time your heel heartthrob turns face, they have established professional wrestling credibility with the fans. The audience will reward exceptional in-ring ability, or the promoter can pair them with or have them be a hot girl(s) as part of their gimmick. That works too.

NOTABLE EXAMPLES

HBK, Sable, Sunny, Stacy Keibler, Ric Flair, Torrie Wilson, Terri Runnels, Bella Twins, American Males, Mandy Rose, The Heart Throbs (Yes, there was a tag team that said screw it and just named themselves the gimmick.)

THE PROFESSION GIMMICK

The old, simplistic version of the profession gimmick is pretty much a forgotten relic of professional wrestling's past. Trying to constantly come up with exciting creative packages for new recruits can be a headache for any writers-block-stricken promoter. With promoters wanting more complex professional wrestling characters, the overly cartoony Village People-esque gimmicks that once populated the landscape are scarce. This new school emphasis has many professional wrestling fans over twelve years old breathing a sigh of relief. Perhaps older fans collectively thought a more mature product would finally allow them to profess their love of professional wrestling to the world. Many longed for the days when they can casually bring up professional wrestling without hearing, "You mean you watch it right now? You mean when you were a kid, right?"

In the not too distanced past, the world of professional wrestling was peppered with profession-based gimmick wrestlers who were both upright and corrupt trade practitioners. The fans were to believe that for whatever reason the evil repossession man decided to spend his nights moonlighting in spandex leotards body-slamming people. The gimmick can be directly centered around one's job, such as the case of the Big Boss Man. It can also be a little more subtle and simply related to a given profession, like Tugboat, who is basically an overgrown sailor. For the smaller regional promotions out there, whenever you are stuck for ideas just look at your territory's economic landscape. If a local sports team uses that profession as a mascot, you're headed in the right direction. If you are in Texas, just go with an oilfield worker or a cowboy. A cheap pop is still a pop, right?

Heel Professions—A heel character can be born out of any job, just insert the world evil in front of it and voila! A savvy promoter will ensure their heel has a suitable profession related prop (towing rope, briefcase, nightstick, etc.) that can most assuredly be used in dastardly ways. This wrestler will require a compelling backstory. Take the evil cop for example. Does he still have his badge? What did he do to get kicked off the force? Can we see his employment file? That might seem like a lot of work, but with a few well-produced vignettes or telling promos, the fans will understand the nature of the character. If you really want to simplify things, just stick to the more detested professions. How can any fan not boo the tax man or the corporate kiss ass?

NOTABLE EXAMPLES

The Mountie, I.R.S., Dr. Issac Yankem DDS, Dr. Britt Baker DMD, Repo Man, The Goon, Duke 'The Dumpster' Droese, 'Cowboy' Bob Orton

Face Professions—There are two ways you can go with this one: rely on a well-respected profession or go with a fun profession. The police officer or soldier can preach about how truth, justice, and the American way will prevail. These gimmicks will attempt to draw admiration from the fans by describing how they strive to serve the community.

The fun profession gimmicks will mostly, but not always (Godfather, we're looking at you), be centered around entertainment for the younger audience. They will incorporate props in comical fashion. A good squirt of water out of the flower or plunger to the face can be counted on for a cheap laugh.

A face profession can also be respected and fun. Who doesn't love a farmer who feeds the community and dumps buckets of slop on his opponents? When choosing a face profession, a promoter simply needs to ask a group of children what they want to be when they grow up, then pick one.

NOTABLE EXAMPLES

The Big Boss Man, Tugboat, Sgt. Slaughter, The Godwinns, Hillbilly Jim, The Smoking Gunns, The Goon, Duke 'The Dumpster' Droese, T.L. Hopper, The Godfather

THE ROCK STAR GIMMICK

There is an old showbiz saying: "Every athlete wants to be a rock star, and every rock star wants to be an athlete." This gimmick can deliver both. The connection between music and professional wrestling is a deep one. Since the 1930s, when, much to the ire of American fans, Lord Patrick Lansdowne came down to the ring to the tune of "God Save the King," professional wrestling and music have been significantly linked. This connection was never more apparent than during the rock 'n' wrestling era where the Music Television Network (MTV) helped put professional wrestling over to the mainstream audience.

The rock star gimmick must be given to a wrestler who has the charisma to pull it off. Given the lack of musical ability among most professional wrestling talent, the rock star gimmick is more about attitude and showmanship than anything else. After all, it's pretty rare you find a real musical talent who can also take a solid steel chair shot.

The rock star gimmick's wardrobe must be carefully cultivated to embellish that unmistakable rock and roll swagger. A quality theme song, despite who performs it, is vital to the success of this gimmick. An entrance music's reception can quickly determine this gimmick's face or heel fate. If you do find a guy with any legitimate musical ability, immediately use this gimmick.

Heel Rock Star—This gimmick will rely on the pompous blustering of their in-ring ability and/or musical talents. If they are actual musicians, they should habitually proclaim how far superior they are than whomever is sitting on top of the latest Billboard charts. This heel will insist on musically performing before most of their matches. This serenade will inevitably draw the ire of the fans irrespective of the quality of the music.

Frequently they will carry a guitar to the ring, both for their musical performances and to inevitably be used to bash their opponents. The heel rock star will often incorporate lyrics about how crappy the fans, their hometown, or local sports teams are. It's cheap heat but at the end of the night it may be the loudest reaction.

NOTABLE EXAMPLES

The Honky Tonk Man, Elias, Jeff Jarrett, Disco Inferno, Fandango, Aiden English

Face Rock Star—The face rock star gimmick based on actual music can be a particularly hard one to pull off. When a grappler is ready to show us their musical talents, we immediately think well this is going to be bad. Usually, we are right. Trying this gimmick with anyone creates a huge uphill battle for that wrestler not to come across as horribly corny.

For this gimmick to work, the wrestler will need at least one catchy tune that the fans can get behind. The music doesn't have to come from the performer themselves, but it definitely needs to be one of the better entrance theme songs on any given roster. You will need an iconic rock star look tailored to whatever genre of music the wrestler is embodying. Other than that, it's pretty simple: be cool.

*Chris Jericho, R-Truth, John Cena, Brodus Clay, The Headbangers,
Men on a Mission, Public Enemy, Edge, Swerve Strickland*

THE LEGACY GIMMICK

Building off past success is integral to any successful business endeavor. In professional wrestling, the combination of fresh faces mixed with nostalgia will instantly spark interest among the community. When legacy professional wrestlers enter, the family business attention-grabbing events are bound to happen.

This gimmick is a great way to start off a rookie. What better introduction to the fans than to emphasize the new comers real-life deep-rooted personal connection to professional wrestling. The pressure on a legacy to live up to the high expectations when stepping into their storied familial wrestling boots can be daunting. Eventually the debuting wrestler will either sink or swim on their own. To their credit, many of these wrestlers are up the task and some even grow to gain more acclaim than their familial predecessors.

Face legacy—These wrestlers will draw upon their authentic appreciation and knowledge of the professional wrestling business. They will preach about how they grew up in the business and are grateful for the opportunity to fulfill their lifelong destiny. This gimmick will focus on their love for the business and their insistence that they will make their own mark on the business through hard work and dedication.

NOTABLE EXAMPLES

Charlotte Flair, Dwayne 'The Rock' Johnson, Cody and Dustin Rhodes, Natalya Neidhart, the Von Erichs

Heel legacy—These wrestlers will drone on about how they are simply destined for greatness because of their athletic pedigree. They will speak about how much better they are than any of their familial predecessors. A heel taking shots at their own family will create a spoiled brat mentality which is sure to draw ire among the fans. We can still hear the boos from when Dominik Mysterio complained that while all his rich friends had new Mercedes Benz, his "dead-beat dad" gifted him a lowly BMW. The heel gimmick will also claim that non legacy wrestlers who were not born into the "right" family are not on their level. They will openly call upon nepotism to advance their placement on the card.

NOTABLE EXAMPLES

Randy Orton, Ted DiBiase Jr., Roman Reigns, The Bloodline, Dominik Mysterio

THE RACIAL STEREOTYPE GIMMICK

According to professional wrestling lore, the influential wrestler turned backstage creative figure known to the world as Michael 'P.S.' Hayes claimed that black wrestlers do not need gimmicks because "being black is their gimmick." It's pretty apparent why this is unquestionably the most controversial gimmick on this list. Perhaps Michael Hayes's antiquated thinking was a stain of the times, but even in modern professional wrestling gimmicks are often tied to a wrestler's ethnic or cultural heritage. After all, many say that the best gimmicks are exaggerated personas of a wrestler's real-life identity.

When done wrong, these gimmicks may be considered racially insensitive or even downright offensive. Being a member of a minority race in America does not by itself make a wrestler fall into this gimmick. It is the portrayal of over exaggerated racial stereotypes that can signal the use of this gimmick. Due to the ever-evolving acceptable social norms this gimmick is more sparingly used and when it is used, it is way different than it once was. Nowadays the negative stereotypes don't go over well. The use of the gang-banging thug that once was a go-to gimmick is a clear example of this.

The use of this gimmick is the hardest and most uncomfortable one for the fans to spot. Is he playing the stereotypical minority gimmick or just being himself? Is it both? Do we want to ask? The whole situation is uneasy.

The heel version of this gimmick will play off the audience's xenophobia and lean in to negative stereotypes. The face version of this gimmick will invite the audience to partake in the celebrated aspects of their culture. Have a Hispanic on your roster? Give him a cape and call him El Matador. For the most part though, just adopt the characteristics of the heel or face foreigner gimmicks.

NOTABLE EXAMPLES

Harlem Heat, Eddie Guerrero, Tatanka, Nation of Domination, Cryme Tyme, New Jack, Los Boricuas, LAX, Street Profits, Hillbilly Jim, Tito Santana

THE PURE WRESTLER GIMMICK

Like your neighborhood all-encompassing lunch buffet, a professional wrestling shows try to provide a little something for everyone. The most important dish in this buffet of violent silliness that is sports entertainment is the actual in-ring wrestling. The pure wrestler gimmicks are no nonsense folks who are great in-ring workers and can deliver quality matches that will satisfy the hardcore purists. Star ratings are everything for this gimmick.

For better or worse, excellent in-ring ability by itself is rarely enough to get a talent over to top guy status. This being the case the pure wrestler may eventually morph into a more complex character once the time is right. If they do, their in-ring reputation as a solid worker will not be forgotten by the professional wrestling faithful.

NOTABLE EXAMPLES

Dean Malenko, Kurt Angle, Chris Benoit, Bryan Danielson, FTR, Kenny Omega

THE UNIQUE FIGHTER GIMMICK

When an athlete from the sports universe arrives on the professional wrestling scene, they bring instant legitimacy to the world of sports entertainment. Whether they're coming from the octagon, the karate dojo, or somewhere else, this wrestler offers a unique move set inside the ring. These athletes may garner mainstream attention that can expand a professional wrestling promoter's audience. Professional wrestler versus boxer, cage fighter, sumo, karate kid, etc. will always garner some mainstream interest.

While the different fighter gimmick does not have to be legitimately trained in any combat sport, it does help. If they aren't, well fake it until you make it. Just like the pure wrestler gimmick, if a unique fighter gimmick wrestler is going to last in the professional wrestling business they will eventually need to morph into a more complex character at some point. The unique fighter gimmick is a hell of a starting point for that transformation or this gimmick can also just be a fun one-off celebrity appearance.

NOTABLE EXAMPLES

Brock Lesnar, Ronda Rousey, Shayna Blazer, Yokozuna, Mr. T, Steve Blackman, Kwang, Sonya Deville, The Oriental Express, The Goon

MOSTLY FACE GIMMICKS

THE RELATABLE FAMILY OF GIMMICKS

THE ALL-AMERICAN HERO GIMMICK

The cheapest pop in professional wrestling: USA! USA! USA! How can any red-blooded American not join in and chant along? Given that the vast majority of shows put on by US based professional wrestling companies are performed in America, it's no surprise that this gimmick quickly came into prominence. You have to try really hard to get a negative reaction when you are saluting the troops and preaching about how great our nation is.

It is no coincidence that Captain America was one of Marvel's first superheroes. He is a heroic patriotic figure that the comic company relied on while building an empire. Displaying bravery, righteousness, and above all patriotic pride is required for this gimmick. After all, the saying is these colors don't run. Waive around the stars and stripes, find the dastardliest foreign heel on your roster, and lock up for an old-fashioned battle of "us versus them." The home team is always on the good side.

NOTABLE EXAMPLES

Hulk Hogan, 'Hacksaw' Jim Duggan, 'The American Dream' Dusty Rhodes, 'The American Nightmare' Cody Rhodes, Lex Luger, John Cena, Sgt. Slaughter, The Patriot, Kurt Angle, U.S. Express, Lacey Evans, Mr. America

THE BLUE-COLLAR TOUGH GIMMICK

He's just a common man. This is another gimmick where fans get to live vicariously through their favorite professional wrestler. In the world of combat fighting, the street tough fighter from humble means who climbs the ladder to big time success is quintessentially the American dream. The *Rocky* movies were able to crank out an Academy Award winning, huge box office successful cinematic franchise around it.

A rise from impoverished roots, working class values, and a take no guff attitude is a sure-fire hit inside the squared circle. This gimmick celebrates the average Joe, the person who fantasizes about standing up to their know-it-all obnoxious boss. Sit back, crack open a few brewskies, and watch this character slap around the big boss.

NOTABLE EXAMPLES

'Stone Cold' Steve Austin, The Sandman, Dudley Boyz, Heavy Machinery, Jon Moxley, Dusty Rhodes, Mr. Kennedy, Hardcore Holly, Terry Funk

THE ULTIMATE UNDERDOG GIMMICK

Who doesn't love to root for an underdog? There is something very admirable about the guy who knows that in all likelihood what he is about to try is not going to end well, but damn it, he's going to have a go at it anyway. This wrestler, whether it is due to lack of ability or some other external factor, will seemingly always have the odds stacked against them. Smaller stature wrestlers, whether intentional or not, will incorporate the use of this gimmick through some form or fashion.

NOTABLE EXAMPLES

The Brooklyn Brawler, Eugene, Santino Marella, Spike Dudley, young Daniel Bryan

THE CARTOON FAMILY OF GIMMICKS

THE COMIC BOOK GIMMICK

The professional wrestling industry was built on people who seemingly have super human abilities. Their sculpted rock-hard bodies make it plausible that they are able to endure insane amounts of violence. A wrestler using this gimmick may appear to have supernatural powers. In countless arenas across the world, professional wrestling fans have witnessed the summoning of lightening, controlling of fire, flickering of the lights, or turning invincible. When critics call the scripted violence that we love cartoonish, this is what they're talking about.

The mystique surrounding these elaborate appearances will have the fans thinking "Well, this guy has to be different from the rest of them. He's special!" At least that's what the professional wrestling powers that be hope for. The over-the-top ring gear and mesmerizing entrance effects are needed to capture that caped crusader vibe. This gimmick's out of this world appearance will easily amuse the younger fans. Merchandise will fly off the shelves. What more can your marketing department want? Just stay away from the bedazzled Star Wars-esque helmets.

NOTABLE EXAMPLES

The Ultimate Warrior, Sting, Hurricane Helms, The Undertaker, Glacier, Rosey (S.H.I.T.), 'The Demon' Finn Bálor, The Road Warriors, Max Moon, The Blue Blazer, The Shockmaster, Nikki Cross (A.S.H), Darby Allin

THE ANAMORPHOUS GIMMICK

Before the late '90s ushered in a more reality-based wrestling product with the attitude era, much of mainstream professional wrestling was heavily marketed to children and thus cartoonish in nature. It seems like the creative guys in the back asked one question when contemplating what gimmick to give their latest baby-face superstar: What can we use to get children to like this guy? Most assuredly, we can thank someone in the back for offering this pearl of wisdom: "Well my kid really loves his dog. Let's give him a pet!" Since then, seemingly every animal that won't induce a heart attack in the insurance underwriters has been worked into the world of professional wrestling. After all, who doesn't love a good mascot?

NOTABLE EXAMPLES

Jake 'The Snake' Roberts, British Bulldogs, Ricky 'The Dragon' Steamboat, 'The Birdman' Koko B. Ware, Luchasaurus, The Gobbledy Gooker, Killer Bees, Gorilla Monsoon

THE FUN FAMILY OF GIMMICKS

THE PARTY GIMMICK

This gimmick relies on energy, enthusiasm, and a "the party starts when I walk in" mantra. Similar to the rock star gimmick, this wrestler will need to rely on a charismatic persona but without the need to be musical or act like they are a megastar. The party gimmick will often use bright upbeat colored ring attire and props. This gimmick often incorporates dancing into their routine and inspires the crowd to join in. Pyro, upbeat music, and props are of extra importance with this gimmick. Having fun is infectious.

NOTABLE EXAMPLES

The Rockers, Private Party, The Freebirds, Street Profits, Hardy Boyz, Naomi, The Midnight Express, Young Bucks, The Rock and Roll Express, The New Day

THE COMEDY GIMMICK

Like its carnival show origins, modern day professional wrestling relies on a variety of acts to entertain its audience. In the major leagues of professional wrestling, when you have multiple hours of television programming to fill, you have to mix it up. The comedy gimmick can provide a needed change of pace for any action-packed card. If you're not constantly changing, whether that be long term or short term, your product is at risk of getting stale.

Some professional wrestling purists may hate the wacky antics a comedy gimmick provides. Do not be deterred, many in the crowd will enjoy the lighthearted laughs and breathing space that this gimmick delivers. In professional wrestling, and in life in general, if you are funny and not a horrible human being, you will be liked.

Let's face it there are only so many ways a guy can entertainingly tell us how he is going to kick someone's ass with a straight face. Jokes will be needed to keep the audience captivated. Any gimmick can deliver some comedic insults at their opponent, but when the comedy is done well it can take over a wrestler's previous gimmick. While this gimmick may seem trivial, it did help launch the career of the biggest star professional wrestling has ever produced in Dwayne 'The Rock' Johnson.

NOTABLE EXAMPLES

Santino Marella, R-Truth, Chris Jericho, Dwayne 'The Rock' Johnson, Orange Cassidy, Eugene, Dude Love, Colt Cabana, Doink the Clown

MOSTLY HEEL GIMMICKS

THE HORROR FAMILY OF GIMMICKS

THE MONSTER GIMMICK

Throughout literary history the evil monster has been a cornerstone of the antagonist role. Whether it is Odysseus clashing with the Cyclops, Beowulf battling Grendel, or Japan versus Godzilla, tales of mankind combating monsters are scattered throughout history. These tales often serve as metaphors for man's perseverance; his resilience against seemingly insurmountable odds; and his struggle to conquer the unknown. These inspiring tales are reminders that good can triumph over evil. They teach us that no matter how big the obstacle in front of us is, we can overcome.

The monster gimmick heavily relies on the common staples of the horror genre. People are fascinated by the macabre; take one look at America's celebration of Halloween and you'll see that this country is no exception. It's easy to see why this popular gimmick always resurfaces. This gimmick has practical applications, if you have a wrestler struggling to develop their promo skills just hide them in a costume. In film and professional wrestling monsters don't really need to talk. Snarling will do.

To effectively pull off this gimmick a promoter will need to pay special attention to the wrestler's wardrobe, entrance music, and special effects. You'll need smoke, fire, lightning, mysterious blackouts, haunting music, and a general chilling appearance. The occasional creepy location promo is pretty much required. The monster gimmick commands the highest production value a promotion can muster. After all, one can spare no expense when making a wrestler mysteriously cause his opponent to vomit green slime. If done right the investment will be well worth it. Many of professional wrestling's most memorable wardrobes, entrances, and special effects revolve around the use of the old reliable monster gimmick.

NOTABLE EXAMPLES

The Undertaker, 'The Fiend' Bray Wyatt, Mankind, Papa Shango, Giant González, Boogeyman, Kane, Mantaur, The Brood, Mordecai, Abyss, Dungeon of Doom, The Yeti, Luchasaurus, House of Black, The Wyatt Sicks

THE PSYCHOPATH GIMMICK

An easy premise to follow, this gimmick creates an unreasonable brute with little regard for humanity. Unlike the monster gimmick, there will be no need for supernatural abilities. The costumes won't need to be quite as elaborate and the promos are relatively simple. Just splice together some nonsensical rambling, throw in a bout of the crazy eyes, toss in a maniacal laugh, and voila! you have your promo.

This gimmick is an easy way to explain a promotion's incorporation of hardcore wrestling. The brutal violence of hardcore matches is perfectly suited for the psychopath gimmick. If you are looking to spice up an undercard match, simply have this gimmick come out and destroy everyone in the ring. No explanation needed because, well, he's a psycho.

NOTABLE EXAMPLES

Psycho Sid, Abdullah the Butcher, 'Dr. Death' Steve Williams, Bray Wyatt, Snitsky, Randy Orton, Lars Sullivan, Waylon Mercy, Cactus Jack, AJ Lee

THE GIANT GIMMICK

These larger-than-life figures captivate imaginations worldwide. Their imposing size adds instant legitimacy and splendor to the character. Once they take that step over the top rope, we feel the proverbial ground shake. Many times, these behemoths are catapulted or even directly debut into main event status. The sheer size of these wrestlers will instantly make them a legitimate threat for whichever top face they meet.

This is the one gimmick where you cannot separate the style of wrestling from the character. The men and women classified as giants in the ring can play a variety of gimmicks, but they really don't need to. If you're seven-foot-plus, you don't need a charismatic personality or scorching promo to get over. Move slowly, look menacing, and seldom speak. David versus Goliath is a classic story that will be perpetually retold, especially inside the squared circle.

NOTABLE EXAMPLES

André the Giant, Big John Studd, King Kong Bundy, Giant González, The Great Khali, Big Show, Omos

THE SUPERIORITY FAMILY OF GIMMICKS

THE ARISTOCRAT GIMMICK

Perhaps the crown jewel of the superiority family of gimmicks. A time-honored gimmick that has been aggravating beer swilling fans ever since modern professional wrestling came into existence. No gimmick offers more of the fabled seven deadly sins than the aristocrat. Pride, greed, envy, and even gluttony are on full display with this character. For the aristocrat gimmick, the devil is in the details. Everything from a wrestler's mannerisms to their vernacular must be done in an air of smugness. A variety of snooty facial expressions is obligatory. Hunter Hearst Helmsley's face perfectly expressed this as he looked down his colossal nose on the fans.

Flaunting an affluent lifestyle full of lavish riches and experiences that most of us only dream of leads to strong feelings of resentment among the "poors." The aristocrat will gripe about how the bleachers are full of commoners who can't comprehend the pressures that wealth and success bring. Whether an aristocrat is born with a silver spoon or is self-made, their braggadocious rants will throw a gasoline-soaked log onto the flames of jeers.

This gimmick must appear in luxurious attire, often paired with expensive jewelry and limousines. Elaborate robes, custom-made suits, Rolex watches, expensive scarves, and alligator shoes all work well.

The aristocrat can easily make use of any excess talent lying around the back. Like a fine wine, the aristocrat gimmick pairs well with an elegantly dressed valet, bodyguard, driver, manservant or personal ring announcer. They can play the antagonist for any face, but are perfectly suited to feud with the blue-collar gimmick.

NOTABLE EXAMPLES

'The Million Dollar Man' Ted DiBiase, Rick Flair, MJF, JBL, Alberto Del Rio, Vince McMahon, Hunter Hearst Helmsley

THE NARCISSIST GIMMICK

This egotistical gimmick will draw instant heat by invoking a self-absorbed tunnel vision view of the world. This character will provide filler material by sluggishly strutting, posing, or otherwise relishing in self-appreciation while stalling the action much to the displeasure of the fans. The narcissist will draw attention to the well sculpted physiques that they have spent years developing. This gimmick may incorporate a variety of mirrors, an exorbitant number of photographers, or constant grooming to draw ire from the fans. The narcissist may plead for no shots to the face or work in other "feminine" behavior.

NOTABLE EXAMPLES

Lex Luger, Gorgeous George, Ric Flair, Mr. Perfect, Tyler Breeze, Bobby Roode, MNM, Adrian Adonis

THE INTELLECTUAL SNOB GIMMICK

A common insulting stereotype about professional wrestling fans is their perceived lack of intelligence. Many non-fans condescendingly refer to them as mouth breathers, boogereaters, feebleminded, or some other "clever" phrase for a simpleton. What better way to play off this disparaging stereotype than with the intellectual snob gimmick?

Bragging about how you are smarter than everyone else in the room is a sure-fire way to get people to hate you. Perhaps, Bobby 'The Brain' Heenan did it best when, referring to professional wrestling fans, he coined the term ham and eggers—a person of low intelligence who always orders the simplest thing on the menu because they lack the intelligence required for a more complex meal. The Brain constantly preached about how using underhanded tactics was simply outsmarting your opponent. To him any upright babyface not willing to go there was an idiot.

Smugness is this gimmick's best friend. Whether it be financially, physically, sexually, or intellectually, claiming you are far superior to anyone on the other side of that ring barrier is a time-tested way to draw major heat. This gimmick will get instant hatred once they state "I am your intellectual superior so you must listen to me about how you should live your life!" The intellectual snob will mockingly speak slowly or condescendingly break things down in the simplest of terms. They will relentlessly insult their opponents and the audience's intelligence. What's two plus two? Thomas Jefferson, sucka!

NOTABLE EXAMPLES

The Genius, 'The Planets Champion' Daniel Bryan, Bobby 'The Brain' Heenan, Dean Douglas, Matt Striker, Damien Sandow, Christopher Nowinski, Chad Gable

THE ROYAL GIMMICK

The royal gimmick is one of the oldest and most common in the world of professional wrestling. It relies on many of the same characteristics as the superiority family of gimmicks. There is just something very contemptuous about a person who was born into arguably the highest level of success. The silver spoon invites lots of hostility. Nothing reeks of privilege more than nobility.

In 1993, the professional wrestling world proclaimed that the royal gimmick was so enduring that it deserved an entire pay-per-view centered around it. The WWF's King of the Ring was born and gave several professional wrestlers a reason to don the crown, grab the scepter, and take a run with this storied gimmick.

It's no surprise that a heel will usually win this regal tournament, if not they will find some other reason to proclaim their majesty. The royal gimmick is well suited to be a short lived or transitional one. It's a fresh gimmick that can be used to give an existing talent a new look and angle. Perhaps, 'Stone Cold' Steve Austin reached the historic levels of popularity he achieved because after winning the King of the Ring he ceremoniously rejected the use of this cheesily reliable gimmick.

NOTABLE EXAMPLES

Jerry 'The King' Lawler, King Corbin, 'The Macho King' Randy Savage, Queen Sherri, King Harley Race, King Booker, Queen Zelina, King Mabel, King Haku, Owen—The King of Harts

THE POWER PLAY FAMILY OF GIMMICKS

THE AUTHORITY FIGURE GIMMICK

The authority figure gimmick is a mainstay of professional wrestling. There is just something about human nature that drives us to rebel against those in charge. In our youths, we would try get away with whatever shenanigans we could when dealing with our parents and teachers. In our adulthood, many distrust politicians, police, judges, basically anyone in charge. Their position of authority by its nature invites never-ending criticism. That extra layer of scrutiny is just part of the game. Perhaps our friendly neighborhood Spider-Man said it best: "With great power comes great responsibility."

There are many advantages to having an authority figure on your promotions roster. Using this gimmick is a sure-fire way to slowly build sympathy for a babyface. Take your hero and continually place them in unfair and seeming unwinnable scenarios. Creatively it's an easy way to incorporate any kind of indecisive finish into a match to extend a feud's lifespan. It's also an easy way to build heat for the heel wrestler who constantly gets an unfair advantage.

The authority figure gimmick can be given to any retired wrestler or any talent who might not be cleared for in-ring competition. It's a way to use that wrestler's screen time worthy talents while giving them a reason to stay away from physicality.

The revolution against the authority is unending. As long as there are wrestlers who are compelled to take advantage of the corporate structure, there will be those who choose to battle against everything the company stands for. Fans may never grow tired of watching their heroes rage against the machine.

NOTABLE EXAMPLES

Kane, Vince McMahon, Baron Corbin, Triple H, Shane McMahon, Stephanie McMahon, Dixie Carter, Eric Bischoff, John Laurinaitis, Matthew and Nicholas Jackson

THE BODYGUARD GIMMICK

In the world of combat sports, a fighter having some imposing people around you to watch their back is an authentic premise. This gimmick is easily paired with any of the "I am better than you and you know it!" gimmicks. This character's inevitable interference in a match will provide easy heat for a heel and protection for any face that needs to take a loss. It's a great way to slowly introduce a rookie giant character without rushing them into the squared circle and risking them cause injury or having a botchfest. The bodyguard gimmick can give a green wrestler a front row seat in watching an established professional work. It is also an easy way to utilize excess talent who "creative has nothing for." This gimmick rarely needs to shoot many promos, we all know bodyguards rarely talk. The pretty much inevitable slow burn turn on the bodyguard's boss is an easy storyline for both the main and secondary heel to partake in.

NOTABLE EXAMPLES

Kevin Nash, APA, Virgil, Wardlow, J & J Security, Mr. Hughes, Chyna, Big Boss Man, Sid, Omos, Satnam Singh

In modern professional wrestling, the simplistic professional wrestler who relies on solely one gimmick in developing their character is pretty much nonexistent. Gimmicks, like people, are best when they are complex. No one wants to be a one dimensional being. Today's best-known professional wrestlers rely on a combination of several gimmicks to produce and maintain a fresh act.

Professional wrestling gimmicks can employ various wrestling styles; however, some styles are particularly tailored to, and in some cases, identical to a particular wrestling gimmick. The next chapter will break down the science of this combination of gimmicks in the legendary careers of some professional wrestling's most storied competitors.

CHAPTER 2

THE MATH AND SCIENCE OF A WRESTLER

Ladies and gentlemen, today we are using the complex academic disciplines of math and science to study the careers of many beloved superstars of the squared circle. Our best efforts will be made to avoid Steiner math. This is the one chapter that is recommended to be read after you have read the gimmicks of professional wrestling. One should also be familiar with the various styles of professional wrestling.

Wrestling styles are various categories used to describe a professional wrestler's core in-ring move set. Just as no wrestler is truly one gimmick, no wrestler is truly one style. The move set a certain professional wrestler uses may be determined by their physical build, athletic abilities, or in-ring experience level. Additionally, as a wrestler's career progresses their individual style evolves highlighting their in-ring strengths and accentuating their gimmick.

Seasoned professional wrestlers may combine a variety of wrestling styles into their matches. This blend may be a result of the wrestler's working with different promotions and trainers, as well as their experiences wrestling in various countries. Notwithstanding, the variety of styles a wrestler uses, any particular professional wrestler has a core style.

When creating professional wrestling, whether it is crafting a promotion, a card, or a single match, there are a number of wrestling styles to be employed. These styles may be associated with a specific geographic region or at time's certain wrestling promotions. The following is a brief breakdown of the main modern-day styles of professional wrestling.

LUCHA LIBRE

Originating in Mexico, this high-flying fast paced style of wrestling has captivated professional wrestling fans worldwide. Lucha libre is highlighted by smaller agile fighters, trio's matches, and rapid-fire offense. Masked heroes flying off the ropes has become an intangible part of the cultural heritage of Mexico and professional wrestling.

JAPANESE: STRONG STYLE (PURORESU) AND KING'S ROAD (ODO)

Focused more on realism than on drama, strong style originated in New Japan Pro-Wrestling. It incorporates a variety of combat sports and is often characterized by stiff strikes and kicks along with traditional submission wrestling. King's Road focuses on in-ring storytelling, often building drama in a match and highlighting the "fighting spirit."

BRAWLER

Basically, professional wrestling's version of street fighting. These wrestlers will use a bar fight smash mouth style of offense. They will rely heavily on the old punch-kick technique. They will often use high impact moves to devastate their opponents. These wrestlers are as home fighting outside of the ring as they are inside it.

MAT TECHNICIAN (TECHNICAL)

A direct descendent from the old school catch-as-catch-can wrestling, this style focuses on grappling techniques and submission holds. Highlighted by the ever-evolving number of submissions holds and frequent reversals. This style relies on the oldest and most historic form of the one true sport.

HIGH FLYING

This style incorporates frequent aerial attacks where a wrestler leaves their feet to perform a variety of high-risk offensive maneuvers. Some of our favorite moves from the dropkick to the big elbow off of the top rope originate from this style. Wrestlers of this style may rely on "spots" to put together their matches.

POWERHOUSE

Big powerful moves performed by massive chiseled bodybuilder-esque individuals or those that are pretty heavy but not quite big enough to be a giant. These wrestlers will rely on classic professional wrestling moves such as the spear, powerbomb, and clothesline. At times these wrestlers will rely on fast impactful action and short matches.

GIANT

The moves associated with this style are usually performed by a seven-foot-plus man or six-foot-plus woman. These wrestlers use slow methodical powerful moves. Using the giant move set, a wrestler will rarely leave their feet. This move-set relies on a punch-kick move set, big throws, and powerful slams. The wrestler's sheer size may limit their move set but to quote big sexy Kevin Nash, "Babe Ruth only had one move and that's out of the park."

HARDCORE

Think standard professional wrestling brawling but with a wide variety of weaponry and some of the craziest bumps you've ever seen. Wrestlers who employ this style are as comfortable with a chair shot as they are with a wristlock. Bumping through tables, ladders, chairs, and whatever else can be thought of will be required for this style. These barbaric bloodfests feature high-risk stunts that have produced some of professional wrestling's most "Oh my God!" moments.

MIXED FIGHTING

These fighters will incorporate boxing, karate, sumo, or another mixed martial art fighting style into their wrestling matches.

Wrestlers utilizing this style will create a unique in-ring move set. This will enable the announcers to consistently remind the fans about the wrestler's combat sports background.

To better understand the legends of professional wrestling, we have created three graphs describing the in-ring careers of some of the greatest of all time. Internet websites, databases, professional wrestling film, and industry books were thoroughly researched to create these graphs.

The data used to create these graphs is compiled from a professional wrestler's active time in any major US-based nationwide professional wrestling promotion. For our purposes a major promotion is considered an organization who (during the age of cable television) has a contract with a major television network, regularly puts on widely discussed pay-per-views, habitually obtains respectable event attendance numbers (an average attendance of five thousand for televised shows is respectable), and has a talent roster with multiple mainstream household names among its ranks.

Any professional wrestling promotion can ascend from a minor promotion to a major one or vice versa. For example, the National Wrestling Alliance (NWA) during the 1980s would be considered a major promotion, but in 2023 it just does not meet the criteria. The status of a promotion at the time a wrestler competed for them will be considered when assessing whether the time counts.

Every time a professional wrestler steps into the ring they put their life on the line for our entertainment. Every match no matter how big or small deserves a certain level of respect.

However, matches outside of the major professional wrestling promotions are just not as well documented. Therefore, to give the most accurate picture possible, time spent in regional, developmental, foreign, or smaller independent promotions will not be counted.

Regarding a wrestler appearing for foreign promotions, such as New Japan Pro-Wrestling, there is a caveat. If that wrestler was under contract with a major promotion but lent out to a foreign promotion, then the time counts. The World Wrestling Federation (WWF) used to do this in the eighties and nineties, and All Elite Wrestling (AEW) continues the tradition today. If the wrestler is working independently abroad or is directly under contract with a foreign promotion, then that in-ring time doesn't count.

For those wrestlers whose in-ring careers predate the emergence of major national professional wrestling promotions and the death of the territories in the 1980s, their time spent and titles won in major promotions will count. The World-Wide Wrestling Federation (WWWF), American Wrestling Association (AWA), and National Wrestling Alliance (NWA) are all old school major professional wrestling promotions. As with everything in this world the further back in time we travel the more blurred history gets. Despite this, our graphs will strive to give the most accurate picture as possible of a professional wrestler's in-ring career.

As discussed, in "The Gimmicks of Professional Wrestling" chapter, the pie graph breaks down how much of each of the classic professional wrestling gimmicks are used in cultivating an individual performer's persona. We are not talking about an individual performer's various gimmick changes over their career. For example, when describing Glen Jacobs's Kane gimmick, the assessment does not include those, yeah, I can see why you think wrestling might be corny, forgetful Dr. Isaac Yankem years. The in-ring time may still count when it comes to analyzing a wrestler's career, but not their ultimate gimmick.

The ultimate gimmick is that undeniable persona that eventually emerges out of one individual performer. Oftentimes a professional wrestler's past gimmicks become incorporated into their new one, adding to the layers of the overall character. This is the case of Chris Jericho, the Undertaker, and countless others. Whether a wrestler's prior gimmicks are considered a part of their ultimate gimmick is determined on a case-by-case basis.

This graph will also label each professional wrestler with their *primary* style of wrestling. Emphasis on primary. Even for those wrestlers whom seem to be able to do it all, a primary style will be given. Don't come at me with that "How can he be a brawler? I've seen him do a moonsault!" nonsense. Remember even Brock Lesnar has hit a shooting star press. Well, sort of hit it.

The face/heel bar graph illustrates what percentage of a professional wrestler's character has been spent playing for either team good or team evil. What team one plays for is an inexact science. The vast majority of the time a professional wrestler's face/heel status is readily apparent. However, sometimes a wrestler finds themselves in the process of a character turn or are hovering in that in-betweener gray world of professional wrestling purgatory. Some wrestlers might protest that they are neither a heel nor a face but just are themselves. That's a nice philosophical musing and I am sure that is true for the real individual. For the character though, in the world of professional wrestling at any given point in time, you're either good or evil. Even for those wrestlers whom some claim have tweener years, those years will be put into one category or the other.

The third graph labeled Golden Times is perhaps the most scientific of these diagrams. Well, at least it logged the most research hours. Here's how it works. We calculate the total time a competitor has spent as an active major league in-ring professional wrestler. The clock starts ticking when a wrestler officially debuts in a major promotion and continues until they are officially retired or are no longer considered an active in-ring competitor.

We calculate the time from their debut until retirement and then subtract any significant amount of time missed throughout their career. This time off can be for extended vacations, injury, drug rehabilitation, filming a movie, abiding by a non-compete clause while switching promotions, scratching themselves, etc. If a wrestler makes a one-off appearance that counts. If a wrestler appears for a major promotion as an unknown jobber that time counts. Any major league matches a wrestler takes part in is considered at least seven days of active wrestling time. More time may be awarded depending on that wrestler's participation in the build for the match or their involvement and availability for a promotion.

If a wrestler spends time being available but only seldom wrestles because of a creative decision, as was the case for Sting during his World Championship Wrestling (WCW) run, all that time still counts. Also, any time you are holding a promotion's gold as a recognized champion, even if you take time off for vacations, injury, or otherwise just seldomly appears, it all still counts. It's just logical that if you're a promotion's recognized champion, then you are active. Our goal here is to only count the time a professional wrestler is available for use as an active member of a major professional wrestling promotion's roster.

After we have calculated the total time for an active major

league in-ring career, we use that timeframe in assessing that respective wrestler's face/heel status and their gimmick. We also use this active in-ring career time to determine each professional wrestler's Golden Time. Golden Time is the total number of days a competitor is a major professional wrestling promotion's title holder.

Throughout the history of professional wrestling, records of title changes have been fuzzy at times. For this reason, we have established our criteria in determining when a title reign counts. We are mostly counting the title reigns and days holding gold as recognized by the professional wrestling promotion awarding that particular title. There are some caveats though, if a wrestler capture's gold but loses it the same night, as in the case of various money in the bank cash ins, that title reign will be counted as one day regardless of how the promotion scores that title reign. We are counting days here not minutes. If you are holding a belt for any part of that particular day, that day counts toward your Golden Time. Additionally, sometimes a promotion, for no real reason, fails to recognize a title change that clearly happened, we will judge these situations on a case-by-case basis. Pre-taped title changes can also create confusion with the title change timeline. For our purposes, the date the title change was presented to the world, i.e. aired on television, will be used for counting title reigns.

The professional wrestlers' title reigns are broken down into five Golden Time categories: Major Gold, Medium Gold, Minor Gold, Tag Gold, and Total Gold. Major Gold is a promotion's top title, i.e. the big gold belt or the World Wrestling Entertainment (WWE) title. In some instances a promotion may have two top titles. This is currently the case in the WWE with each of the respective brand split top titles.

Medium Gold is a promotion's mid-card belts, i.e. the intercontinental title and the US title. Additionally, pre-national regional heavyweight titles or world titles for a lesser brand that exists under a major league promotion's umbrella will be considered medium gold. An example of this is the Florida heavyweight championship under the NWA.

Minor Gold is a promotion's third tier of title, i.e. WWE's hardcore title or WCW's television title. The FTW title, the Million Dollar belt, or any other non-recognized titles are barred from consideration. Tag Gold is any major promotion's traditional tag team titles, other multi-man titles like trios' titles are out. The same pre-national regional rules apply for tag gold, just without the tiered system. Tag gold is tag gold.

Total Gold is the total time a professional wrestler has spent carrying any major promotion's eligible titles. In addition to the total number of days spent in golden time, we have calculated the percentages of a wrestler's total active major league in-ring career spent in each respective Golden Time category. All results are calculated up until January 1, 2024. Here are thirty scientifically devised—well, sort of—graphs to help you further enjoy the world of professional wrestling:

BRUNO SAMMARTINO

STYLE: MAT TECHNICIAN

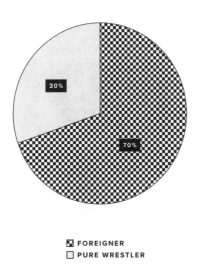

30%

70%

■ FOREIGNER
☐ PURE WRESTLER

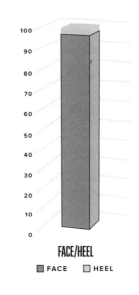

100
90
80
70
60
50
40
30
20
10
0

FACE/HEEL

■ FACE ☐ HEEL

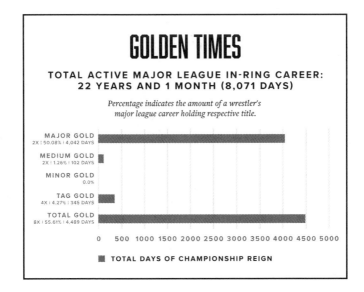

GOLDEN TIMES

TOTAL ACTIVE MAJOR LEAGUE IN-RING CAREER:
22 YEARS AND 1 MONTH (8,071 DAYS)

*Percentage indicates the amount of a wrestler's
major league career holding respective title.*

MAJOR GOLD
2X | 50.08% | 4,042 DAYS

MEDIUM GOLD
2X | 1.26% | 102 DAYS

MINOR GOLD
0.0%

TAG GOLD
4X | 4.27% | 345 DAYS

TOTAL GOLD
8X | 55.61% | 4,489 DAYS

0   500 1000 1500 2000 2500 3000 3500 4000 4500 5000

■ TOTAL DAYS OF CHAMPIONSHIP REIGN

ANDRÉ THE GIANT

STYLE: GIANT

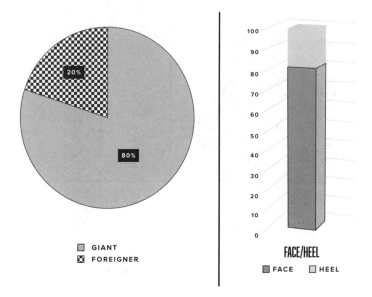

GIANT — 80%
FOREIGNER — 20%

FACE/HEEL

FACE   HEEL

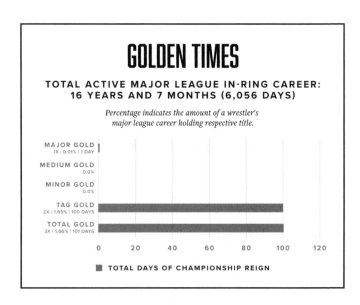

GOLDEN TIMES

TOTAL ACTIVE MAJOR LEAGUE IN-RING CAREER:
16 YEARS AND 7 MONTHS (6,056 DAYS)

*Percentage indicates the amount of a wrestler's
major league career holding respective title.*

MAJOR GOLD
1X | 0.01% | 1 DAY

MEDIUM GOLD
0.0%

MINOR GOLD
0.0%

TAG GOLD
2X | 1.65% | 100 DAYS

TOTAL GOLD
3X | 1.66% | 101 DAYS

TOTAL DAYS OF CHAMPIONSHIP REIGN

RIC FLAIR

STYLE: MAT TECHNICIAN

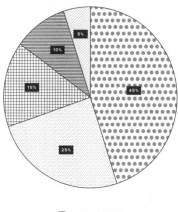

- ☑ ARISTOCRAT
- ☐ ROCK STAR
- ☐ HEARTTHROB
- ☐ NARCISSIST
- ☐ AUTHORITY FIGURE

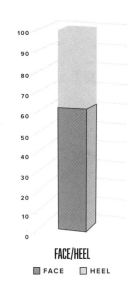

FACE/HEEL

- ☐ FACE   ☐ HEEL

GOLDEN TIMES

TOTAL ACTIVE MAJOR LEAGUE IN-RING CAREER:
31 YEARS AND 3 MONTH (11,406 DAYS)

*Percentage indicates the amount of a wrestler's
major league career holding respective title.*

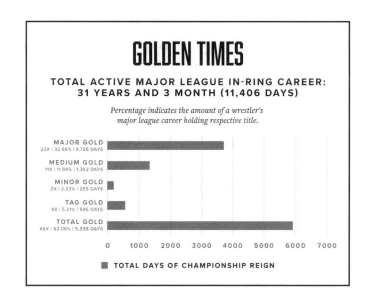

MAJOR GOLD
23X | 32.66% | 3,726 DAYS

MEDIUM GOLD
11X | 11.94% | 1,362 DAYS

MINOR GOLD
2X | 2.23% | 255 DAYS

TAG GOLD
9X | 5.21% | 595 DAYS

TOTAL GOLD
45X | 52.06% | 5,938 DAYS

0   1000   2000   3000   4000   5000   6000   7000

■ TOTAL DAYS OF CHAMPIONSHIP REIGN

HULK HOGAN

STYLE: POWERHOUSE

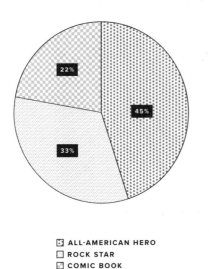

- ▨ ALL-AMERICAN HERO
- ☐ ROCK STAR
- ☐ COMIC BOOK

22%

45%

33%

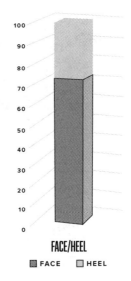

FACE/HEEL

■ FACE ☐ HEEL

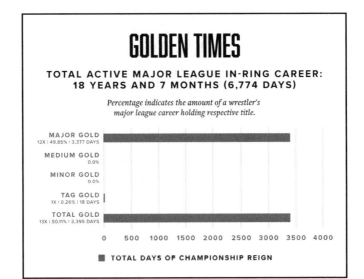

GOLDEN TIMES

TOTAL ACTIVE MAJOR LEAGUE IN-RING CAREER:
18 YEARS AND 7 MONTHS (6,774 DAYS)

*Percentage indicates the amount of a wrestler's
major league career holding respective title.*

MAJOR GOLD 12X | 49.85% | 3,377 DAYS	
MEDIUM GOLD 0.0%	
MINOR GOLD 0.0%	
TAG GOLD 1X | 0.26% | 18 DAYS	
TOTAL GOLD 13X | 50.11% | 3,395 DAYS	

0   500   1000 1500 2000 2500 3000 3500 4000

■ TOTAL DAYS OF CHAMPIONSHIP REIGN

BRET 'THE HITMAN' HART

STYLE: MAT TECHNICIAN

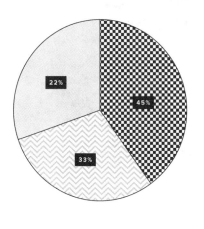

- **FOREIGNER**
- **LEGACY**
- **PURE WRESTLER**

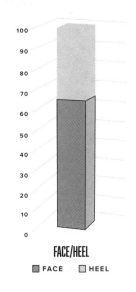

FACE/HEEL

- **FACE**
- **HEEL**

GOLDEN TIMES

TOTAL ACTIVE MAJOR LEAGUE IN-RING CAREER:
14 YEARS AND 10 MONTHS (5,404 DAYS)

Percentage indicates the amount of a wrestler's major league career holding respective title.

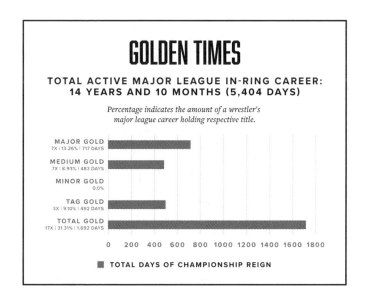

MAJOR GOLD
7X | 13.26% | 717 DAYS

MEDIUM GOLD
7X | 8.93% | 483 DAYS

MINOR GOLD
0.0%

TAG GOLD
3X | 9.10% | 492 DAYS

TOTAL GOLD
17X | 31.31% | 1,692 DAYS

0 200 400 600 800 1000 1200 1400 1600 1800

TOTAL DAYS OF CHAMPIONSHIP REIGN

'THE HEARTBREAK KID' SHAWN MICHAELS

STYLE: HIGH FLYER

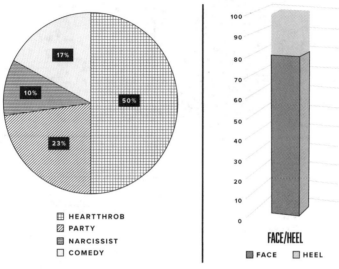

- ▦ HEARTTHROB
- ▨ PARTY
- ▤ NARCISSIST
- ▢ COMEDY

FACE/HEEL

■ FACE   □ HEEL

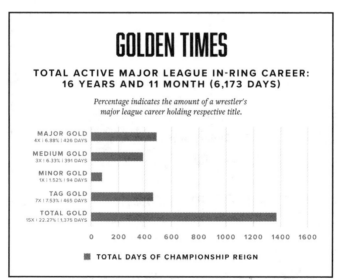

GOLDEN TIMES

TOTAL ACTIVE MAJOR LEAGUE IN-RING CAREER: 16 YEARS AND 11 MONTH (6,173 DAYS)

Percentage indicates the amount of a wrestler's major league career holding respective title.

MAJOR GOLD
4X | 6.88% | 426 DAYS

MEDIUM GOLD
3X | 6.33% | 391 DAYS

MINOR GOLD
1X | 1.52% | 94 DAYS

TAG GOLD
7X | 7.53% | 465 DAYS

TOTAL GOLD
15X | 22.27% | 1,375 DAYS

■ TOTAL DAYS OF CHAMPIONSHIP REIGN

'THE MACHO MAN' RANDY SAVAGE

STYLE: HIGH FLYER

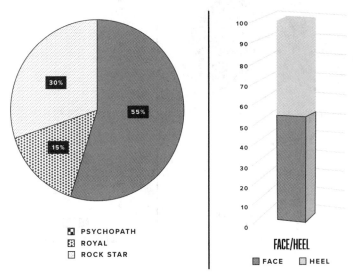

- 30%
- 55%
- 15%

PSYCHOPATH
ROYAL
ROCK STAR

100
90
80
70
60
50
40
30
20
10
0

FACE/HEEL

FACE   **HEEL**

GOLDEN TIMES

TOTAL ACTIVE MAJOR LEAGUE IN-RING CAREER:
12 YEARS AND 5 MONTHS (4,520 DAYS)

*Percentage indicates the amount of a wrestler's
major league career holding respective title.*

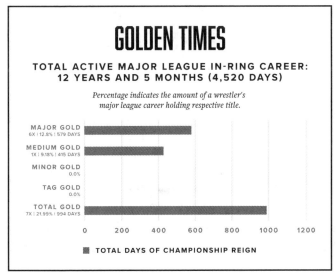

MAJOR GOLD
6X | 12.8% | 579 DAYS

MEDIUM GOLD
1X | 9.18% | 415 DAYS

MINOR GOLD
0.0%

TAG GOLD
0.0%

TOTAL GOLD
7X | 21.99% | 994 DAYS

0   200   400   600   800   1000   1200

TOTAL DAYS OF CHAMPIONSHIP REIGN

MICK FOLEY

STYLE: HARDCORE

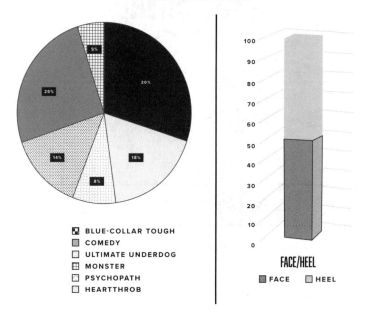

- **BLUE-COLLAR TOUGH**
- **COMEDY**
- **ULTIMATE UNDERDOG**
- **MONSTER**
- **PSYCHOPATH**
- **HEARTTHROB**

FACE/HEEL

- **FACE**
- **HEEL**

GOLDEN TIMES

TOTAL ACTIVE MAJOR LEAGUE IN-RING CAREER: 8 YEARS AND 1 MONTH (2,942 DAYS)

Percentage indicates the amount of a wrestler's major league career holding respective title.

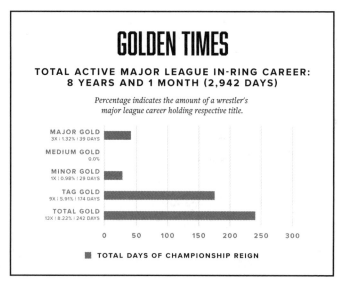

MAJOR GOLD
3X | 1.32% | 39 DAYS

MEDIUM GOLD
0.0%

MINOR GOLD
1X | 0.98% | 29 DAYS

TAG GOLD
9X | 5.91% | 174 DAYS

TOTAL GOLD
13X | 8.22% | 242 DAYS

TOTAL DAYS OF CHAMPIONSHIP REIGN

STING

STYLE: POWERHOUSE

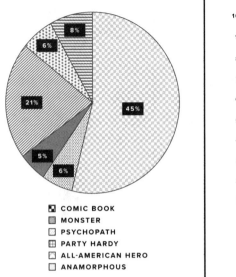

- ▨ COMIC BOOK
- ▧ MONSTER
- ▢ PSYCHOPATH
- ▦ PARTY HARDY
- ▨ ALL-AMERICAN HERO
- ▢ ANAMORPHOUS

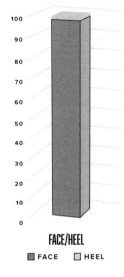

FACE/HEEL

- ▨ FACE ▢ HEEL

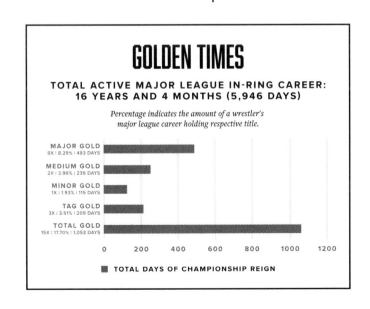

GOLDEN TIMES

TOTAL ACTIVE MAJOR LEAGUE IN-RING CAREER:
16 YEARS AND 4 MONTHS (5,946 DAYS)

*Percentage indicates the amount of a wrestler's
major league career holding respective title.*

MAJOR GOLD
9X | 8.29% | 493 DAYS

MEDIUM GOLD
2X | 3.96% | 236 DAYS

MINOR GOLD
1X | 1.93% | 115 DAYS

TAG GOLD
3X | 3.51% | 209 DAYS

TOTAL GOLD
15X | 17.70% | 1,053 DAYS

▨ TOTAL DAYS OF CHAMPIONSHIP REIGN

THE ULTIMATE WARRIOR

STYLE: POWERHOUSE

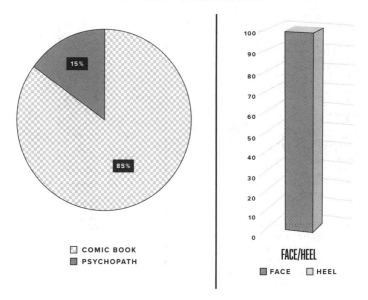

COMIC BOOK
PSYCHOPATH

FACE/HEEL

FACE   HEEL

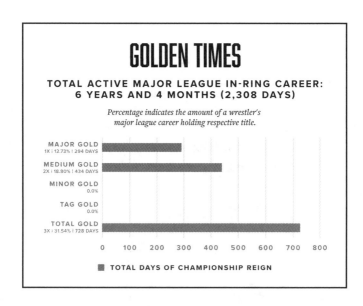

GOLDEN TIMES

TOTAL ACTIVE MAJOR LEAGUE IN-RING CAREER:
6 YEARS AND 4 MONTHS (2,308 DAYS)

*Percentage indicates the amount of a wrestler's
major league career holding respective title.*

MAJOR GOLD
1X | 12.73% | 294 DAYS

MEDIUM GOLD
2X | 18.80% | 434 DAYS

MINOR GOLD
0.0%

TAG GOLD
0.0%

TOTAL GOLD
3X | 31.54% | 728 DAYS

TOTAL DAYS OF CHAMPIONSHIP REIGN

EDDIE GUERRERO

STYLE: LUCHA LIBRE

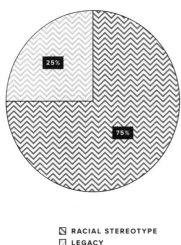

- ⬚ RACIAL STEREOTYPE
- ⬚ LEGACY

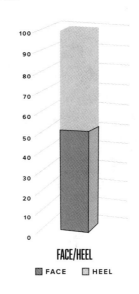

FACE/HEEL

- ▨ FACE
- ▨ HEEL

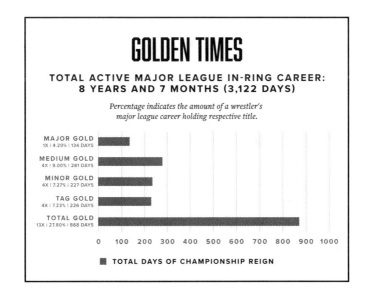

GOLDEN TIMES

TOTAL ACTIVE MAJOR LEAGUE IN-RING CAREER:
8 YEARS AND 7 MONTHS (3,122 DAYS)

Percentage indicates the amount of a wrestler's major league career holding respective title.

MAJOR GOLD
1X | 4.29% | 134 DAYS

MEDIUM GOLD
4X | 9.00% | 281 DAYS

MINOR GOLD
4X | 7.27% | 227 DAYS

TAG GOLD
4X | 7.23% | 226 DAYS

TOTAL GOLD
13X | 27.80% | 868 DAYS

0   100   200   300   400   500   600   700   800   900   1000

■ TOTAL DAYS OF CHAMPIONSHIP REIGN

THE UNDERTAKER

STYLE: GIANT

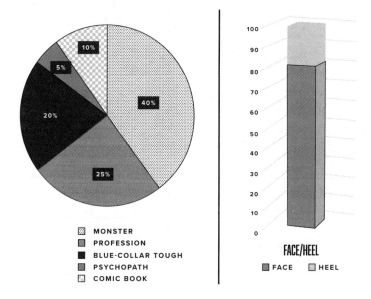

MONSTER — 10%
PROFESSION — 40%
BLUE-COLLAR TOUGH — 20%
PSYCHOPATH — 25%
COMIC BOOK — 5%

FACE/HEEL

FACE   HEEL

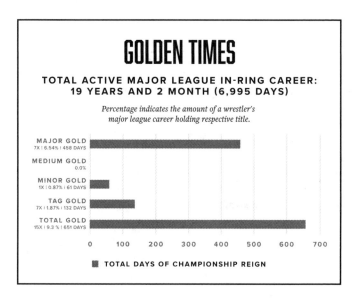

GOLDEN TIMES

TOTAL ACTIVE MAJOR LEAGUE IN-RING CAREER:
19 YEARS AND 2 MONTH (6,995 DAYS)

*Percentage indicates the amount of a wrestler's
major league career holding respective title.*

MAJOR GOLD
7X | 6.54% | 458 DAYS

MEDIUM GOLD
0.0%

MINOR GOLD
1X | 0.87% | 61 DAYS

TAG GOLD
7X | 1.87% | 132 DAYS

TOTAL GOLD
15X | 9.3 % | 651 DAYS

TOTAL DAYS OF CHAMPIONSHIP REIGN

KEVIN NASH

STYLE: GIANT

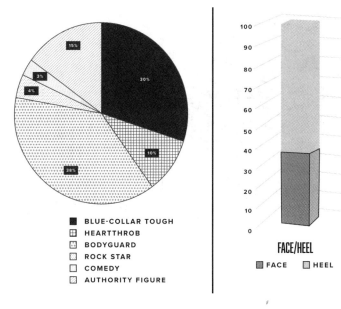

- ■ BLUE-COLLAR TOUGH
- ⊞ HEARTTHROB
- ▨ BODYGUARD
- ▫ ROCK STAR
- ▫ COMEDY
- ▨ AUTHORITY FIGURE

FACE/HEEL

▨ FACE   ▫ HEEL

GOLDEN TIMES

TOTAL ACTIVE MAJOR LEAGUE IN-RING CAREER:
10 YEARS AND 11 MONTHS (3,992 DAYS)

*Percentage indicates the amount of a wrestler's
major league career holding respective title.*

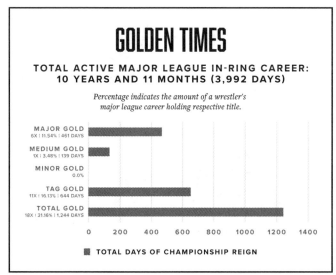

MAJOR GOLD
6X | 11.54% | 461 DAYS

MEDIUM GOLD
1X | 3.48% | 139 DAYS

MINOR GOLD
0.0%

TAG GOLD
11X | 16.13% | 644 DAYS

TOTAL GOLD
18X | 31.16% | 1,244 DAYS

■ TOTAL DAYS OF CHAMPIONSHIP REIGN

'STONE COLD' STEVE AUSTIN

STYLE: BRAWLER

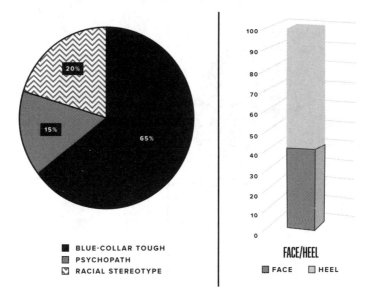

20%

15%

65%

■ BLUE-COLLAR TOUGH
■ PSYCHOPATH
◪ RACIAL STEREOTYPE

FACE/HEEL

■ FACE   □ HEEL

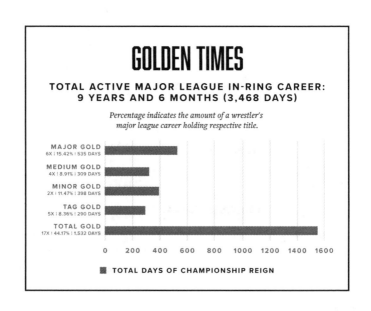

GOLDEN TIMES

TOTAL ACTIVE MAJOR LEAGUE IN-RING CAREER:
9 YEARS AND 6 MONTHS (3,468 DAYS)

*Percentage indicates the amount of a wrestler's
major league career holding respective title.*

MAJOR GOLD
6X | 15.42% | 535 DAYS

MEDIUM GOLD
4X | 8.91% | 309 DAYS

MINOR GOLD
2X | 11.47% | 398 DAYS

TAG GOLD
5X | 8.36% | 290 DAYS

TOTAL GOLD
17X | 44.17% | 1,532 DAYS

■ TOTAL DAYS OF CHAMPIONSHIP REIGN

BOOKER T

STYLE: BRAWLER

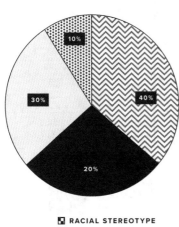

- ▦ RACIAL STEREOTYPE
- ■ BLUE-COLLAR TOUGH
- □ COMEDY
- ❖ ROYAL

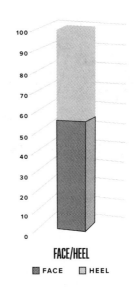

FACE/HEEL

▦ FACE   ▦ HEEL

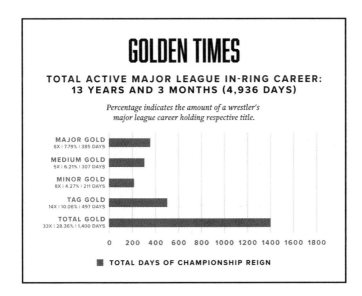

GOLDEN TIMES

TOTAL ACTIVE MAJOR LEAGUE IN-RING CAREER: 13 YEARS AND 3 MONTHS (4,936 DAYS)

Percentage indicates the amount of a wrestler's major league career holding respective title.

MAJOR GOLD
6X | 7.79% | 385 DAYS

MEDIUM GOLD
5X | 6.21% | 307 DAYS

MINOR GOLD
8X | 4.27% | 211 DAYS

TAG GOLD
14X | 10.06% | 497 DAYS

TOTAL GOLD
33X | 28.36% | 1,400 DAYS

0   200   400   600   800   1000   1200   1400   1600   1800

■ TOTAL DAYS OF CHAMPIONSHIP REIGN

KANE

STYLE: GIANT

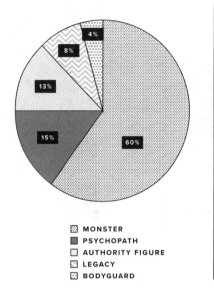

- ▨ MONSTER
- ▦ PSYCHOPATH
- ▧ AUTHORITY FIGURE
- ▨ LEGACY
- ▨ BODYGUARD

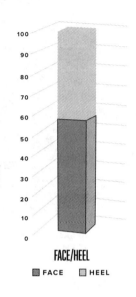

FACE/HEEL

- ▨ FACE
- ▨ HEEL

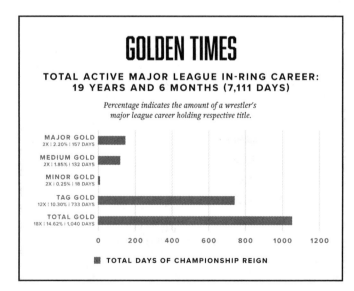

GOLDEN TIMES

TOTAL ACTIVE MAJOR LEAGUE IN-RING CAREER: 19 YEARS AND 6 MONTHS (7,111 DAYS)

*Percentage indicates the amount of a wrestler's
major league career holding respective title.*

MAJOR GOLD
2X | 2.20% | 157 DAYS

MEDIUM GOLD
2X | 1.85% | 132 DAYS

MINOR GOLD
2X | 0.25% | 18 DAYS

TAG GOLD
12X | 10.30% | 733 DAYS

TOTAL GOLD
18X | 14.62% | 1,040 DAYS

▨ TOTAL DAYS OF CHAMPIONSHIP REIGN

TRIPLE H

STYLE: POWERHOUSE

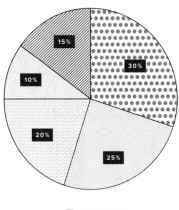

- ▦ ARISTOCRAT
- ▢ AUTHORITY FIGURE
- ▨ ROCK STAR
- ▢ COMEDY
- ▨ PARTY

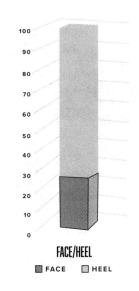

FACE/HEEL

■ FACE   ▨ HEEL

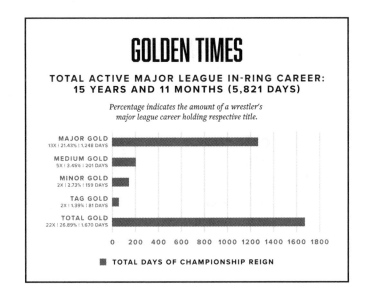

GOLDEN TIMES

TOTAL ACTIVE MAJOR LEAGUE IN-RING CAREER:
15 YEARS AND 11 MONTHS (5,821 DAYS)

*Percentage indicates the amount of a wrestler's
major league career holding respective title.*

MAJOR GOLD
13X | 21.43% | 1,248 DAYS

MEDIUM GOLD
5X | 3.45% | 201 DAYS

MINOR GOLD
2X | 2.73% | 159 DAYS

TAG GOLD
2X | 1.39% | 81 DAYS

TOTAL GOLD
22X | 26.89% | 1,670 DAYS

0   200 400 600 800 1000 1200 1400 1600 1800

■ TOTAL DAYS OF CHAMPIONSHIP REIGN

EDGE

STYLE: HIGH FLYER

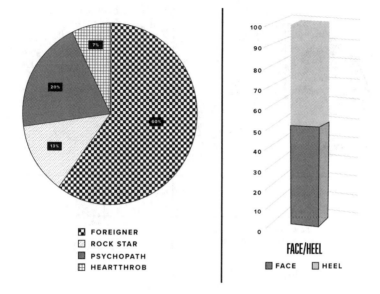

FOREIGNER
ROCK STAR
PSYCHOPATH
HEARTTHROB

7%
20%
13%
60%

100
90
80
70
60
50
40
30
20
10
0

FACE/HEEL

FACE HEEL

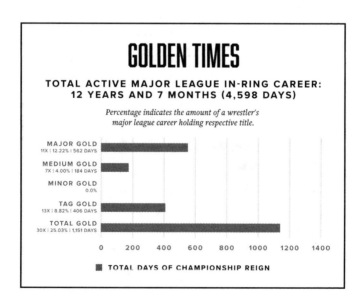

GOLDEN TIMES

TOTAL ACTIVE MAJOR LEAGUE IN-RING CAREER:
12 YEARS AND 7 MONTHS (4,598 DAYS)

*Percentage indicates the amount of a wrestler's
major league career holding respective title.*

MAJOR GOLD
11X | 12.22% | 562 DAYS

MEDIUM GOLD
7X | 4.00% | 184 DAYS

MINOR GOLD
0.0%

TAG GOLD
13X | 8.82% | 406 DAYS

TOTAL GOLD
30X | 25.03% | 1,151 DAYS

0   200   400   600   800   1000 1200 1400

TOTAL DAYS OF CHAMPIONSHIP REIGN

REY MYSTERIO

STYLE: LUCHA LIBRE

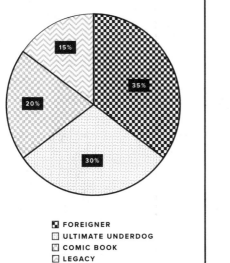

- 35%
- 30%
- 20%
- 15%

■ FOREIGNER
□ ULTIMATE UNDERDOG
▨ COMIC BOOK
▧ LEGACY

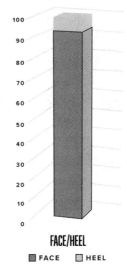

FACE/HEEL

■ FACE   ▨ HEEL

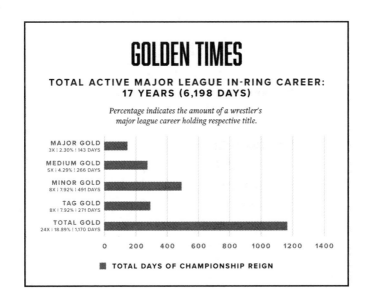

GOLDEN TIMES

TOTAL ACTIVE MAJOR LEAGUE IN-RING CAREER: 17 YEARS (6,198 DAYS)

Percentage indicates the amount of a wrestler's major league career holding respective title.

MAJOR GOLD
3X | 2.30% | 143 DAYS

MEDIUM GOLD
5X | 4.29% | 266 DAYS

MINOR GOLD
8X | 7.92% | 491 DAYS

TAG GOLD
8X | 7.92% | 271 DAYS

TOTAL GOLD
24X | 18.89% | 1,170 DAYS

0   200   400   600   800   1000   1200   1400

■ TOTAL DAYS OF CHAMPIONSHIP REIGN

CHRIS JERICHO

STYLE: MAT TECHNICIAN

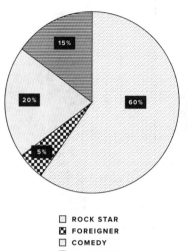

- ░ ROCK STAR
- ▨ FOREIGNER
- ▢ COMEDY
- ▤ NARCISSIST

15%
20%
5%
60%

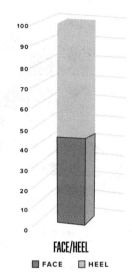

FACE/HEEL

▨ FACE   ▢ HEEL

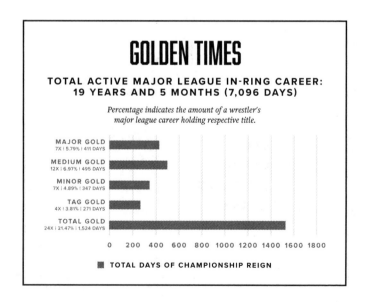

GOLDEN TIMES

TOTAL ACTIVE MAJOR LEAGUE IN-RING CAREER: 19 YEARS AND 5 MONTHS (7,096 DAYS)

Percentage indicates the amount of a wrestler's major league career holding respective title.

MAJOR GOLD
7X | 5.79% | 411 DAYS

MEDIUM GOLD
12X | 6.97% | 495 DAYS

MINOR GOLD
7X | 4.89% | 347 DAYS

TAG GOLD
4X | 3.81% | 271 DAYS

TOTAL GOLD
24X | 21.47% | 1,524 DAYS

0   200   400   600   800   1000   1200   1400   1600   1800

▨ TOTAL DAYS OF CHAMPIONSHIP REIGN

THE ROCK

STYLE: POWERHOUSE

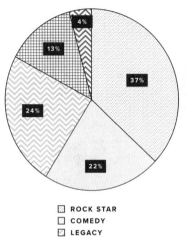

- ▦ ROCK STAR
- ☐ COMEDY
- ▨ LEGACY
- ⊞ HEARTTHROB
- ◩ RACIAL STEREOTYPE

4%

13%

37%

24%

22%

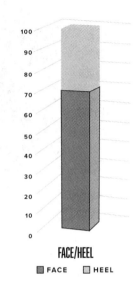

FACE/HEEL

- ▨ FACE
- ☐ HEEL

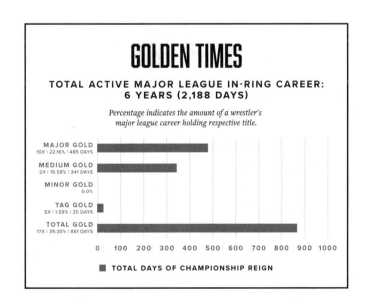

GOLDEN TIMES

TOTAL ACTIVE MAJOR LEAGUE IN-RING CAREER: 6 YEARS (2,188 DAYS)

Percentage indicates the amount of a wrestler's major league career holding respective title.

MAJOR GOLD
10X | 22.16% | 485 DAYS

MEDIUM GOLD
2X | 15.58% | 341 DAYS

MINOR GOLD
0.0%

TAG GOLD
5X | 1.59% | 35 DAYS

TOTAL GOLD
17X | 39.35% | 861 DAYS

0   100   200   300   400   500   600   700   800   900   1000

■ TOTAL DAYS OF CHAMPIONSHIP REIGN

GOLDBERG

STYLE: POWERHOUSE

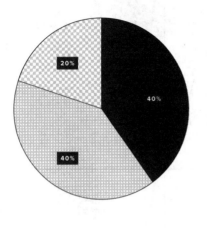

- ▨ BLUE-COLLAR TOUGH
- ▤ DIFFERENT FIGHTER
- ▦ COMIC BOOK

20%
40%
40%

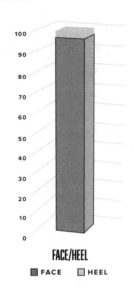

FACE/HEEL

■ FACE   □ HEEL

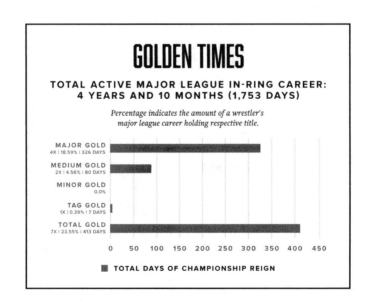

GOLDEN TIMES

TOTAL ACTIVE MAJOR LEAGUE IN-RING CAREER:
4 YEARS AND 10 MONTHS (1,753 DAYS)

*Percentage indicates the amount of a wrestler's
major league career holding respective title.*

MAJOR GOLD
4X | 18.59% | 326 DAYS

MEDIUM GOLD
2X | 4.56% | 80 DAYS

MINOR GOLD
0.0%

TAG GOLD
1X | 0.39% | 7 DAYS

TOTAL GOLD
7X | 23.55% | 413 DAYS

0   50   100 150 200 250 300 350 400 450

■ TOTAL DAYS OF CHAMPIONSHIP REIGN

KURT ANGLE

STYLE: MAT TECHNICIAN

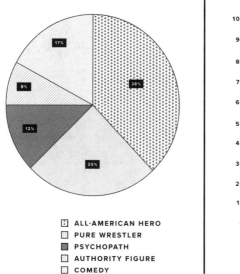

- ⊞ ALL-AMERICAN HERO
- ☐ PURE WRESTLER
- ▨ PSYCHOPATH
- ▨ AUTHORITY FIGURE
- ☐ COMEDY

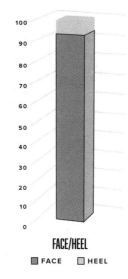

FACE/HEEL

▨ FACE   ☐ HEEL

GOLDEN TIMES

TOTAL ACTIVE MAJOR LEAGUE IN-RING CAREER:
7 YEARS AND 7 MONTHS (2,759 DAYS)

*Percentage indicates the amount of a wrestler's
major league career holding respective title.*

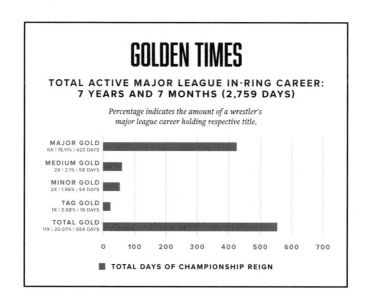

MAJOR GOLD
6X | 15.11% | 423 DAYS

MEDIUM GOLD
2X | 2.1% | 58 DAYS

MINOR GOLD
2X | 1.95% | 54 DAYS

TAG GOLD
1X | 0.68% | 19 DAYS

TOTAL GOLD
11X | 20.07% | 554 DAYS

▨ TOTAL DAYS OF CHAMPIONSHIP REIGN

RANDY ORTON

STYLE: BRAWLER

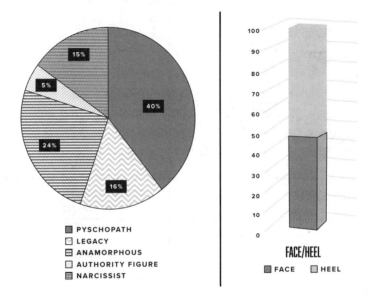

15%
5%
40%
24%
16%

- PYSCHOPATH
- LEGACY
- ANAMORPHOUS
- AUTHORITY FIGURE
- NARCISSIST

FACE/HEEL

FACE   HEEL

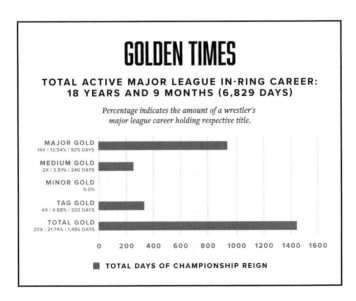

GOLDEN TIMES

TOTAL ACTIVE MAJOR LEAGUE IN-RING CAREER:
18 YEARS AND 9 MONTHS (6,829 DAYS)

Percentage indicates the amount of a wrestler's major league career holding respective title.

MAJOR GOLD
14X | 13.54% | 925 DAYS

MEDIUM GOLD
2X | 3.51% | 240 DAYS

MINOR GOLD
0.0%

TAG GOLD
4X | 4.68% | 320 DAYS

TOTAL GOLD
20X | 21.74% | 1,485 DAYS

TOTAL DAYS OF CHAMPIONSHIP REIGN

BROCK LESNAR

STYLE: POWERHOUSE

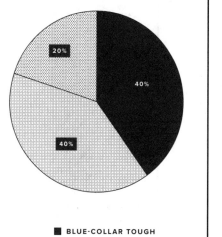

- ■ BLUE-COLLAR TOUGH
- ▦ DIFFERENT FIGHTER
- ▦ MONSTER

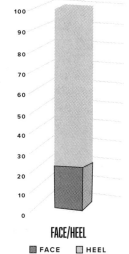

FACE/HEEL

- ■ FACE
- ▢ HEEL

GOLDEN TIMES

TOTAL ACTIVE MAJOR LEAGUE IN-RING CAREER: 9 YEARS AND 8 MONTHS (3,524 DAYS)

Percentage indicates the amount of a wrestler's major league career holding respective title.

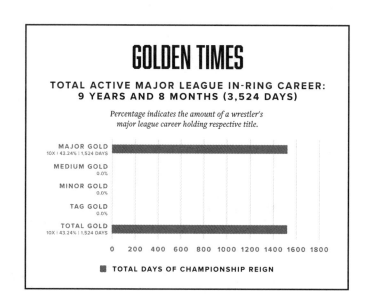

MAJOR GOLD 10X	43.24%	1,524 DAYS	
MEDIUM GOLD 0.0%	
MINOR GOLD 0.0%	
TAG GOLD 0.0%	
TOTAL GOLD 10X	43.24%	1,524 DAYS	

0   200   400   600   800   1000 1200 1400 1600 1800

■ TOTAL DAYS OF CHAMPIONSHIP REIGN

BATISTA
STYLE: POWERHOUSE

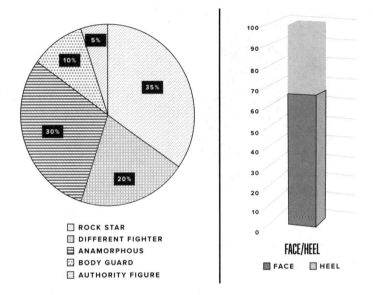

- ROCK STAR
- DIFFERENT FIGHTER
- ANAMORPHOUS
- BODY GUARD
- AUTHORITY FIGURE

5%
10%
35%
30%
20%

FACE/HEEL

FACE   HEEL

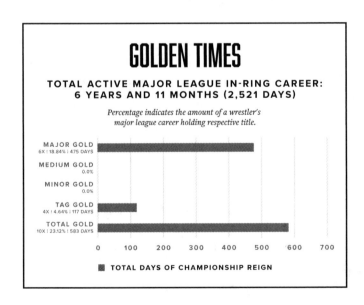

GOLDEN TIMES

TOTAL ACTIVE MAJOR LEAGUE IN-RING CAREER:
6 YEARS AND 11 MONTHS (2,521 DAYS)

Percentage indicates the amount of a wrestler's major league career holding respective title.

MAJOR GOLD
6X | 18.84% | 475 DAYS

MEDIUM GOLD
0.0%

MINOR GOLD
0.0%

TAG GOLD
4X | 4.64% | 117 DAYS

TOTAL GOLD
10X | 23.12% | 583 DAYS

0   100   200   300   400   500   600   700

TOTAL DAYS OF CHAMPIONSHIP REIGN

JOHN CENA

STYLE: POWERHOUSE

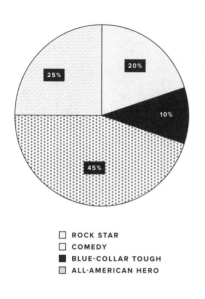

- ☐ ROCK STAR
- ☐ COMEDY
- ■ BLUE-COLLAR TOUGH
- ▨ ALL-AMERICAN HERO

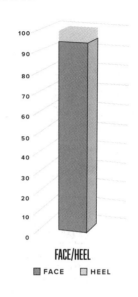

FACE/HEEL

▨ FACE   ☐ HEEL

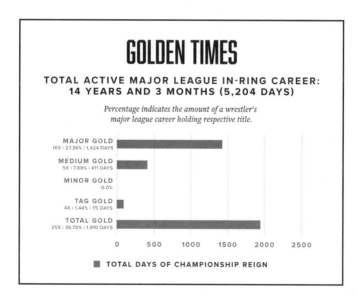

GOLDEN TIMES

TOTAL ACTIVE MAJOR LEAGUE IN-RING CAREER:
14 YEARS AND 3 MONTHS (5,204 DAYS)

*Percentage indicates the amount of a wrestler's
major league career holding respective title.*

MAJOR GOLD
16X | 27.36% | 1,424 DAYS

MEDIUM GOLD
5X | 7.89% | 411 DAYS

MINOR GOLD
0.0%

TAG GOLD
4X | 1.44% | 75 DAYS

TOTAL GOLD
25X | 36.70% | 1,910 DAYS

■ TOTAL DAYS OF CHAMPIONSHIP REIGN

BRYAN DANIELSON

STYLE: MAT TECHNICIAN

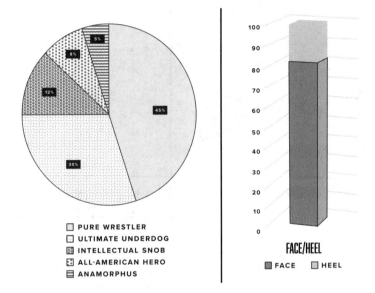

PURE WRESTLER
ULTIMATE UNDERDOG
INTELLECTUAL SNOB
ALL-AMERICAN HERO
ANAMORPHUS

FACE/HEEL

FACE   HEEL

GOLDEN TIMES

TOTAL ACTIVE MAJOR LEAGUE IN-RING CAREER:
9 YEARS AND 2 MONTHS (3,330 DAYS)

Percentage indicates the amount of a wrestler's major league career holding respective title.

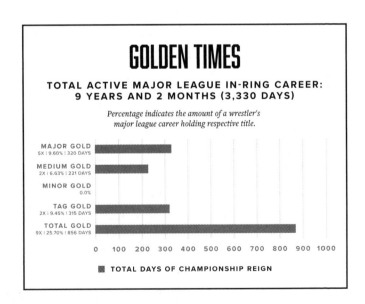

MAJOR GOLD
5X | 9.60% | 320 DAYS

MEDIUM GOLD
2X | 6.63% | 221 DAYS

MINOR GOLD
0.0%

TAG GOLD
2X | 9.45% | 315 DAYS

TOTAL GOLD
9X | 25.70% | 856 DAYS

TOTAL DAYS OF CHAMPIONSHIP REIGN

CM PUNK

STYLE: MAT TECHNICIAN

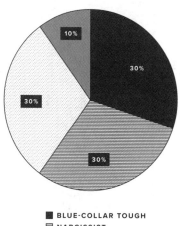

- ■ BLUE-COLLAR TOUGH
- ▦ NARCISSIST
- ☐ ROCK STAR
- ☐ PSYCHOPATH

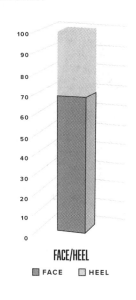

FACE/HEEL

- ▦ FACE
- ☐ HEEL

GOLDEN TIMES

TOTAL ACTIVE MAJOR LEAGUE IN-RING CAREER:
8 YEARS AND 11 MONTHS (3,246 DAYS)

Percentage indicates the amount of a wrestler's major league career holding respective title.

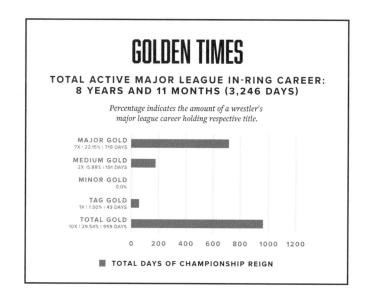

MAJOR GOLD
7X | 22.15% | 719 DAYS

MEDIUM GOLD
2X |5.88% | 191 DAYS

MINOR GOLD
0.0%

TAG GOLD
1X | 1.50% | 49 DAYS

TOTAL GOLD
10X | 29.54% | 959 DAYS

0   200   400   600   800   1000   1200

■ TOTAL DAYS OF CHAMPIONSHIP REIGN

ROMAN REIGNS

STYLE: POWERHOUSE

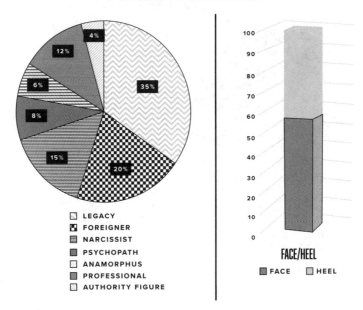

- ☐ LEGACY
- ▨ FOREIGNER
- ☰ NARCISSIST
- ▨ PSYCHOPATH
- ☐ ANAMORPHUS
- ▨ PROFESSIONAL
- ▨ AUTHORITY FIGURE

35%
4%
12%
6%
8%
15%
20%

FACE/HEEL

☐ FACE ☐ HEEL

GOLDEN TIMES

TOTAL ACTIVE MAJOR LEAGUE IN-RING CAREER: 10 YEARS (3,663 DAYS)

Percentage indicates the amount of a wrestler's major league career holding respective title.

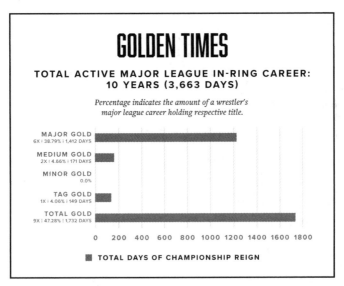

MAJOR GOLD
6X | 38.79% | 1,412 DAYS

MEDIUM GOLD
2X | 4.66% | 171 DAYS

MINOR GOLD
0.0%

TAG GOLD
1X | 4.06% | 149 DAYS

TOTAL GOLD
9X | 47.28% | 1,732 DAYS

0 200 400 600 800 1000 1200 1400 1600 1800

▨ TOTAL DAYS OF CHAMPIONSHIP REIGN

CHAPTER 3
THE KAUFMANS

The worlds of professional wrestling and cinema have had a long storied intertwined history together. *The Godfather* is considered one of, if not, the greatest film of all time. Among that exceptional cast was the Zebra Kid, aka Lenny Montana, who was cast as the memorable mobster Luca Brasi. Montana was able to hold his own with some acting greats and ever since professional wrestlers have been cast in everything from serious dramatic roles to spandex clad superheroes.

When Vince McMahon Jr. decided to put all his chips on the professional wrestling mega event known as WrestleMania, he looked toward Hollywood to hedge his bet. McMahon brought in popular television star Mr. T to tag with his company's biggest babyface, Hulk Hogan. The two herculean stars battled against Rowdy Roddy Piper and Paul Orndorff in the super card's main event. In an effort to give the big match a promotional boost, the unlikely pairing hosted *Saturday Night Live* the night before. Since the success of that historic weekend, the intersecting of Hollywood and professional wrestling has only grown.

At times professional wrestlers will cross over into Hollywood and, vice versa, Hollywood stars will cross over into the world of professional wrestling. For a professional wrestler to get that exclusive upper echelon household name stardom, they must have broad mainstream appeal. Nothing is more mainstream than appearing on the screens we constantly watch. Whether it's a brief cameo, a reoccurring role or even a leading role, countless professional wrestlers from the Bushwhackers to Bret Hart have used the world of television and film to increase their profile. Throughout the years both the world of professional wrestling and film and television have continuously borrowed from one another to captivate audiences.

In 1982, *Rocky III* provided that far-reaching audience for a promising professional wrestling talent going by the name of Hulk Hogan. His portrayal of Thunderlips elevated his career both in film and inside the squared circle. Toward the back end of his career, Hogan shrewdly leaned into his mainstream recognition, adopting the heel moniker of Hollywood Hulk Hogan. The moniker had a multitude of purposes. It served as a fresh heelish way for Hogan to flex his superiority to the audience. It also left fans wondering if Santa with Muscles really thought he was Mr. Hollywood. Boosted by his Hollywood credentials, Hogan was arguably professional wrestling's biggest star both in and out of the ring, this was the case until a young charismatic newcome propelled professional wrestling's Hollywood box office success to another level.

To the dismay of many film critics and classically trained thespians, Dwayne 'The Rock' Johnson is one of Hollywood's biggest box office draws. In the June 7, 2001, issue of *Rolling Stone*, the Rock became the first and only professional wrestler to grace one of pop culture's most iconic magazine covers. The tag line advertised the *Rolling Stone* article as a talk with Hollywood's next action hero. Boy did they get that right. It wasn't long before the Rock's undeniable charm, good looks, and athletic physique propelled him to the top of the movie star stratosphere. He is one of, if not the most, recognizable celebrities in the world and yet at his core he's still very much a professional wrestler.

The blend of Tinsel town and the world of the squared circle was exquisitely depicted in the 1999 Andy Kaufman biopic *Man on the Moon*. Jim Carrey's brilliant portrayal of Kaufman's gonzo comedy act gave us a glimpse into the iconic comedian's humorous blend of reality, comedy, and performance art. Andy was a master of the worked shoot long before most professional wrestling fans ever uttered the term. Kaufman and his professional wrestling coconspirator Jerry 'The King' Lawler, knew that professional wrestling, film, comedy, and sports were all essentially the same thing: entertainment.

Professional wrestling has the *Pro Wrestling Illustrated* awards. Motion pictures has the Oscars. Television has the Golden Globes. And now we have the Kaufmans, a prestigious award honoring the intermingling of professional wrestling, film, and television.

OUTSTANDING FIGHT IN A MOTION PICTURE
AND THE NOMINEES ARE:

☐ *Hulk Hogan v. Slyvester Stallone (*Rocky III*)*

☐ *John Cena v. Vin Diesel (*F9: The Fast Saga*)*

☐ *Dwayne 'The Rock' Johnson v. The Rebels (*The Rundown*)*

☐ *Dave Bautista v. Chung Tin-chi (*Master Z: IP Man Legacy*)*

☐ *Rowdy Roddy Piper v. Keith David (*They Live*)*

★★★★★

AND THE WINNER IS:

Rowdy Roddy Piper v. Keith David (They Live)

In John Carpenter's cult classic, our drifter hero, Nada, played by Rowdy Roddy Piper, discovers that America's ruling class is actually aliens in disguise. The number one debuting box office film was a commentary of Carpenter's dissatisfaction with Reaganomics and the commercialization of our culture. It entertainingly comments on the exploitation of the working class by the elites. Today, as we see numerous worker union's strike for a better cut of the profits, it is clear that the issues addressed in the film still resonate. Putting the thought-provoking social commentary aside for minute, that fight scene is something else.

Inspired by John Wayne's fight in *The Quiet Man*, Carpenter didn't rely on over-the-top special effects or uber unrealistic action sequences that defy the laws of physics. Instead, Carpenter put his trust in professional wrestling. Piper and David's famous "Alley Brawl" is a gritty realistic fight that brilliantly incorporates professional wrestling moves to achieve it's status as a six minute masterpiece. The two men use random weapons, eye gouging, biting, and below the belt shots to enhance the fights realism. Anything goes when you have no idea how far the other guy is willing to take it. In between all the flying fists the men execute backbody drops, drop toe holds, and suplexes in a way that somehow only adds to the fights' genuine feel. Complete with false finishes, the alley brawl serves as a stellar example of just how good a professional wrestling cinematic fight can be.

OUTSTANDING ANIMATED PERFORMANCE
AND THE NOMINEES ARE:

- [ ] John Cena (Ferdinand)
- [ ] Dwayne 'The Rock' Johnson (Moana)
- [ ] The Big Show - Paul Wight (The Jetsons & WWE: Robo-WrestleMania!)
- [ ] Rowdy Roddy Piper (Green Lantern: Emerald Knights)
- [ ] John Cena (Scooby Doo! WrestleMania Mystery)

★★★★★

Dwayne 'The Rock' Johnson (Moana)

Disney and the Rock-just feel like an unstoppable combination. If box office success is any indication, *Moana* is clearly the best picture in this category. It's the story of a teenage girl finding herself while exploring her culture. Moana learns about her heritage with the help of some island magic. The film lives up to the high-quality level of cinema you would expect from the entertainment juggernaut. Dwayne does a superb job of bringing his trademark wit and electric energy to the big screen in this animated performance. He even does a pretty decent job of belting out one of those catchy Disney tunes.

No other nominated movie was a big enough box office success to merit a live-action remake. Though, we are still hoping that the live-action *Scooby Doo! WrestleMania Mystery* eventually happens. The tentatively scheduled 2025 live action remake of *Moana* featuring Dwayne Johnson is sure to be a fun, action-packed ride. If the *Moana* remake is a success, it may lead to more future joint projects. It's a low blow to humanity that the Rock and Disney have yet to connect in the Marvel Universe. As they say in the world of professional wrestling, never say never.

OUTSTANDING COMEDIC PERFORMANCE
AND THE NOMINEES ARE:

- [ ] *The Big Show / Paul Wight* (The Waterboy)
- [ ] *Chris Jericho* (MacGruber)
- [ ] *Dwayne 'The Rock' Johnson* (Be Cool)
- [ ] *Dave Bautista* (Stuber)
- [ ] *John Cena* (Trainwreck)

★★★★★

AND THE WINNER IS:

John Cena (Trainwreck)

In 2012, on the *Howard Stern Show,* comedian Amy Schumer raucously and hilariously opened up about her real-life dating experiences, including her relationship with former World Wrestling Entertainment (WWE) superstar Dolph Ziggler. The two had plenty of what Schumer called "too athletic sex . . . that felt like they were wrestling." She went on to talk about how she got wrapped up in the fun of professional wrestling but ultimately the unlikely duo parted ways. Out of her reality the 2015 movie *Trainwreck* and John Cena's future role was born.

In 2024, on the *Howard Stern Show,* Cena stated that Schumer based his breakout character on an ex-boyfriend whom she had way too athletic sex with. Cena plays Schumer's beefed up, looking like "Mark Wahlberg ate Mark Wahlberg," very sensitive boyfriend. John brings unintentional homosexualized trash talk and a desperate desire to make Schumer his CrossFit queen to his short but memorable performance. For the record, we do not know for sure if Cena's character was based on or inspired by Dolph Ziggler. But we can speculate that maybe John used the role as a rib on Dolph—after all, there may have been some bad blood over their respective romances with Nikki Bella. Lots of unanswered questions here. What we do know is that Cena reportedly improvised his lines and managed to work in a Koko B. Ware reference. The Kaufmans award extra points for that.

OUTSTANDING GUEST APPEARANCE IN A TELEVISION SITCOM

AND THE NOMINEES ARE:

- [ ] *Rowdy Roddy Piper* (It's Always Sunny in Philadelphia)
- [ ] *King Kong Bundy* (Married with Children)
- [ ] *The Bushwhackers* (Family Matters)
- [ ] *Bret 'The Hitman' Hart* (The Simpsons)
- [ ] *Vader* (Boy Meets World)

★★★★★

AND THE WINNER IS:

Vader (Boy Meets World)

For those of growing up in the 1990's professional wrestling and *Boy Meets World* accompanied us from adolescence to adulthood. *Boy Meets World* is a coming-of-age sitcom that follows the life of an eleven-year-old boy in middle school named Corey Matthews. The series follows his young life up until he marries his lifelong love Topanga and moves away from his home town. During the 1990s, professional wrestling progressed from superheroes battling dungeons full of evil baddies to a landscape full of beer drinking anti-heroes, scantily clad women, and invading too cool gangs. It was a time when we shed our childhood innocence and started to understand the world from a more mature perspective.

In 1995 Leon White, aka the man they call Vader, made his acting debut on the beloved '90s sitcom *Boy Meets World*. In three episodes of the series, White played Francis 'Frankie' Stecchino, Sr. the father of the show's resident school yard bully Frankie Jr. His first appearance comes when Corey 'The Corey' Matthews joins the school's wrestling team and beats Frankie Jr.'s friend, Joey the Rat. In frustration, Joey demands an unsanctioned rematch and Corey bests him again. After the match, Vader steps into the ring but is backed down by the intervening school principal Mr. Feeny. In his second appearance, Vader briefly returns to encounter Feeny at the principal's office after his son gets into trouble for acting out because his friends have moved away.

Vader's final appearance comes in the memorable "Sixteen Candles and Four-Hundred-Pound Men" episode. In this episode, Corey is torn between helping his friend Frankie Jr. connect with his dad and attending Topanga's sweet sixteen birthday party. Frankie Jr., while an imposing man, is a sensitive soul who has little interest in professional wrestling. Frankie Sr. is the all too familiar professional wrestler who wants nothing more than for his sons to follow in his massive footsteps.

When the big wrestling match comes to town, Frankie Jr. calls upon wrestling fan Corey to join Vader's corner and help Frankie Jr. advise his father. Problem is, the match is the same night as Topanga's party. Corey agrees to attend both events and devises a *Flintstones*-modeled plan to go back and forth between the two events. Vader ultimately wins the match but Topanga busts Corey. After she realizes his intentions were well meaning, she forgives him, and the two share a special dance inside an empty arena wrestling ring. Vader's performance reminds us all that common interests, professional wrestling included, can strengthen all of our relationships.

OUTSTANDING GUEST APPEARANCE IN A TELEVISION DRAMA

AND THE NOMINEES ARE:

☐ *Lita (*Dark Angel*)*

☐ *Edge (*Haven*)*

☐ *Kane (*Smallville*)*

☐ *Cody Rhodes (*Arrow*)*

☐ *Rob Van Dam (*The X-Files*)*

★★★★★

AND THE WINNER IS:

Lita (Dark Angel)

When legendary film maker James Cameron made his television debut he teamed up with screenwriter and producer Charles H. Eglee and co-created *Dark Angel*. The science fiction drama starred Jessica Alba and continued Cameron's tradition of creating empowered female characters. The show opened big and had an overall positive first season both commercially and critically. Due to a drop of viewership, the show being a big budget production, and the network wanting to move on to other projects, the series was cancelled.

In 2002, Lita played the role of Thula, the leader of a clan of warriors named the Phalanx, who entered the series during its finale. Thula had little screen time and even fewer lines. Lita did get to flex her combat skills when she partook in a battle royal action sequence, which included everything from weaponized mannequin body parts to desks crashing upon fallen bodies. Ultimately, Jessica Alba's super solider character would defeat her. Alba's character, despite being the hero, pulled a classic heel move and handcuffed Lita around a pillar. It would have been a fun little part that helped say goodbye to a short-lived but loved series had the whole experience not jeopardized Lita's entire professional wrestling career.

During production Lita performed her signature hurricanrana move but was unable to fully rotate and landed awkwardly on her neck. Reports suggest that the stunt double she was working with dropped her while they were rehearsing the move. Lita sustained three cracked vertebrate and was out of in-ring action for seventeen months. It was a tough setback for a rising star who only a year earlier made her WrestleMania debut. For all her sacrifices to entertain us, the Kaufmans salute you.

OUTSTANDING TAG TEAM PERFORMANCE IN A MOTION PICTURE

AND THE NOMINEES ARE:

☐ Dwayne 'The Rock' Johnson and Zac Efron (Baywatch)

☐ Dwayne 'The Rock' Johnson and Sean Williams Scott (The Rundown)

☐ Dwayne 'The Rock' Johnson and Kevin Hart (Central Intelligence)

☐ Dwayne 'The Rock' Johnson and Mark Wahlberg (Pain and Gain)

☐ Dwayne 'The Rock' Johnson and Jason Statham (Hobbs and Shaw)

★★★★★

AND THE WINNER IS:

Dwayne 'The Rock' Johnson and Sean Williams Scott
(The Rundown)

Ever since the Rock and Sock connection angle graced our televisions, Dwayne Johnson has appreciated a good buddy pairings' box office potential. About five months after ending his full-time professional wrestling career, the Rock won the weekend box office when *The Rundown* opened as the number one movie in America. It was the Rock's second leading role but his first without any franchise support. *The Scorpion King* was his first leading role, but it had *The Mummy* franchise and all of its fans to lean on.

The film opens with an intense fight scene between Dwayne Johnson and a gang of football players. Soon after the fight Johnson is sent to Brazil to retrieve a mob boss's wayward son and the film quickly becomes an *Indiana Jones* meets *Rambo* mashup. In the jungle the Rock battles everyone from local rebels to corrupt foreign miners. While Sean Williams Scott aka Stifler's comedy feels corny and dated, the Rock's action sequences are a thrilling rollercoaster ride. The film has some acting heavyweights with Rosario Dawson and Christopher Walken playing major roles, but it is Dwayne 'The Rock' Johnson who carries this team. Johnson proved to the major movie studios that he can take any tag partner and turn it into a winning team.

OUTSTANDING BABYFACE PERFORMANCE IN A MOTION PICTURE

AND THE NOMINEES ARE:

- [ ] *Hulk Hogan (*No Holds Barred*)*
- [ ] *John Cena (*Peacemaker*)*
- [ ] *Dwayne 'The Rock' Johnson (*G.I. Joe: Retaliation*)*
- [ ] *Dave Bautista (*Guardians of the Galaxy*)*
- [ ] *Jesse 'The Body' Ventura (*Predator*)*

★★★★★

AND THE WINNER IS:

Hulk Hogan (No Holds Barred)

Train, say your prayers, and take your vitamins, there isn't a more wholesome babyface message in the history of professional wrestling than Hulk Hogan's immortal demandments. In his first leading role, Hogan changes out of the familiar red and yellow and wears baby blue and white as he steps into the boots of Rip Thomas. When Rip spurns the business propositions of the evil television network executive Mr. Brell, all hell breaks loose.

The Rip Hulk fights off would be rapists, has his family brutalized, and battles harden ex-cons just as one might expect a Saturday morning cartoon star to do. Mr. Brell recruits Zeus to be his champion and fight Hogan to the death. The feud culminates in a no-holds-barred championship match. Rip Hulk, looking like a golden-haired, furless Chewbacca, saves the girl, avenges his family, and kills the bad guys. Rip em'. It's all a badly-acted, campy, ultraviolent, feel-good story that only a true babyface can deliver.

OUTSTANDING HEEL PERFORMANCE IN A MOTION PICTURE
AND THE NOMINEES ARE:

- [ ] *Kane (*See No Evil*)*
- [ ] *Samoa Joe (*Twisted Metal*)*
- [ ] *Nathan Jones (*Mad Max: Fury Road*)*
- [ ] *Kurgan (*300*)*
- [ ] *Dave Bautista (*Master Z: The IP Man Legacy*)*

★ ★ ★ ★ ★

Dave Bautista (Master Z: The IP Man Legacy)

It's a longstanding tradition for North American wrestlers to travel to Asia, particularly Japan, to gain international fame, collect a solid paycheck, and help build the local promotions' stars. The North American wrestlers are welcomed as foreigners called *gaijin* and more often than not are cast in the heel role. Stan Hansen, Bruiser Brody, and Abdulla the Buther all became top heels in Japan as they embraced the role of the bulky menacing gaijin. This Chinese marital arts film set in Hong Kong, *Master Z: The IP Man Legacy* cast Dave Bautista as its main villain and built upon the tradition established by their Pacific Ocean neighbors.

The effects of imperialism and the exploitive culture that surround it are central themes in this action-packed martial arts movie. Under the bright neon lights of a popular entertainment district, an opium epidemic plagues the streets of Hong Kong. Using the cover of a steakhouse owner and philanthropist Owen Davidson, played by Bautista, is a sinister drug smuggling syndicate boss.

Bautista uses his corrupt influence to frame Cheung Tin-chi's (the film's hero) right-hand man Fu after his family's interference with his illegal drug dealings. In an unfair fight, where Fu is handcuffed, Dave executes a Batista bomb on Fu, killing him. The hero learns of this and the Animal is now the final boss on his quest for vengeance and justice.

Cheung Tin-chi comes to the steakhouse for revenge, a fight ensues and Bautista's brute strength is tested against the hero's lightning-fast Wing Chun kung fu attacks. During a pivotal point of the fight, Bautista attempts another devastating power bomb only this time Cheung Tin-chi uses a hurricanrana to reverse it. Even Kung Fu experts can expand their fighting repertoire with some professional wrestling moves. Cheung Tin-chi dropkicks Bautista out of a window and emerges victorious. The evil foreigners are defeated and the local population rejoices as justice finally prevails. Bautista did his duty and the local hero went over.

LIFETIME ACHIEVEMENT AWARD
El Santo

AND THE WINNER IS:

El Santo

Rodolfo Guzmán Huerta, aka El Santo, starred in at least fifty-three films throughout his twenty year plus professional wrestling and film career. After establishing a successful lucha libre career, El Santo grew larger than life starring in a comic book that ran for over thirty-five years. The masked legend playing a professional wrestler moonlighting as a superhero battled every kind of villain there is. Over the course of his storied career El Santo became as iconic to Mexican culture as Superman is to America.

Well before the American professional wrestling superstars invaded the DC or Marvel cinematic universe, El Santo expanded his entertainment career and battled the forces of evil on the silver screen. His thespian range extended from battling vampires to mummies to werewolves. Basically, if a demonic creature has their costume inside a Spirt Halloween store, chances are El Santo fought it.

After close to five decades of staying true to kayfabe and never being publicly seen without his mask, El Santo appeared on a televised Mexican talk show and shockingly unmasked himself. Ten days later he passed away. His funeral was among the largest Mexico has ever seen. A giant statue of El Santo was erected in his hometown. Today El Santo is widely known as one of the greatest legends of Mexican sports and in all of professional wrestling.

OUTSTANDING USE OF A WRESTLING MOVE IN FILM
AND THE NOMINEES ARE:

- [ ] *Dwayne 'The Rock' Johnson—Rock Bottom (Furious 7)*
- [ ] *Hulk Hogan—Atomic Leg Drop (Rocky III)*
- [ ] *'Macho Man' Randy Savage—Flying Elbow Drop (Spider-Man)*
- [ ] *Jerry 'The King' Lawler—Pile Driver (Girls Gone Dead)*
- [ ] *Dave Bautista—Batista Bomb (Man in the Iron Fists)*

★ ★ ★ ★ ★

AND THE WINNER IS:

Dwayne 'The Rock' Johnson (Furious 7)

The year was 2017, I was sitting in a packed movie theater with my brother in-law, our wives went to another theater to watch a film with more emotion and less horsepower. Ironically, this movie elicited the most emotional reaction I've ever experienced sitting in those leather reclining seats while soaking in that popcorn-filled air. It wasn't one of those sad movie moments that make you ponder your morality, but it was truly moving.

Dwayne 'The Rock' Johnson and Jason Statham were battling it out in an epic fight. Statham surprises Johnson with a desk flip followed by a flying kick to the chest. From then on, it's Johnson's raw power versus Statham's educated quick strike attacks. Things are about even when the Rock grabs Statham and hits him with the rock bottom. The impact is so hard the camera tilts to the side. It took everything in me to not jump out of my seat and yell "Rock bottom!" in the loudest JR voice I could muster. That dear reader must have been what Roger Ebert was referring to when he said, "Art is the closest we can come to understanding how a stranger really feels."

OUTSTANDING PERFORMANCE BY AN ACTOR INSIDE THE SQUARED CIRCLE

AND THE NOMINEES ARE:

☐ *Andy Kaufman v. Jerry 'The King' Lawler (*Memphis Wrestling*)*

☐ *David Arquette v. Nick Gage (CZW)*

☐ *Mr. T and Hulk Hogan v. Rowdy Roddy Piper and 'Mr. Wonderful' Paul Orndorff (WWE)*

☐ *Stephen Amell and Pac (Neville) v. Cody Rhodes and Wade Barrett (WWE)*

☐ *Johnny Knoxville v. Sami Zayn (WWE)*

★★★★★

AND THE WINNER IS:

David Arquette (CZW)

For most of us, it baffles our mind when we hear that a forty-seven-year-old established actor worth millions of dollars wants to risk his body inside of a professional wrestling ring. Our confusion grows when we find out that this actor doesn't want to participate in just a regular professional wrestling match but he wants to do a bloody deathmatch. It gets even worse when we learn that his opponent is real life convicted felon and the deathmatch legend known as Nick Gage. Once we learn that all this madness is set to go down inside a three hundred person capacity venue, what's left of our brains turn to mush.

The whole insane story is told in the 2020 documentary *You Cannot Kill David Arquette*. Ever since 2000 when Arquette won the World Championship Wrestling (WCW) heavyweight title, David has felt he owed a huge debt to the world of professional wrestling. Arquette never made a dime from that infamous WCW title debacle. Instead he donated the money to the families of several tragedy-stricken professional wrestlers. Despite his generosity, many professional wrestling fans hated the fact that an unworthy actor won the prestigious belt and it took it out on Arquette. In 2018, Arquette, who was still searching for redemption in the eyes of professional wrestling fans, found one hell of a way to try and win them over.

The match's brutality can make even the most seasoned professional wrestling fans squeamish. Arquette throws fists, hits a hurricanrana, flying cross bodies, and gets in some serious chair shots against Gage. Arquette gets thrown through tables, sliced with a pizza cutter, and pummeled with fluorescent lightbulbs. During all this carnage, Arquette's neck was badly cut, causing him to end the match and be rushed to the hospital. If that's not enough to earn some respect among professional wrestling fans, then nothing is.

OUTSTANDING DOCUMENTARY ON PROFESSIONAL WRESTLING

AND THE NOMINEES ARE:

- [ ] Beyond the Mat
- [ ] Hitman Hart: Wrestling with Shadows
- [ ] André the Giant
- [ ] The Resurrection of Jake the Snake
- [ ] Wooooooo! Becoming Ric Flair
- [ ] Dark Side of the Ring - Benoit

★ ★ ★ ★ ★

AND THE WINNER IS:

Beyond the Mat

Perhaps the most competitive category in the coveted Kaufman awards. There is a minefield of documentaries depicting the lives and stories surrounding the world of professional wrestling. *Beyond the Mat* is a groundbreaking documentary that paved the way for the whole behind the scenes of professional wrestling documentary genre. Once you get past the narrator's unfamiliarity with the professional wrestling business, it is apparent that this documentary's inside look into the often ruthless world of professional wrestling is something special.

The world of professional wrestling has a plethora of captivating characters but if you really want to expose the brutality of the business who better to revolve your story around than wrestling legends Jake 'the Snake' Roberts, Terry Funk, and Mick Foley. Jake is a man seemingly born into the dark side of the ring and subsequently plagued by substance abuse addiction. His troubled soul clings to the past, as his present self is plagued by addiction and struggles to produce anything of value.

Terry Funk is that all too familiar old-timer who is still willing to risk it all for one more shot of in-ring adrenaline. The hardcore Texas legend struggles to reluctantly hang up his boots. Mick Foley is that professional wrestler who, arguably, takes it too far inside of the ring, much to the detriment of his body and his family's mental health. The cringe-worthy scenes of Mick Foley's children screaming in terror as their dad is hammered eleven times by unprotected stiff chair shots to the head is about as real as any scripted program ever gets. All three men display the undeniable pain that a life of professional wrestling can cause.

Vince McMahon's perpetual struggle to develop new characters in an ever-evolving business offers an intriguing glimpse into the creative side of professional wrestling. Watching him light up like a kid at Christmas as he pitches the puke gimmick to Droz never gets old. The never-ending pool of new talent helps us somewhat understand why guys like Jake, Terry, and Mick do the dangerous things they do. Yet despite all the brutality and sorrow, the three legendary wrestlers in this documentary just love it to death. The world of professional wrestling is like a drug, with all the same highs and lows.

OUTSTANDING SUPPORTING ACTOR
AND THE NOMINEES ARE:

- [ ] *Hulk Hogan (*Rocky III)
- [ ] *Jerry 'The King' Lawler (*Man on the Moon)
- [ ] *Dave Bautista (*Guardians of the Galaxy)
- [ ] *André the Giant (*Princess Bride)
- [ ] *Lenny Montana (*The Godfather)

★ ★ ★ ★ ★

AND THE WINNER IS:

André the Giant (Princess Bride)

Another very competitive field in the prestigious Kaufman awards. All of these five men have a compelling case for walking away with the golden Andy. These major Hollywood productions all sought squared circle veterans to round out their colorful casts of characters. From serious biopics to Marvel juggernauts and everything in between, these films showcase the acting range professional wrestlers bring to the silver screen.

When acclaimed director Rob Reiner decided to bring William Gold's fairytale fantasy novel to a live-action portrayal, perhaps no human on Earth was more suited to be cast in this mythical world than André the Giant. Reiner stated that André's in-ring instincts made him a natural actor. André the Giant's authentic depiction of the imposing Fezzik was a vital part to the success of one of the most iconic fantasy movies of all-time. When we first meet Fezzik he is hired muscle for the cunning Sicilian, Vizzini, a man who very much feels like an old school professional wrestling heel manager. As the film progresses, André switches alliances and turns face. The Eighth Wonder of the World is now aiding the hero on his quest to save the princess.

One exchange in the film highlights the essence of André the Giant, Billy Crystal yells to a knocking André: "I'll call the brute force." "I'm on the brute force," André replies. Crystal opens his front door window, gazes at the immense André, and quips, "You are the brute force." If you disagree with this winner, go ahead and grab the Andy out of André's 16-inch hands.

OUTSTANDING PERFORMANCE BY AN ACTRESS IN A MOTION PICTURE

AND THE NOMINEES ARE:

- ☐ *Mercedes Moné (*The Mandalorian*)*
- ☐ *Awesome Kong (GLOW)*
- ☐ *Ronda Rousey (*The Expendables 3*)*
- ☐ *Becky Lynch (*Young Rock*)*
- ☐ *Eve Torres (*Skiptrace*)*

★ ★ ★ ★ ★

Awesome Kong (GLOW)

During the 1980s, David McLane created an empowering all-female professional wrestling promotion known as the Gorgeous Ladies of Wrestling (GLOW). If the National Wrestling Alliance (NWA) was professional wrestling's Tim Burton's Batman, then GLOW was the Adam West version. GLOW was an exciting new promotion full of goofy comedy, on the nose gimmicks, and B-movie flash. Rather than recruiting experienced professional wrestlers, McLane sought out entertainers from a variety of genres to be his stars. Once he had his roster in place, he turned to professional wrestling legend Mando Guerrero to train his ladies. McLane found a venue to serve as his studio, put together a production team, found outlets to syndicate his programming, and the promotion was off and running.

Out of this unreal true story, Netflix created a fictionalized version of the groundbreaking promotion with aptly titled *GLOW* show. Kia Stevens, or more commonly known to professional wrestling fans as Awesome Kong, takes on the role of a struggling single mother who finds work in the crazy world of 1980's professional wrestling. Kong adopts the heel gimmick of the Welfare Queen, a black woman who leans in to America's racial prejudices and flaunts her abuse of the social services system. Her struggle with providing for her family and preserving her dignity is a compelling empathy inducing dilemma. Kong's passionate portrayal spotlights America's racial prejudices and the professional wrestling industries subsequent capitalization of them.

OUTSTANDING PERFORMANCE BY AN ACTOR IN A MOTION PICTURE

AND THE NOMINEES ARE:

- [ ] *Dwayne 'The Rock' Johnson (*Hobbs and Shaw*)*
- [ ] *Hulk Hogan (*No Holds Barred*)*
- [ ] *Dave Bautista (*Stuber*)*
- [ ] *John Cena (*12 Rounds*)*
- [ ] *Rowdy Roddy Piper (*They Live*)*

★ ★ ★ ★ ★

AND THE WINNER IS:

Dwayne 'The Rock' Johnson (Hobbs and Shaw)

There is no argument that Rock's filmography is the most impressive of anyone that has ever stepped foot inside the squared circle. The question may not have been so much as would Dwayne 'The Rock' Johnson wins this category but rather which movie would he win it for. Luke Hobbs in *Hobbs and Shaw* is a certified badass violently reconnecting with his past both professionally and personally.

In *Hobbs and Shaw*, the Rock mixed his Samoan badass gimmick with the franchise's fast paced action and created a big screen triumph. Johnson teaming with Statham seeks his estranged families help in battling the evil terrorists who are hunting them down. Roman Reigns is chief among those Samoans who answer his call. Years before Roman started calling himself the Tribal Chief, the Rock helped the Big Dog see the box office potential of tapping into his cultural heritage. When it comes to being a kick ass action movie star, not many have done it bigger or better than Dwayne 'The Rock' Johnson.

OUTSTANDING MOTION PICTURE ON PROFESSIONAL WRESTLING

AND THE NOMINEES ARE:

- [ ] The Wrestler
- [ ] Fighting with My Family
- [ ] The Iron Claw
- [ ] Heels
- [ ] Nacho Libre
- [ ] No Holds Barred

★★★★★

AND THE WINNER IS:

The Wrestler

This film artfully crafts a gritty portrayal of an all too familiar professional wrestling life full of pain and sorrow. *The Wrestler* was marvelously cast with Mickey Rourke, Marisa Tomie, and Evan Rachel Woods all delivering masterful performances. In

Rourke's case it would, arguably, be the finest work of his seasoned acting career. If any professional wrestler lasts as long in the business as Rourke's Randy 'The Ram' Robinson character did, they may find themselves dealing with many of the same struggles highlighted in the film.

The Ram copes with trying to succeed in a physical profession while having a worn-down body, a drug dependency, and a disenfranchised family. The aging wrestler is unable to move past his glory days and gracefully accept the times he lives in. Any actor can attest that a film set has a certain romantic air about it, the same is true for a professional wrestler stepping into that big arena. Droves of people eagerly line up just to see you. When the bright lights are turned on and the crowd roars, perhaps nothing is as intoxicating. It can be quiet, the fall to end up working at your local grocery store a few short years later. When you clock out and plop down on the couch with an intensely aching body, one can start to think about whether it was all worth it.

Marisa Tomie's aging stripper character is struggling with her body not attracting the customers as it once did. Her character brilliantly illustrates just how universal the problems facing professional wrestlers are. For some, their body and all it offers is an essential part of their identity. When that body starts failing them, it can be a tough adjustment. We all get old, but for those who rely on their bodies to make a living the process can become a particularly arduous one.

Notwithstanding these universalities, the pure brutality of the hardcore match between the Ram and Necro Butcher showcases just how unique the world of professional wrestling is. The Ram's finisher, an off the top rope dive, demonstrates the sacrifices wrestlers make for the pop of the crowd. It is no coincidence that the move is strikingly similar to Chris Benoit's diving head-butt. Just witnessing all this violence is enough to make the viewer reach for a bottle of pain killers.

Many moments in the movie do an exceptional job of depicting the bright and dark sides of professional wrestling. Rourke shows the pure joy the Ram gets when hanging out with the boys in the back, performing in the ring, and reliving his past glory. He also shows the deep sorrow the Ram deals with in failing to make amends with his family because he can't resist the addictive drug lifestyle. We sympathize with the Ram as he realizes that his past professional wrestling success isn't as important to most people as he would like to believe it is. It's powerful and saddening when we see Ram appreciate that the only worthwhile relationship he has had throughout his entire life is the one with the squared circle.

TIMELINE OF SIGNIFICANT ROLES IN
PROFESSIONAL WRESTLING CINEMATIC HISTORY

ALIAS THE CHAMP
Gorgeous George (Himself),
Various Wrestlers
1949

SOME LIKE IT HOT
Mike Mazurki
(Spats' Henchman)
1959

YOU ONLY LIVE ONCE
Peter Maivia
(Car Driver/Henchmen)
1967

PARADISE ALLEY
Terry Funk (Frankie 'The Thumper'),
Various Wrestlers
1978

THE MUPPET MOVIE
Hard Boiled Haggerty
(Lumberjack)
1979

INDIANA JONES: RAIDERS OF THE LOST ARK
Pat Roach
(Giant Sherpa)
1981

PREDATOR
Jesse Ventura
(Blain)
1987

THE PRINCESS BRIDE
André the Giant
(Fezzik)
1987

THEY LIVE
Roddy Piper
(Nada)
1988

TEENAGE MUTANT NINJA TURTLES II: THE SECRET OF THE OOZE
Kevin Nash (Super Shredder)
1991

SUBURBAN COMMANDO
Hulk Hogan (Shep Ramsey),
The Undertaker (Hutch)
1991

3 NINJAS
Toru Tanaka
(Rushmore)
1992

MAN ON THE MOON
Jerry Lawler (Himself)
1999

READY TO RUMBLE
WCW Roster at time
2000

X-MEN
Tyler Mane
(Sabertooth)
2000

THE GODFATHER
*Lenny Montana
(Luca Brasi)*

1972

**THE CASTLE OF
MUMMIES
OF GUANAJUATO**
*Blue Demon, El Santo,
Mil Mascaras*

1973

THE WRESTLER
*Verne Gagne (Mike Bullard),
Various Wrestlers*

1974

ROCKY III
*Hulk Hogan
(Thunderlips)*

1982

**CONAN THE
DESTROYER**
*André the Giant
(Dagoth)*

1984

BODY SLAM
*Roddy Piper
(Quick Rick Roberts)*

1986

ROAD HOUSE
*Terry Funk
(Morgan)*

1989

NO HOLDS BARRED
*Hulk Hogan (Rip),
Various Wrestlers*

1989

PROBLEM CHILD
*Kerry Von Erich
(Neo-Nazi)*

1990

ED WOOD
*George 'The Animal' Steele
(Tor Johnson)*

1994

**DIE HARD WITH
A VENGEANCE**
*Ludviga Borga (Roman),
Damien DeMento (Erik)*

1995

THE WATERBOY
*Paul 'Big Show' Wight
(Captain Insano)*

1998

**HIGHLANDER:
ENDGAME**
*Edge
(Lachlan)*

2000

**THE
MUMMY
RETURNS**
*Dwayne 'The Rock' Johnson
(Scorpion King)*

2001

**THE
SCORPION
KING**
*Dwayne 'The Rock' Johnson
(Scorpion King)*

2002

TIMELINE OF SIGNIFICANT ROLES IN
PROFESSIONAL WRESTLING CINEMATIC HISTORY

SPIDER-MAN
Randy Savage
(Bone Saw McGraw)
2002

SLAVES OF THE REALM
Sable (Shira)
2003

THE RUNDOWN
Dwayne 'The Rock' Johnson
(Beck)
2003

SEE NO EVIL
Kane
(Jacob Goodnight)
2006

THE MARINE
John Cena
(John Triton)
2006

300
Kurrgan
(Uber Immortal—Giant)
2006

MACGRUBER
Chris Jericho (Frank Korver),
Various Wrestlers
2010

THE EXPENDABLES
Steve Austin
(Paine)
2010

FAST FIVE
Dwayne 'The Rock' Johnson
(Luke Hobbs)
2011

CONFESSIONS OF A WOMANIZER
Nikki Bella (Erica),
Brie Bella (Sally)
2014

PRO WRESTLERS VS ZOMBIES
Roddy Piper (Himself),
Shane Douglas (Himself),
Various Wrestlers
2014

GUARDIANS OF THE GALAXY
Dave Bautista
(Drax)
2014

GIRL ON THE THIRD FLOOR
CM Punk
(Don Koch)
2019

FAST & FURIOUS PRESENTS: HOBBS & SHAW
Dwayne 'The Rock' Johnson
(Luke Hobbs),
Roman Reigns (Mateo)
2019

THE SUICIDE SQUAD
John Cena
(Peacemaker)
2021

THE PUNISHER
Kevin Nash
(The Russian)
2004

BE COOL
Dwayne 'The Rock' Johnson
(Elliot Wilhelm)
2005

THE LONGEST YARD
Bill Goldberg (Battle),
Kevin Nash (Guard Engleheart),
Steve Austin (Guard Dunham)
2005

THE CONDEMNED
Steve Austin
(Jack Conrad)
2007

THE WRESTLER
Ernest Miller (The Ayatollah),
Various Wrestlers
2008

TOOTH FAIRY
Dwayne 'The Rock' Johnson
(Derek)
2010

WARRIOR
Kurt Angle
(Koba)
2011

MAGIC MIKE
Kevin Nash
(Tarzan)
2012

PITCH PERFECT
Lana
(Barden Bella)
2012

MADMAX:
FURY ROAD
Nathan Jones
(Rictus Erectus)
2015

BUMBLEBEE
John Cena
(Agent Burns)
2018

FIGHTING WITH
MY FAMILY
Dwayne 'The Rock'
Johnson (Himself),
Zelina Vega (AJ Lee),
Various Wrestlers
2019

BLACK ADAM
Dwayne 'The Rock' Johnson
(Black Adam)
2022

THE COLLECTIVE
Mercedes Moné
(Nikita)
2023

THE IRON CLAW
Maxwell Jacob Friedman
(Lance Von Erich),
Various Wrestlers
2023

CHAPTER 4

RACE AND THE RING

Professional wrestling is pretty far from what mainstream society would consider a serious cultural art form. Many people think it's just gigantic dudes grunting and slamming each other around and sure, there is plenty of that! But there is so much more. No, it's not the same experience as watching an Oscar worthy film that really tugs on your heartstrings or listening to a powerful ballad that makes one contemplate the ills of society. It's different but that's kind of the joy of it. We can escape from the seriousness of life and wrap ourselves up in their crazy world of professional wrestling.

No one is arguing that professional wrestling is akin to Shakespeare, yet any promoter who offers a wrestling show to the world surely has some kind of moral obligation to society. There are lessons gathered from every piece of cultural art we consume. Art in all forms often helps formulate public opinions. If you're going to offer up a work of art to the masses, some consideration should be placed into what that content, whether intentional or not, promotes. Professional wrestling is no exception.

Professional wrestling is full of stories depicting racist backstage incidents. With so many people involved in the production of professional wrestling and the ever-evolving racial climate in

America it's no surprise that such stories exist. The truth of many of those incidents is disputed. For this discussion, we're not going to focus on the transpirings of the various backstage locker rooms. We are going to focus on the actual product being offered up for public consumption: the shows. Professional wrestling's history is full of racially insensitive storylines and gimmicks that repeatedly occur inside of the squared circle. It is a little harder to dispute what actually happened when it's on videotape and broadcast for the world to see.

Race and the ring is an ever-evolving state of affairs. Society has come a long way from the days of segregation. Is it fair to judge any fictional character or storyline regardless of when it was created by contemporary standards? That's a challenging question. I would submit that yes, it is. However, the critique of the work fails if it does not account for the times in which it was created, the overall value of the product created, and the outright offensiveness level of the work as perceived when it was created and by modern standards.

The Simpsons is critically acclaimed, many hail it as one of the greatest television show ever created. Whether we wanted to admit it or not, that loving yet dysfunctional yellow family taught us many lessons over the years. We laugh and learn from the characters, from the well thought out moral compass of Lisa to the less reasoned yet hysterical logic of Homer. Does *The Simpsons* portray racial and ethnic stereotypes? Absolutely. The documentary titled *The Problem with Apu* highlighted some of the hurt that people feel from these seemingly innocent comical portrayals. Apu was not alone in *The Simpsons'* stereotype rolodex. Cookie Kwan (the real-estate agent of Asian descent), Bumblebee man (the star of a Spanish language sitcom of Latino descent), Fat Tony (the mob boss of Italian descent), and Groundskeeper Willie (the Scottish groundskeeper at Springfield Elementary) are just a few of the overly exaggerated ethnic caricatures that occupy Springfield.

Do we acknowledge that *The Simpsons* has problematic aspects to it? Well, what doesn't? Do we still love it? Well, if thirty plus years of being on the air is any indicator . . . yeah, we do. That's the thing about art as a reflection of society, it doesn't have to be perfectly politically correct to still be good. *The Simpsons* is eerily good at being reflective of the past, predicting where society may be headed, and commenting on the topical issues of the day. The world viewed through the lens of *The Simpsons* is enough material for a series of books.

While professional wrestling doesn't come close to the mainstream critical acclaim *The Simpsons* has garnered, its television presence does share a similar longevity. Like *The Simpsons*, the often cartoon world of professional wrestling teaches us, well . . . something? Sometimes they beat us over the head with whatever it is they're selling, like when Hulk Hogan clad in the red, white, and blue beats down the evil foreigner. Sometimes we have to think a little harder. *Wait, should I cheer for Bret or Austin here?* Whether it is the wholesome training, say your prayers, and eating your vitamins or the more jaded don't trust anyone philosophy, there are some worthwhile life lessons to soak in when you're watching action-figure-esque adults pummel each other.

Remember the old adage that ponders if art is a reflection of reality or if reality is a reflection of art. Probably both are right to some degree. What does race and professional wrestling say about us? What do we say about professional wrestling and race? The collaborative venture that is sports entertainment for better or worse echoes the problems in society. Race is no exception.

The history of professional wrestling in America is reflective of the larger racial issues that plagued and continue to plague our society. Whether intentional or not, what happens in the world of professional wrestling is a mirror of the fan's desires, their tolerances, and in some cases their bigotry. In the golden age (1940s–1950s), dark-skinned professional wrestling fans were forced to segregate from the white audience members. They were made to sit in the venue's upper decks. Usually, due to local laws, the wrestling promoters' hands were tied regarding the situation.

During this time, African-American wrestlers were not even allowed to play the heel. The promoters of the day legitimately feared that a black heel using dastardly heel tactics against a white babyface would cause a riot. The Fabulous Moolah, at the time known as 'Slave Girl' Moolah, was serving as a valet and was paired with a dark-complexioned Mexican dubbed the Elephant Boy whom was billed as hailing from "darkest Africa." On one occasion in Oklahoma, she kissed him on the cheek, spurring a fan to rush to the ring and slash her with a knife. It was as real as reality gets.

In the early days of modern-day professional wrestling, several pioneering superstars paved the way for all minorities in the business. Bearcat Wright was an immensely popular wrestler who is well remembered for being a pioneer against racial segregation. It is well known that he refused to wrestle on cards that were segregated or in front of segregated crowds. Five days before Martin Luther King Jr.'s "I have a dream" speech, Bearcat broke through the racial tensions and captured the World Wrestling Association (WWA) world heavyweight championship from 'Classy' Freddie Blassie. Though it's a significant moment, this accomplishment is not considered a major world championship win as, contrary to its name, the World Wrestling Association was more of a regional promotion rather than a national or worldwide one.

Houston Harris, commonly known to wrestling fans as Bobo Brazil, is another wrestler often credited with breaking down the racial segregation barriers in professional wrestling. Brazil won over fans of all races despite at times being banned from certain restaurants, hotels, and even wrestling venues due to segregation. He is credited with preforming in Atlanta's first racially integrated match and would later serve as a mentor to fellow black wrestler Rocky 'Soulman' Johnson.

Bobo was not alone in paving the way for the black community. Standing at 6'9", the 'Big Cat' Ernie Ladd was one of the first African-Americans to take on the hated heel persona. He wasn't the only person of color in the heel locker room, the half African-American, half Blackfoot Indian, 100 percent heel known as Abdullah the Butcher terrorized babyfaces up and down the wrestling territories. Abdullah was so hated he was considered a special attraction capable of drawing fans to the show. The 'Junkyard Dog' Sylvester Ritter and The Soul Patrol, a tag team consisting of Rocky Johnson and Tony Atlas, were heavily over fan favorites. These men were pivotal in showing the professional wrestling industry that African-American wrestlers could play a wide variety of characters.

Latinos also had a powerful impact on the industry with professional wrestling greats such as Gory Guerrero, Pepper Gomez, Miguel Peréz Sr., Argentina Apollo and Pedro Morales all leaving their mark on American professional wrestling. Miguel Peréz Sr. and Argentina Apollo are credited as the first tag team champions in World Wrestling Entertainment (WWE) history. The Puerto Rican native Pedro Morales had one of the longest WWE world championship runs, holding the major gold from February 8, 1971, until December 1, 1973, a whooping 1,027-day reign. This long reign is a clear sign that Morales had crossover appeal and was loved by more than just those in the Latino community.

Professional wrestling is now and has been for some time an international game. During the sixties and seventies, other nationalities and races were also represented and offered great contributions to the world of American professional wrestling. Wahoo McDaniel, High Chief Peter Maivia, The Sheik, Giant Baba, Mr. Fuji, The Wild Samoans, The Iron Sheik, and many more have left their legacies on the industry. The professional wrestling world's need for a diverse cast of characters meant there was room for all, but for anyone of color that usually meant they were routinely saddled with a race-related gimmick.

Though not the first gimmick with deep racial undertones, Kamala the Ugandan Giant is widely regarded as one of the most racist gimmicks in the business. James Harris, an African-American southern farmer, portrayed the painted African savage who came down to the ring carrying a spear, wearing a tribal mask and a leopard print skirt known as Kamala. The Ugandan Giant was so uncivilized, in the professional wrestling storyline that is, that he needed a handler to compete in any organized sporting event. The controversial, yet beloved by many, character would pat his belly and grunt while the over stimulation of modern society continuously startled him. At the time it was thought that he was a perfect monster and foreign menace foil for any all-American protagonist to battle with.

While the African wild man Kamala can certainly be interpreted as offensive, he was far from being the only "savage" portrayed in the ring. The beastly Samoan wrestler was a common occurrence in the ring. Paired with wrestling manager great Captain Lou Albano, the Wild Samoan's left absolutely no doubt about what their gimmick was all about. Similarly, John Nord portrayed a savage Viking known as the Berserker and was also paired with a handler. The Icelandic Norseman was managed by a stereotypical evil Asian character named Mr. Fuji. While the wild savage gimmick has come in many shapes and colors, it is telling that none have evoked the same racial controversy as Kamala. Perhaps it's America's shameful history with slavery. Real racism can be powerfully hurtful. It's no wonder that white guilt can invoke deep feelings of shame.

Akeem the 'African Dream' was another controversial gimmick to come out of the 1980s. George Gray was a white wrestler most commonly known to fans as the One Man Gang. When it came time for a new gimmick, through his smooth-talking African-American manager Slick, Gray announced that he was originally from Africa and planned to re-embrace his roots. From an on-location set dubbed "the deepest darkest parts of Africa," surrounded by tribal dancers chanting around a fire, and now speaking in a stereotypical jive accent, Akeem the 'African Dream' made his debut. Akeem embraced his new heritage by adopting perceived black mannerisms and shucking and jiving in the ring. It's commonly believed that whole tasteless gimmick was meant to be an insult to the 'American Dream' Dusty Rhodes. It was offensive to a lot more people than just the Rhodes family, but, hey, at least Akeem wasn't in blackface. While one can argue, excuse, or even justify the racial insensitivity of these eighties professional wrestling gimmicks, other controversial race related events in professional wrestling history are not so debatable.

In 1990, perhaps the most racist match ever put on by a major promotion went down on the industry's biggest stage: WrestleMania. The fan favorite was the 'Hot Rod' Rowdy Roddy Piper squaring off against the ill-tempered African-American heel known as Bad News Brown. The segment opens with a half black faced painted Piper, calling himself the Hot Scott, cutting a backstage promo where he insults Bad News Brown's "bug eyes with gnarly veins and big dilated nostrils." The camera's cut to the announcing team composed of Gorilla Monsoon, Jesse 'The Body' Ventura, and 'Mean' Gene Okerlund, who joke about Pipers' new split personality and claim that he is so well loved by the Canadian crowd that he could be Prime Minister.

The match begins with Piper using his blackened arm to bust out his best disco moves as he shucks and jives around the ring. The boys in the booth laugh and applaud at, as they put it, Pipers' mind games. The action begins, the crowd, now unquestionably aware of Pipers' new look, enthusiastically cheer him on. The two men brawl back and forth until Bad News gets the upper hand. Brown slaps a trapezius vice grip hold on Piper and calls out Piper's blackface appearance as he shouts, "So you want to be a black, huh." Piper escapes the hold and the two continue to brawl back and forth until Hot Rod pokes his thumb in Bad News's eye. Classic heel move. Bad News retaliates causing the referee to immediately check on Piper's well-being, but no one ever checks on Brown.

For some inexplicable reason, Piper pulls a "Michael Jackson" glove out of his wrestling tights. The announcers speculate about the legality of such a move as the fight spills out of the ring. Piper grabs a steel chair and swings it widely at Brown. He misses. The referee, although much quicker than a standard ten count, rules the match a double count out. The two men throw blows all the way up the ramp and stumble to the backstage.

Racial taunting. Unjust rulings. Mass apathy. That's a lot of problematic racial issues to unpack here. Now why Vince McMahon, a man who considers Martin Luther King Jr. one of his personal heroes, approved this match is beyond comprehension. Even if the rumors that claim that McMahon originally wanted Bad News to win but settled on a double count out after Piper refused to lose is true, it still does not account for why this outright racism was on full display in the middle of one of his rings. Now it's been rumored that Piper was a racist, a claim which he denies. Yet in front of sixty-seven thousand fans Piper had no problem insulting both the physical features and the perceived cultural traits of Black people. If he is not racist as he had claimed, he somehow managed to let out his racist fantasy for the whole world to see, in under fifteen minutes.

This match unintentionally provides an allegory for the African-American struggle with the American justice system. While on its face both competitors seem to be on a level playing field, they clearly are not. When Brown uses a poke to the eye it's highlighted and despised. When Piper does it, that same poke to the eye is downplayed and justified. If you are saying "Well, that's not because of race. It is just because Piper is the face and Brown is the heel," a blackface painted wrestler using heel tactics doesn't exactly scream hero status. And if Piper is the hero, why was he the first to use the old thumb to the eye tactic in the first place?

After Piper blatantly pulls out a glove from his trunks, Jesse Ventura and Gorilla Monsoon epitomize the role of the juror. They almost instinctively search for any plausible explanation to exonerate Piper of all culpability. Well, the referee must have checked that glove in the back, they lament. Yes, I know, it's just because Piper is the face, right?

Later on in the match, Piper grabs the old, trusty steel chair and madly swings it at Brown. Referee Davis calls for the bell. Any rational professional wrestling fan would assume that he is calling for a disqualification on Piper, right? After all the bell rang right after his steel chair shot attempts. But no, that would be too just for this match. Instead, the ref calls for a premature double count out. An ending where on paper no one wins but in reality, we all see who clearly lost.

The match feels like America, a land where to many it felt like a black man seemingly just can't win. Bad News was pitted not just against Piper but against Piper, the announcer, the commentators, the crowd, and the booker. Even when Brown was clearly in the right, the best he could hope for was a draw. No one seemed to appreciate this match for what it really was: a true double turn. A match where Piper was exposed as the true heel, a role he famously played in the past, and where Bad News heroically persevered despite everything working against him. It's an unsurprising shame that whether it was because of the powers that be or Piper not wanting to do business, Bad News's arm was never raised in victory. We will though. Bad News, you won that match.

Piper versus Bad News at WrestleMania was perhaps the most racist moment a major league wrestling company ever broadcast, but it was far from the only one. Ironically, when Virgil, the Million Dollar Man's black manservant, was finally ready to turn on his abusive, slaveowner-esque boss, it was Piper who was called upon to train and equip him to fight off the oppressor. Maybe Piper was trying to make amends with the black community when he was appointed as Virgil's white savior?

American professional wrestling has a troubled history of

overtly portraying minorities as racially stereotypical characters or in many cases as downright criminals. In 1993, Harlem Heat, the legendary tag team made up of real-life brothers Booker T and Stevie Ray, was originally packaged as a pair of shackled prisoners. Col. Rob Parker, a man who looked very much like a white plantation owner, had apparently won their services in a card game. The antebellum slave look was quickly abandoned but that fact that it existed at all is reflective of the racial insensitivities of the times.

In 1997, five years after being the first African-American wrestler to win a major world championship, Ron Simmons, now known as Faarooq, and saddled with a reinvented gimmick lead the "Bigger, Badder, Better, and Blacker" version of the faction known as the Nation of Domination. The original manager of the faction was a Johnnie Cochran inspired attorney/professional wrestling manager called Clarence Mason. Clarence, a black man, reportedly requested to leave the group partly because he was uncomfortable with Faarooq making racist remarks during his promos. In front of the camera, racial tensions rose as the Nation feuded with Los Boricuas (a Puerto Rican stable led by Savio Vega) and the Disciples of Apocalypse (a whiter biker gang group led by Crush). It was what many say was professional wrestling's worst feud of the year.

A few months later a *Raw* show opens with Good Ol' JR stating that nowhere on Earth will you feel this kind of freedom of expression. The Nation feels that expression as they continue to deal with hate. In the show, their locker room has been vandalized with Uncle Tom Go Home!, a no KFC sign, a scratched out Malcom X writing, Homie Stay Home, and We Hate You! all written on the walls. Vince McMahon himself steps into the middle of the ring and gives the Nation a half-hearted apology for last week's incident but defends his company claiming there is no racism in the World Wrestling Federation (WWF). Due to the pro-Canada evidence found inside the room, the Nation quickly blames the Hart Foundation for these hateful acts. Faarooq says, "It all started with a boat ride, but it's going to end with a black fist right on the side of your white ass!"

The Hart Foundation comes out to address these allegations, and the live audience receives them as heroes. Bret comes out and says, "First of all brothers we accept!" After preaching about his Canadian values of racial equality, Bret blames Shawn Michaels and D-Generation X. DX appear on the Titantron and Shawn calls Bret the Grand Wizard. DX accuses the Hart Foundation of using the N-word and Shawn has about as comically fake an outraged face as one can make. The whole thing is uncomfortable to watch.

As time goes by, up-and-coming superstar The Rock seizes leadership away from Faarooq, and the Nation moves away from its militant focus. The new, hipper Nation has now become more inclusive, recruiting former Hart Foundation member Owen Hart into its ranks. The group, now full of swagger, slowly moves away from race-based storylines yet still retains its "by any means necessary" motto. Lead by a young charismatic performer in the Rock and booked to feud with the uber popular D-Generation X, the Nation was finally ready for some more substantial storytelling. Then X-Pac showed up to *Raw* in blackface. The DX parody started out comedically playing off the individual characteristics of the Nation members, blackface aside, it didn't feel like they were simply making fun of the black community. Then X-Pac gets handed the mic and does his best Fat Albert impression. Maybe that's why "Go away heat" and "X-Pac heat" have become synonymous. The '90s were something else.

During this "edgy" decade, an African-American wrestler portraying a gangsta gimmick known as New Jack was constantly greeted by angry fans yelling the N-word at him. The black thug version of the often-used outlaw wrestling gimmick was repeatedly presented without any regard to racial sensitivity. In the 2000s, a pair of African-American wrestlers known as Cryme Tyme were similarly packaged with the gangsta gimmick. They'd come out looking like 50 Cent music video extras and danced around the ring shouting the latest rap slang. Around this time, MVP entered into a feud with the All-American Jack Swagger, which was played up as the obnoxious privileged blue-chip athlete against the rehabilitated black ex-con. These repeated portrayals of the black thug didn't go down in "we don't answer to the mainstream" indies (independent wrestling promotions) but in professional wrestling promotions with American nationwide television contracts.

In 2003, Booker T found himself in another racially charged storyline. This time main event player Triple H cut a promo on Booker, telling him that "Somebody like you doesn't get to be world champion. People like you don't deserve it. That's reserved for people like me." If anyone was questioning whether that comment was a racially motivated, Hunter cleared it up when he started referencing Booker T's "nappy hair."

The two future Hall-of-Famers racially infused feud led to a championship title match at WrestleMania XIX. There was no justice for Booker though, like Bad News thirteen years earlier, Booker would not have his hand raised that night. No gold went around his waist. Triple H, a man who has lost thirteen WrestleMania matches, retained the title and buried any shot at redemption for one of World Wrestling Entertainment's (WWE) most cringe-worthy storylines. Why is it that Triple H was involved in some of professional wrestling's most racially charged moments?

The black community may have been the most apparent use of the racial stereotype gimmicks seen in professional wrestling, but it was certainly not alone. Legendary Mexican wrestler Konnan spent much of his stateside career portraying a Latino gang-banger who shouted, "Órale! Arriba La Raza!" The Mexicools, a trio of three wrestlers known as Super Crazy, Psiscois, and Juventud, rode to the ring on a Juan Deer-titled riding lawn mower. For a time, whenever you saw a Latino on professional wrestling television, it felt like an us against them storyline. This feeling was never more apparent than when John Bradshaw Layfield or JBL, in character, infamously railed against bilingualism and multiculturalism in America. He took it so far as shooting segments where he "hunted down" illegals at the border.

Despite Mexico's status as one of the most influential countries in the world when it came to professional wrestling in America, Latinos still struggled with having to rely on leaning into racial stereotypes. Even the legendary Eddie Guerrero was frequently reduced to incorporating negative Latino stereotypes into his character. He played the heel in a domestic-abuse angle with Chyna and eventually his life's motto grew into the immensely popular "I lie, cheat, and steal!" slogan.

Some may argue that these racially reliant gimmicks are just exaggerated versions of the personalities of the wrestlers portraying them, which is common in the world of profession-al wrestling. It can be argued that these gimmicks are simply reflective personas of the people playing them and therefore they are not as problematic as others may claim.

There may be some truth to that. R-Truth, the Street Profits and other hip-hopish gimmicks are portrayed by individuals who in actuality love the hip-hop culture. I'm sure that Eddie Guerrero really did enjoy mamacitas and cruising around in a lowrider, after all it's a pretty dope flex. But the race gimmick problem becomes more apparent when minorities are disproportionately called upon to play the role of criminals or thugs. At best it can feel like lazy creative work and at worst it's insulting and downright offensive. One thing is for sure though, the latent fears that much of white America has toward people of color has been exploited inside the professional wrestling ring time and time again.

Does the professional wrestling show's script reflect the fantasies of the fans or are the fans reactions reflecting the fantasies of professional wrestling bookers? Like a circus maze of mirrors, they may reflect themselves. It's no surprise that over the years many racist fan-created signs have been peppered throughout arenas across America. From referencing jungle fever to telling a Hispanic wrestler to mow my lawn, the language people use is shocking. The signage is nothing compared to the nasty racial slurs' fans have spewed inside these arenas.

When a professional wrestling company uses racially insensitive storylines and gimmicks, is it practically encouraging this behavior from its fans? Isn't fan engagement what these companies seek in building a dedicated audience? Is it any surprise then that those in the crowd holding up a tasteless sign or shouting vulgar racial slurs at the professional wrestlers will just think they are only playing along?

Throughout history many of professional wrestling's most

powerful and influential figures have found themselves embroiled in racial controversy. Ric Flair, Roddy Piper, Michael Hays, Dusty Rhodes, and countless other well-known names have been accused of racist behavior. Hulk Hogan was temporarily evicted from the WWE for a viral racist rant. Even Vincent K. McMahon, in a misguided comedic attempt, used the N-word right in front of Booker T on national TV. Why is it always Booker T?

The fact that these legends may have exhibited some bigoted behavior in the past should be understood for what it was. It does not mean that they need to be erased from professional wrestling history, all of their behavior whether good or bad is a part of their legacy. Hopefully, they will evolve, and if they are unwilling to do so, well, with today's climate it may be time to step aside from current dealings in the professional wrestling industry. History should be reflected upon, not erased, censored, or forgotten.

Despite all of this, few minorities walk away in protest from the professional wrestling business. The fame and glory of being a major league wrestler makes this decision entirely understandable. There are levels to professional wrestling glory, and winning a major wrestling title is a good indicator of what level one is on. Given the predominantly white power structure of professional wrestling and its predetermined outcomes, it's not surprising that minorities have been historically underrepresented when it comes to winning major gold. When a professional wrestler wins a major title, it's a signal to the world that this person is a valued and trusted part of the company. If things go right, they may very well become the face of the company. It took a long time for the promoters to see any persons of color as the potential face of their enterprise.

Since Ron Simmons historic title run in 1992, more than a handful of African-American wrestlers have captured major gold. Charismatic performers such as the Rock, Eddie Guerrero, and Booker T have shown that they are capable of carrying the big gold and being a face of the company. Since then, Kofi Kingston, Big E, Bobby Lashley, Sasha Banks, Naomi, and Bianca Belair have all respectively won major gold.

In 2021, WrestleMania's four major title matches consisted of three African-American's, one Japanese, one Samoan, one Australian, one Canadian, and one Caucasian American. That's diversity, and the fact that three out of four of the title winners were not white—well, given the history of professional wrestling in America, it's remarkable. Now many of the biggest stars in professional wrestling are people of color. Bayley, Asuka, Thunder Rosa, Jade Cargill, and Sammy Guevara are just a few of the minority wrestlers whom have held gold and built a large, inclusive fanbase.

In 2024, the Samoan powerhouse Roman Reign truly does sit at the head of professional wrestling's table. His historic run has been cited as the some of the best storytelling professional wrestling has ever done. In January of 2024, Dwayne 'The Rock' Johnson was appointed to the board of directors of TKO Group, the publicly traded company that is now the parent company of the WWE. Finally, people of color have become instrumental in professional wrestling decision making at the highest level.

Far too often people of color in professional wrestling have dealt with everything from racial insensitivity to outright bigotry. No one should feel like their gimmick perpetuates negative racial stereotypes. No one should feel that they are undervalued on account of their skin color. No one in the wrestling ring, or around it, should feel that it's acceptable to make a racial slur or hold up a racially offensive sign.

As larger segments of society move away from apathy toward racist behavior so too has professional wrestling. In today's environment, in the collaborative effort that is professional wrestling, there is more consideration taken in creating a racially-harmonized product. This suggests that racial harmony inside the wrestling ring is progressing. Wrestlers of all ethnicities are represented across nationally-televised wrestling shows now more than ever. Hopefully, this combination of representation and sensitivity will foster an atmosphere of inclusiveness. One where people of every skin color can enjoy the wondrous spectacle that is professional wrestling without having to look past that one storyline or gimmick that makes a person question whether they are really in on the fun after all.

CHAPTER 5
THE SQUARED CIRCLE PRESIDENTS: PART ONE

In a way professional wrestling and presidential politics share the same goal: get the masses to do exactly whatever it is you want them to do. They both are two worlds built around illusions and the cult of personality, yet the two worlds rarely intertwine. When they do come together, it is often in the form of political pundits comparing a loathed brass politician to the latest heel professional wrestler.

In 1998, Jesse 'the Body' Ventura shocked the world when, as a third-party candidate, he was elected Governor of Minnesota. Ventura and his "Don't vote for politics as usual" campaign combined grassroots politics with television debate victories to win the election. There is no doubt that the Body's charming no-nonsense personality was cultivated by his years of being in front of professional wrestling television cameras. While certainly a historic rarity, Ventura is not the only professional wrestler to achieve success in the political realm.

The legendary Antonio Inoki became an elected official in Japan and even convinced Saddam Hussein to free Japanese hostages prior to the onset of the Gulf War. Since 2018, Glen Jacobs, aka Kane, aka the Devil's Favorite Demon, is carrying the professional wrestling political torch forward as the mayor of Knox County, Tennessee. Other professional wrestling legends such as Ric Flair, Hulk Hogan, and Dwayne 'The Rock' Johnson have all openly discussed their respective political aspirations on national non-wrestling television.

Today the intermingling of politics and professional wrestling continues as we elect a professional wrestler to lead the professional wrestling industry. Just as every four years we elect a President to serve as the face of the nation, a worthy professional wrestler will be proclaimed as the face of the business for their respective term.

From the 1980s on, every four years we will elect a professional wrestler to lead the industry and ensure that the sports entertainment business is thriving. In the November of the year before each election, two candidates will engage in the ultimate fall brawl with the leadership of the professional wrestling world at stake. Charisma, reputation (both inside and outside of the locker room), character, experience, leadership, drawing power, and political savvy will all be considered.

Candidates will be judged on their established record and potential to lead for the next four years. Now, when looking at any given election, we have to ignore the future and what we know, that is how it will all eventually pan out. A professional wrestler's accomplishments and credentials will only be considered up until mid-November of the year preceding the election. For example, for the election of 1980, each candidates' credentials and resume will only be looked at from prior to mid-November of 1979. Starting in 1980, "Hail to The Chief" will be the new entrance music for the one wrestling superstar elected as the President of the Squared Circle.

PRESIDENTIAL ELECTION FOR 1980

The 1980s were pivotal in creating what modern day professional wrestling is all about and finding the right leader during this transformative time is crucial. With the talent booms of the 1970s, there were plenty of horses to hitch your wagon to. In November of 1979, when professional wrestling fans popped open a couple cold ones and talked about who was the top dog in the world of professional wrestling, a few names probably came up more than others: Dusty Rhodes, Bruno Sammartino, André the Giant, Harley Race, Terry Funk, Bob Backlund, and The Sheik.

At the time, the professional wrestling scene was slowly transitioning from being a loosely allied system of local territories with many influential power brokers, into a national multimedia powerhouse controlled by a few major nationwide promotions. Only two wrestlers will get to vie for the right to lead the world of professional wrestling during the period that saw the greatest transformation in the history of the business.

ANDRÉ THE GIANT V. HARLEY RACE

CAMPAIGN FOR ANDRÉ THE GIANT

In the 1970s, the 'Eighth Wonder of the World' André the Giant was both literally and figuratively the largest attraction in the world of professional wrestling. Perhaps no other wrestler racked up the miles traveled like André did during the seventies. André traveled all over the world, almost never losing and always astonishing audiences. If money was any indication of success or importance, André easily won that category among his peers. He was one of the top grossing professional wrestlers, taking in about $400,000 a year, which would equate to about $3 million by today's standards.

In 1976, André crossed over into mainstream show business, making his Hollywood debut in *The Six Million Dollar Man*. It would become one of the most loved episodes of the series. Back in those days, it was a rarity for any professional wrestler to have mainstream appeal, but when André burst onto the national scene, how could anyone not notice? He would appear on the *Tonight Show*, fight well known boxer and real-life inspiration for Sylvester Stallone's Rocky Balboa character Chuck Wepner, and even be "recruited" by the Washington Redskins.

In the territory system of the 1970s, promoters were constantly looking to increase their bottom line. A surefire way to accomplish this goal was by booking the most popular attraction available. Standing at 7'4" and weighing north of 400 lbs., no one attracted more attention and astonishment from the fans than the Giant. When André came to town, it was a must-see event. He was voted the most popular wrestler by *Pro Wrestling Illustrated* in 1977, and finished as runner up in 78 and 79. With an impressive resume and having the upmost respect of his peers, it'll be a tall task to top the Giant.

CAMPAIGN FOR HARLEY RACE

In November of 1979, Harley Race was a well-respected, grizzled veteran of the squared circle. Harley was a four-time National Wrestling Alliance (NWA) heavyweight champion. Race also toured the world collecting an impressive number of regional titles along the way. In 1979, he was named *Pro Wrestling Illustrated* wrestler of the year. On October 13, 1978, in Houston, Texas, Race body slammed André the Giant, an honor bestowed on only a few legendary wrestlers.

During a trip to Japan, Race gained electoral steam when he captured his fourth NWA heavyweight championship on November 7, 1979. If you are looking for a genuine tough guy to protect the business and defend it to the death, Harley is your man. According to professional wrestling lore, the entire locker room, including André, respected and feared hard-nosed Harley. Race could protect the title from any screwy finishes and protect the business from anyone who dared to question a professional wrestler's ability to fight.

THE PROJECTED WINNER IS . . .

At the time no professional wrestler was more globally recognized than André the Giant. Some may argue that the Giant wasn't exactly representative of your average professional wrestler. They may think that if you're not over seven-foot-tall, studying André's wrestling techniques offered little lessons. As the saying goes, you can't teach big. But any learned individual can appreciate that no matter your size, much can be gained by studying André's ability to connect with people.

Harley on the other hand was a professional wrestler's wrestler. Race has the grappling technique, unmatched toughness, and a healthy level of respect for the business in his corner. While Race had all the locker room respect in the world, he just didn't have that crossover superstar appeal. Harley didn't have that leading-man look that Hollywood was after. One of Harley's strongest talking points for his presidential campaign is his toughness, but you have to wonder: In a real fight are you going to bet against a young André the Giant?

A close matchup pitting two tough-as-nails wrestlers both in their mid-thirties against each other. Race was a long reigning champion but the Giant said it best himself: "There are many champions, but there is only one André!"

André the Giant wins.

PRESIDENTIAL ELECTION FOR 1984

During the decade of greed, professional wrestling was in the middle of a drastic transformation. The business was morphing from mainly regional attractions to having large promotions with national audiences. Summoning the Gordon Gekko greed is good philosophy. Vincent Kennedy McMahon maneuvered his way into becoming the full owner of the World Wide Wrestling Federation (WWWF).

On February 21, 1980, McMahon officially incorporated his new company appropriately named Titan Sports. McMahon and Titan Sports entered an agreement with the four owners of Capitol Wrestling, the company who owned the WWWF. Vince McMahon Sr., Gorilla Monsoon, Arnold Skaaland, and Phil Zacko agreed to allow Titan Sports to fully buy their shares of WWWF in a series of four scheduled balloon payments. There was a catch though. If McMahon defaulted on any payment, the original four owners would retain all their shares and keep any money that had been paid up to that point. It was a risky endeavor with McMahon paying for a company with money he didn't have, but, hey, that was what the eighties was all about.

By June of 1982, McMahon was able to make his payments, acquired the WWWF, and launched a full out invasion of the professional wrestling territories. Titan Sports rebranded its wrestling promotion and subsequently withdrew it from the NWA. McMahon took his promotion nationwide, and in September of 1983, the World Wrestling Federation (WWF) debuted its national television programing on the aptly named USA Network. It was an ambitious promotion that sought to move away from authentic wrestling and toward a more theatrical product. McMahon was all-in on what many thought were unthinkable goals.

The NWA was an organization comprised of a group of allied regional professional wrestling promotions. At the time, the alliance was still squeezing the headlock it had slapped on the world of professional wrestling and any non-affiliated organizations. It controlled professional wrestling in most of the United States and had deep ties with the television industry and various athletic commissions. The NWA had a long and storied history but was constantly plagued by infighting resulting from the competing interests within its ranks. It sought to counterbalance any cartoonish depictions of professional wrestling with undeniable gritty violence.

Out of these two visions for professional wrestling emerged two sports entertainers with an abundance of charisma and polar opposite styles of wrestling:

RIC FLAIR V. HULK HOGAN

CAMPAIGN FOR RIC FLAIR

In 1981, former actor Ronald Reagan became the President of the United States of America. In that same year, Ric Flair beat Dusty Rhodes to win his first NWA world heavyweight championship. It was a year where the importance of being entertaining, no matter your profession was readily apparent. Ric and Ron broke that television era cult of personality ground that continues to be built on today.

1981 was a breakthrough year for Flair, he captured his first *Pro Wrestling Illustrated* wrestler of the year award. In 1982 and 1983, Ric Flair won Dave Meltzer's *Wrestling Observer Newsletter* wrestler of the year award. In 1983, the NWA presented the, pay-per-view predecessor to WrestleMania, event called Starrcade. The tagline for the big event was a Flare for Gold and featured Harley Race against Ric Flair in the main event. Flair had a glorious performance which ended with him donning the big gold title belt while a crimson mask covered his trademark golden hair. The brilliantly bloody match was awarded the *Wrestling Observer Newsletter* match of the year.

Prior to 1984, Flair held the NWA world heavyweight championship five times over. During his title reigns there was no lack of quality opponents as Ric feuded with the likes of Ricky Steamboat, Roddy Piper, Jimmy Snuka, Greg Valentine, and the original Nature Boy Buddy Rogers. Flair spent much of the early 1980s traveling around the NWA circuit, defending and challenging for the world title. In 1984, Ric was in his mid-thirties, at the peak of his game, and a bigger attraction than Space Mountain.

CAMPAIGN FOR HULK HOGAN

The year was 1983 and the tide that would become HulkaMania was steadily rising. Hogan was gaining recognition by working for New Japan Pro-Wrestling, Continental Wrestling Association, National Wrestling Alliance, and Georgia Championship Wrestling. The blonde bruiser spent most of the '84 presidential election cycle wrestling for Verne Gagne's American Wrestling Association (AWA). There he quickly became a fan favorite and was booked in a main event feud with the promotion's biggest star Nick Bockwinkel. For whatever reason (some say it's because Gagne didn't respect Hogan's wrestling ability, others say Hogan refused because he knew the move would tie him to Gagne to Hogan's financial detriment) Hogan never captured the AWA title. However, he did capture New Japan Pro-Wrestling's IWGP heavyweight championship by defeating the legendary Antonio Inoki.

Hogan was already a major in-ring player and now his crossover power was becoming more apparent. In 1982, Hulk appeared in Sylvester Stallone's major Hollywood motion picture *Rocky III*. Appearing in the blockbuster film alongside one of Hollywood's biggest stars gave Hogan's growing star power significant credibility. Boxer versus wrestler encounters rarely live up to the hype, but the showdown between these two icons was one of the few exceptions. Hogan's surging popularity and drawing power make him an undeniably formidable candidate.

THE PROJECTED WINNER IS . . .

Hogan was on the rise, but Vincent K. McMahon had not yet sculpted him into the worldwide phenomenon that we all know. Flair was trusted by most of the power players in the NWA to carry their signature title for a majority of the early eighties. The Nature Boy was limousine riding and jet flying all over America, putting on exciting bar-setting matches. In 1976, Flair was in a plane crash and broke his back in three places. Four months later he was back in the ring defending his title. His technical prowess, resiliency, and respect for the professional wrestling business earned Flair a lot of respect among his peers. The alligator-shoe-wearing, kiss-stealing son of a gun elevated his game and was headlining professional wrestling cards all over America.

Flair wins.

PRESIDENTIAL ELECTION FOR 1988

This historic election cycle was the first for a new era of professional wrestling. The old school professional wrestling territories were suffering a death by a thousand cuts. By 1987 the regional territories were starting to resemble Abdullah the Butcher's shredded forehead. By election day, body slams were being broadcast nationwide on network and cable television.

In 1985, the Super Bowl of professional wrestling, WrestleMania, was born. WrestleMania's success transformed just exactly what a professional wrestling mega-event could be. During the 1980s Mr. McMahon's development of larger-than-life characters along with the intermingling of pop culture transformed the sports entertainment landscape. McMahon's rock and wrestling Music Television (MTV) cross promotional venture made professional wrestling mainstream cool.

The NWA, an organization held together through perpetually strained alliances and backroom agreements by the major regional promoters, was led by Jim Crockett Promotions and struggled to compete with McMahon's growing national expansion. The NWA created its own super cards, shared wrestling talent, and secured national television deals all in an attempt to directly compete with the WWF. This election would boil down to the NWA versus WWF, with each organization's marquee player vying to lead the professional wrestling world. This is the rematch the world's been waiting for . . .

RIC FLAIR V. HULK HOGAN

CAMPAIGN FOR HULK HOGAN

In the three WrestleManias that occurred prior to this election, the immortal one was the man headlining them all. None of those events were bigger than WrestleMania III, where in Pontiac, Michigan, professional wrestling's biggest match went down on March 29, 1987. In what is still considered one of, if not the, most important match in the industry's history, Hulk Hogan squared off against the legendary André the Giant. The torch was unofficially passed when Hogan body slammed and pinned André. The slam heard around the world highlighted what many already knew: HulkaMania was running wild.

Between 1984–1987, Hogan exploded onto the mainstream pop culture scene. From Saturday morning cartoons to late night television shows and many time slots in between, the Hulkster was everywhere. He was a superstar bigger than any professional wrestler that preceded him. In 1985, Hogan became the first and still only professional wrestler to ever grace the cover of *Sports Illustrated*. In November of 1987, the Hulkster was on his 47th consecutive month as WWF champion, a truly immortal reign. Hogan's worldwide fame and inarguable status as the face of professional wrestling's largest promotion would cause any campaign manager to wonder: Whatcha gonna do, brother?

CAMPAIGN FOR RIC FLAIR

Since his 1983 presidential election victory, Ric Flair continues to rack up accomplishments. The Nature Boy pulled off the unprecedented achievement of winning three consecutive *Pro Wrestling Illustrated* wrestler of the year awards. In 1984, 1985, and 1986, Flair took home the prestigious honor and in 1987 Naitch finished second. By 1986, Ric Flair was a five-time consecutive winner of the *Wrestling Observer Newsletter* wrestler of the year award.

By mid-November of this election year, Flair was a nine-time world champion and no one doubted that it was only a matter of time before he crossed into that double-digit status. In an on-the-nose move, Jim Crockett crafted the famed big gold belt seemingly specifically designed for his golden boy.

In 1985, the Nature Boy became the leader of one of the greatest factions of all time with the formation of the Four Horsemen. Leading this legendary faction is exemplary of the "a rising tide lifts all boats" boisterous leadership that Ric Flair brought to the table. This election cycle was perhaps the most formative for the development of slick Ric's signature swag.

During his reelection campaign, there is no doubt that Ric lived up to his saying "all the women want to be with me, all the men want to be like me." If his sexual exploit numbers are anywhere near what he claims, the man is in Wilt Chamberlin's company. Decades later his slogans, yells, and struts continue to be paid homage to. A wrestler's professional wrestler like no other, if anyone can go head-to-head with HulkaMania, its Flair. Wooooo!

THE PROJECTED WINNER IS . . .

It still stings that we never got the televised late eighties/early nineties Hogan versus Flair feud that we deserved. Never before or since have two men been at the peak of the business, found themselves working for the same company, and yet for whatever reason there was no big pay-per-view or even regular television payoff. It was the greatest possible WrestleMania headlining feud that never was.

Anyone who wins three *Pro Wrestling Illustrated* wrestler of the year awards during a four-year election cycle must be a shoe in for the upcoming election, right? Well, the only problem for Flair is that in each of those three years, Hulk Hogan finished second and the one year he lost, the closest year to this election, Hogan won.

While the margin of wrestling ability between Hogan and Flair is debatable, most would agree that Ric was a better in-ring performer. Flair reached that next level of over that every professional wrestler strives for. He was technically sound and could deliver widely entertaining promos. Most of the boys in the back most would probably attest that Flair was the better wrestler. Then those same boys would see the paycheck increases on the houses Hogan worked and could easily overlook any lack of technical proficiency.

By November of 1987, McMahon and his biggest star Hulk Hogan sat on the throne of the professional wrestling world. The two had effectively crushed the little lords that once populated the vibrant NWA empire. Hogan was the biggest thing that professional wrestling had ever seen. As formidable an opponent as Flair is, no one could match Hogan's star power in the late eighties.

Hogan wins.

PRESIDENTIAL ELECTION FOR 1992

By 1992, the plug was pulled on the life support machine hooked into the territory system and only two major players remained. The WWF and World Championship Wrestling (WCW) were the last two American nationwide organizations left in the professional wrestling world. Once again, the industry searched for its leader among the major players. A few potential leaders surfaced during the primary race: Ric Flair, Hulk Hogan, the 'Macho Man' Randy Savage, Sting, and the Ultimate Warrior.

In August of 1991, Ric Flair was in the midst of a career transition as he jumped ship from the familiar WCW, the promotion which succeeded the NWA, to the WWF. Given the WWF's reputation regarding the booking of former NWA talent, questions arose about whether Flair would be properly used. Many voters recall the toned-down Road Warriors WWF presentation and the polka dot clad version of the 'American Dream' Dusty Rhodes. Nothing is guaranteed in this world and the same is true for sports entertainment. Given the freshness of Flair's move, it's all an uncertain situation.

After the 1988 election, the Ultimate Warrior was pushed to the moon. At that year's Summer Slam he ended the Honky Tonk Man's historic 454-day intercontinental title reign in 27 seconds. At WrestleMania VI, Warrior accomplished the once unthinkable feat of cleanly defeating Hulk Hogan. At the following year's WrestleMania, he defeated the 'Macho Man' Randy Savage, ending the Macho one's professional wrestling career and presidential campaign hopes.

Heading into 1991 the Warrior seemed destined to lead the

professional wrestling world. Then during the Summer of 1991, the Warrior hit the self-destruct button and tried to squeeze more money out of the most powerful man in professional wrestling. At Summer Slam, Warrior refused to work the main event of one of the company's marquee pay-per-view events unless he received more money in cash. For the sake of his show, Mr. McMahon gave in to the Warrior's demands but subsequently handed him his walking papers and effectively ended his campaign hopes.

In the fall of 1991, Hulk Hogan was still Hulk Hogan, with all of the issues involving his primary competitors, Hulk easily secures a primary nomination. Sting was on the rise in WCW, quickly becoming a major player. Flair, having already suffered an election defeat and now in the midst of a career transition, is edged out by the Stinger.

HULK HOGAN V. STING

CAMPAIGN FOR HULK HOGAN

Following his Presidential victory in 1988, HulkaMania was running as wild as ever. Hogan started off his first presidency by headlining a National Broadcast Company (NBC) special called *The Main Event* against André the Giant. The famous WrestleMania III rematch drew a record setting 33 million viewers. It is still, and probably always will be, the highest rated professional wrestling event ever broadcast. At this point, Hogan had nothing left to prove regarding his mcgastar power, he was unquestionably the main man.

When you have a superstar that is this over, it's only natural for promoters to try to use him to bolster the other talent on his roster. Hogan, being the team player, gave Randy Savage the Hulkster rub, teaming up with him to create the star-studded tag team known as the Mega Powers. Of course, the team eventually imploded, leading to Hogan taking the WWF title from Savage. Notwithstanding this, at least to some degree, Hulk still elevated Randy.

Hogan went on to create his own monster opponent when he starred in professional wrestling's first major motion picture, the cult classic *No Holds Barred*. Tom Lister Jr., aka Zeus, was put in a number of cross promotional high-profile matches. During their feud, Hogan did the unthinkable and actually made Zeus look like a decent competitor.

At WrestleMania VI, Hogan continued to elevate talent when he lost cleanly to the Ultimate Warrior. The match, despite featuring two men whom many consider to not be technically proficient wrestlers, won the *Professional Wrestling Illustrated* match of the year award. Whether Warrior deserved the honors or not, Hogan was a team player looking out for the long-term success of the professional wrestling business.

Hogan also feuded with various heels, giving them all a boost of legitimacy simply by sharing the ring with the Hulkster. Earthquake, Sgt. Slaughter, and the Big Boss Man all got pushes in their professional wrestling status. In the fall of 1991, Hogan was already in the process of helping create WWF's next heel monster when he entered a feud with a young Undertaker. At this point the Deadman only had one year with the WWF under his belt, but with Hogan selling for him, he was instantly a credible main event player.

By 1991, Hogan was doing in professional wrestling what

Michael Jordan was doing in basketball: winning and making everyone around him better. Perhaps that's why Rodman decided to share the stage with both of these cultural icons? Six years later, Hulk Hogan appeared on the *Tonight Show* with Jay Leno and announced his presidential run for the United States of America. Maybe he wouldn't have been laughed out of the building if the world appreciated his ability to elevate those around him. Then again, we are all most certainly better off because nothing ever came of it.

CAMPAIGN FOR STING

In 1988, Sting was booked into a prolonged feud with the Four Horsemen. At the first ever Clash of the Champions, the Stinger wrestled Flair to an epic time-limit draw. The future icon had proven himself a box office draw as the NWA's Clash of the Champions I earned a 7.8 rating. According to Dave Meltzer, it was the most watched match in the history of the NWA.

In 1989, the NWA presented Starrcade: Future Shock. The pay-per-view event featured an iron man round-robin tournament and asked who will survive to become the wrestler of the 1990s? Sting pinned The Great Muta and Ric Flair to win the tournament and earned himself a future title match. Following the tournament, Sting tore his left patella tendon, sidelining his title hopes for months. The Stinger soon bounced back.

In July of 1990, Sting defeated Ric Flair at the Great American Bash to capture his first NWA world heavyweight championship. After Sting dropped the title back to Flair, he had a critically acclaimed tag team match partnering with Lex Luger against the Steiner Brothers at Super Brawl. The match won the *Pro*

Wrestling Illustrated match of the year award. Sting had the look and attitude of a major player. Who can forget that rad, bright, colorful face paint that surfer Sting made cool? It was all the rage in the late eighties.

THE PROJECTED WINNER IS . . .

Yes, Hogan was one of a few WWF wrestlers used to monetarily capitalize on the Gulf War. Yes, the seemingly unbeatable Hulkster took a major clean loss to the arguably unworthy Ultimate Warrior at WrestleMania VI. Yes, Hogan was practically the poster child for the professional wrestling steroid scandal that led to WWF's ringside doctor, Dr. Zahorian's, conviction and the eventual federal trial of Vince McMahon. Yes, despite years of being the face of professional wrestling, Hogan's in-ring ability had not really improved much. And yes, Hogan had just released the commercial and critical failure of a film known as *Suburban Commando*.

But still, it's just too hard to elect any professional wrestler that was once saved by Robocop at a pay-per-view.

Hogan wins.

PRESIDENTIAL ELECTION FOR 1996

In the mid-nineties the professional wrestling landscape was continuing its constant evolution. In large part, the 1994 federal trial *United States v. McMahon et al.*, McMahon was the catalyst for this change. McMahon was charged with conspiracy to distribute steroids, possession of illegal steroids with intent to distribute, and embezzlement for allegedly using money from Titan Sports Inc. to purchase illegal steroids. McMahon was ultimately acquitted of all charges but the negative publicity had lingering effects. At least partially because of the steroid scandal, the larger-than-life physiques, while still present, were not being as heavily promoted as before.

If there was ever a four-year time span full of corny childish gimmicks, 1992-1996 was it. Dungeons full of supernatural characters and a plethora of profession-based gimmicks were widespread throughout the industry's landscape. It felt like the Super-friends and the Village People threw an ice cream party and broadcasted it to the world. Professional wrestling attendance and profits overall were trending downward while this hokey goofiness was trending up.

Despite all of this, televised professional wrestling was on the rise. On January 11, 1993, the WWF moved away from its weekly hybrid talk show/wrestling show called *Prime Time Wrestling* and debuted its match center weekly episodic show called *Monday Night Raw*. WCW followed suit and debuted its live weekly television show called *Monday Night Nitro*. There was also an increase in the amount of major professional wrestling pay-per-views held per year. It was a strange time where the creative aspect of professional wrestling felt stale, while at the same time the amount of creative material being asked for reached unprecedented levels. Out of this strangeness a few good men were called upon to lead the professional wrestling world forward. Out of those men our candidates are . . .

BRET 'THE HITMAN' HART V. 'THE HEARTBREAK KID' SHAWN MICHAELS

CAMPAIGN FOR BRET HART

There is a strong argument to make that no wrestler has ever cared more about the professional wrestling business than Bret 'The Hitman' Hart. He grew up in it, thrived in it, lived it, and became obsessed with it. He respected legitimate tough guys, loathed fake ones, and was bound by blood to uphold the professional wrestler's strict code of honor, if ever such a thing ever existed.

Perhaps no one strove harder to make the bell-to-bell ringwork the absolute best it could possibly be. Aside from being a very talented performer, Bret tended to his craft with an obsessive seriousness which helped him create many in-ring masterpieces. His first rate matches against Mr. Perfect, Roddy Piper, Ric Flair, and the 'British Bulldog' Davey Boy Smith are all testament to that. In his book *Hitman*, Bret Hart sums it up perfectly when he says, "I was recognized as being an artist and a storyteller. If Hulk Hogan was the Elvis of wrestling, I was the Robert DeNiro."

In the Fall of 1992, the Hitman won his first major title, the WWF championship defeating the legendary Ric Flair. Hart lead the company forward as its champion until the following year's WrestleMania. It didn't help Bret's status when, at the largest toga-themed professional wrestling show ever produced, the WWF made him look like a school yard wimp who got something stuck in his eyes and needed his big buddy to come fight for him during his main event title match. Nonetheless, Hart proved that he was a main event player capable of carrying the company's biggest show.

At the following year's WrestleMania, Bret Hart captured his second WWF championship this time his was the last match on the card and he finally defeated the biggest bully on the block, Yokozuna. Bret was voted *Pro Wrestling Illustrated* wrestler of the year and was ranked number one in the "PWI 500" both in 1993 and 1994. The same publication deemed that Bret was part of the feud of the year with his brother Owen. The Hitman received the coveted Meltzer five-star rating for his Summer Slam cage match with his brother.

In November of 1995, Hart was a major player, loved by fans, revered by critics, and respected by peers. At this point Bret had spent years in the major title picture and was prime to fulfill his lifelong dream of being the face of professional wrestling.

CAMPAIGN FOR SHAWN MICHAELS

Many consider Shawn Michaels to be the greatest in-ring performer to ever lace up a pair of wrestling boots. While many of his best matches were still ahead of him, anyone watching could see the pure wrestling talent he possessed. Shawn had it all inside the ring. He had the athletic ability, ring psychology, and work rate to make his matches rank among the very best. It was his superb bell-to-bell work that made many a legendary professional wrestler speak his name when questioned about who your greatest match was against.

In 1992, Shawn adopted his now synonymous moniker, the Heartbreak Kid. The following year Shawn won his first

Pro Wrestling Illustrated match of the year award for his match against his old tag team partner Marty Jannetty. While Jannetty is a talented wrestler, he isn't considered in the upper echelon of professional wrestling work rate talent like Owen is.

After a few years of finding his footing and putting on excellent matches, HBK won the intercontinental title. Shawn had his true main event player moment when he faced Razor Ramon at WrestleMania X. The famed ladder match received the coveted Meltzer five-star rating and was voted the *Pro Wrestling Illustrated* and the *Wrestling Observer Newsletter* match of the year. The match is still regarded as revolutionary for being the gold standard for ladder matches. While Shawn hasn't won any major gold at this point in his career, the evidence that he is a main event player was undeniable.

THE PROJECTED WINNER IS . . .

In October of 1995, a month before the election, Shawn Michaels was legitimately assaulted and forced to forfeit his intercontinental title at that month's WWF pay-per-view titled In Your House. Shawn was a victim in the October 1995 incident; however, his lifestyle choices may have been partially responsible as to why he had not held any major gold at this point. He was also relatively young and had already been fired once over behavioral issues.

On that same October in 1995, at the In Your House pay-per-view, Bret continued to show up and deliver stellar matches, picking up another win on the road to his big Survivor Series 1995 WWE championship title win. In the fall of 1995, Shawn had all the raw talent and potential to lead the professional wrestling world, but Bret has the resume, respect, and craftsmanship to carry this election. When this chapter in the bitter Hart versus Michaels rivalry is over, Michaels personal instability is just too much to overcome. The Hitman comes out on top, and Bret fulfills his lifelong dream. How can a guy who grew up in a legendary professional wrestling family that actually had a wrestling bear living under their house be destined for anything less?

Hitman wins.

PRESIDENTIAL ELECTION FOR 2000

The year 1999 was a complex one in the world of professional wrestling. Some argue that this was the worst year professional wrestling has ever seen, tragic events most notably the in-ring death of the beloved Owen Hart, WCW's internal chaos headlined by the infamous "Finger poke of doom," and the WWF's tasteless storylines, take your pick between eating your own pet or disgracing your opponent's father's funeral among others—all went down as the millennium came to an end. Yet despite all the tragedy and inner turmoil, the professional wrestling industry had never been hotter.

WWF was practically printing money and launched its second primetime weekly television show with the debut of *Smackdown*. Even the smaller Philadelphia based and locally owned Extreme Championship Wrestling (ECW) promotion got a major television network deal. 1999 was quite a year, and its presidential powerhouse election would be a hell raising electrifying event. Our candidates are . . .

'STONE COLD' STEVE AUSTIN V. DWAYNE 'THE ROCK' JOHNSON

CAMPAIGN FOR 'STONE COLD' STEVE AUSTIN

By November of 1999, the Texas Rattlesnake had a solid decade of professional wrestling experience under his belt. Steve Austin's portrayal of the no-nonsense, beer drinking, hell raising anti-hero Stone Cold character grew so popular that it arguably ushered in a new era for all of professional wrestling: the attitude era. Austin was no overnight success; Steve honed his craft for years wrestling in WCW and ECW before signing on with WWF. Once in the WWF, Austin's popularity generically grew at a steady pace. It was the organic rise that fans were clamoring for after years and years of having management's chosen clean cut babyface forced down their throat. Stone Cold's natural rise reached a point where it was undeniable that he will be considered one of the most popular superstars ever.

In 1996, Austin put on a brilliant match with Bret 'The Hitman' Hart at WrestleMania 13. The match showcased a slow and subtle double-turn. After Austin was finished with one of the all-time greatest feuds against Bret, he captured his first world championship by defeating Shawn Michaels at WrestleMania XIV. Austin's time was here. This was apparent when he entered into arguably the all-time greatest feud and wrestling storyline ever against WWF owner Vince McMahon.

The world lived vicariously through Austin as he took no bull from anyone, including his boss.

In 1998 and 1999, Austin brought the coveted *Pro Wrestling Illustrated* wrestler of the year award back to the Lone Star state. The publication also ranked the Texas Rattlesnake as the number one wrestler in the "PWI 500" for both of those years. The *Wrestling Observer Newsletter* named Stone Cold the wrestler of the year in 1998. With such high accolades achieved in between elections it seemed that nothing would derail Austin's victory. Unless something dastardly, like getting intentionally hit by a car, would knock him off course.

CAMPAIGN FOR THE ROCK

In November of 1996, the Rock formally entered the televised world of professional wrestling when he competed in his debut match at Survivor Series. The blue chipper, as they were calling him, son of Rocky Johnson and grandson of the High Chief Peter Maivia, was seemingly destined for greatness in the professional wrestling business.

Over the late nineties the Rock's persona gradually transformed from the crowd chanting "Die Rocky Die!" into the now-customary huge pop the People's Champion is welcomed with. Dwayne comically lashed out at the fans who mocked him and dethroned the veteran Ron Simmons to become the leader of the Nation of Domination stable.

The Rock's naturally entertaining personality would shine even brighter as he entered epic feuds with the likes of Triple H and Mankind. In 1998, Dwayne Johnson captured major gold and the following year the Rock was so influential that one of WWF's flagship shows *Smackdown* was named after one of his iconic catchphrases. In September of 1999, the Rock gave us one final campaign push when he and Mankind put on the iconic "This is Your Life" segment on *Raw*. The segment is still the highest rated one that the decades old television show has ever produced.

THE PROJECTED WINNER IS . . .

This election campaign features two once in a lifetime talents vying for the right to be the face of the professional wrestling industry. The Rock's charisma is undeniable, but perhaps no one was ever hotter than 'Stone Cold' Steve Austin. If the pops these two are receiving are any indication no matter how this election turns out the professional wrestling world will be in good shape. The question is are both these two men willing and able to carry the professional wrestling torch forward for the next four years. Even though the Rock's mainstream crossover power was readily apparent, having already began his journey to onscreen stardom by guest starring in the second highest rated episode in season one of *That '70s Show*, he is just not winning an election against the most over wrestler in the history of professional wrestling.

The winner is 'Stone Cold' Steve Austin. Oh hell yeah!

CHAPTER 6

ALL IN THE FAMILY

Carrying on the family business through multiple generations feels like an ancient tradition. At the age of seven, Spartan boys were sent to military training for the rest of their childhood. Their entire upbringing was centered around their future military participation. The world of professional wrestling doesn't seem too far from Sparta. They train early, bleed often, and sacrifice their bodies. They embody the spirit of the modern-day warrior.

There are many wrestling bloodlines that are centered around carrying on the legacy of performing inside the squared circle. Professional wrestling is known as a tight knit community, one full of many famous families who carry on the craft generation after generation. It takes a lot of people who are willing to sacrifice their blood, sweat, and tears to create a professional wrestling dynasty.

A well-known wrestling family offers many benefits to a promotion. They have long standing business ties, can instantly become a stable or tag team, and there is a certain level of trust and respect for the business that is presumed. The greatest benefit though, as history has shown, is that professional wrestling families produce some of the greatest wrestlers the world has ever seen.

Second generation wrestlers, more often than not, know the written and unwritten rules of the business well before they ever lace up a pair of wrestling boots. A legacy's entire life can revolve around all things professional wrestling. They understand the social norms of the industry and are less likely to go into business for themselves. Going rouge might be a little tougher if your entire family is intricately tied to the trade.

Professional wrestling is not the only business full of public figures whose family ties are prevalent. Film, music, sports, politics, television, and many other platforms are all peppered with famous families looking to expand their family's legacy. Growing up in an intoxicating lime light can seduce many to follow the bright spotlight. The doors opened by nepotism make the journey to fame that much more plausible.

It's been said that the advantage of patronage exists in almost every aspect of society. Many believe sports is the last true meritocracy. A famous family might get you a try out, but you won't make the team if you can't make a winning impact on the game. Professional wrestling perpetually straddles that balancing scale between theater and sports. This balance is apparent when comparing professional wrestling families to other non-wrestling related famous families. Naturally this begs the question: Which famous families are the most comparable to our well-known professional wrestling ones?

MCMAHON/THE ROYAL FAMILY— HOUSE OF WINDSOR

If there is one famous family who for decades has garnered constant worldwide attention, it's the English royal family. In the world of professional wrestling, like it or not, the McMahons are that royalty. Since the early 1900s, starting with Jess McMahon, the McMahon family has been promoting professional wrestling. In the 1950s, Vincent J. McMahon took the reins of the family business and established the Capitol Wrestling Corporation. Vince Sr.'s control of professional wrestling in New York City, the most profitable regional territory, helped cement his position as one of the most influential promoters in the world. Capitol Wrestling Corporation evolved into the World Wide Wrestling Federation (WWWF), which would eventually be rebranded into a company that became synonymous with professional wrestling itself, the World Wrestling Federation (WWF). By 1970, Vince Sr.'s company was building momentum and repeatedly selling out arenas.

In the 1980s, Vincent Kennedy McMahon took over his father's wrestling business and it wasn't long before he redefined the industry. Over time, Vince took his father's promotion from an influential regional territorial leader to an undeniably powerful worldwide juggernaut. McMahon's dedication to creating polished television programs, marketable superstars, and captivating storylines captured the audiences' attention. This dedication to high production values combined with McMahon's shrewd business dealings paved the way for WWF dominance. The WWF eventually was rebranded once again, this time as World Wrestling Entertainment (WWE).

Once Shane and Stephanie joined the business, it was evident that the tradition of McMahons in professional wrestling would continue. In 2003, Triple H and Stephanie McMahon married. Hunter joined the family, ensuring that the next generation of Connecticut blue bloods carried on the storied McMahon legacy. For the past five decades the McMahon's have been the most influential family in the professional wrestling world.

The House of Windsor has also been exerting their worldwide

influence since the early 1900s. Currently the Royal family serves as the monarch of sixteen sovereign states including the United Kingdom, Canada, and Australia. Throughout the years, no family has garnered more worldwide attention. Royal weddings, funerals, coronations, and other major life events are met with spectacular global fanfare. In 2021, an interview with Prince Harry and Megan Markel garnered a remarkable 17.1 million viewers in America alone.

Both of these families have withstood major scandals and have held on to their prominent position in the public eye. Time will tell whether the McMahons maintain their royal status. But even Cody Rhodes acknowledged their regal legacy when he claims, through his in-ring musical entrance, that wrestling has more than one royal family.

In the latest chapter of the Book of McMahon, Vince, plagued by scandalous publicity, temporarily bequeathed the professional wrestling throne to Stephanie McMahon. Soon thereafter Vince reasserted himself into the company's dealings. In 2023, Vince McMahon did the once unthinkable act of selling his company. Perhaps he foresaw that the worst of his scandalous storm was yet to come.

The new owners, TKO Group Holdings, passed the creative torch to Triple H, but many still wondered what may linger of Vince's influence. At this point, who is really in charge of the company? The scandals and internal power struggles feel like they were ripped out of the pages of *Game of Thrones*. Drama aside, just as the House of Windsor is still the most recognized royal family, in professional wrestling no family is more widely recognized than that of House McMahon.

ANOA'I-MAIVIA / KARDASHIAN-JENNER

The head turning physiques of these two large families helped launch these families into household name status. Their respective business acumen has enabled them to establish exceptional careers with lasting legacies. The eye-popping wow factor of these booty and the beast families caught the world's attention, but it took much more to keep us watching. Both families are headlined by some of pop culture's most iconic personas and both boost a number of famous members who standout as megastars in their own right. Through physical training and mental determination, these families have kept their surname in the spotlight for multiple generations.

While technically the Anoa'i family is not in the same bloodline as High Chief Peter Maivia and his descendants, their shared Samoan heritage, blood oath, and lasting professional wrestling connections, including the High Chief Peter Maivia's training of Afa and Sika, makes them practically family. Like with many things in professional wrestling, we just accept it as reality.

Two of the top five most followed Instagram accounts in the world are held by the Kardashian's Kylie Jenner and the Anoa'i–Maivia family's Dwayne 'The Rock' Johnson. The Kardashian-Jenner family has five members in the top twenty most followed Instagram accounts. Both of these families are home to some of the most watched celebrities in the world. Everyone with access to social media or a television smells what these families are cooking. While the Kardashian-Jenner clan has spent decades dominating the reality television scene, the Bloodline had a historic championship run in WWE.

It is pretty much undisputed amongst the professional wrestling community that Roman Reigns is currently sitting at the head of professional wrestling's table. Roman has one of the longest running title reigns in professional wrestling history. Jimmy and Jey Uso hold the record for the longest reign with the WWE's tag team straps, while Solo Sikoa is impressing many as the family's new monster enforcer.

Rodney Anoa'i, better known to wrestling fans as Yokozuna, stood out from his family by rising to fame using a unique Japanese sumo wrestler gimmick, one that had no reliance on his Samoan roots. Yoko was different from what the world expected of him and was rewarded for it with a world championship run. Much like the Anoa'i-Maivia family, when people picture a Kardashian-Jenner family member, they have a certain image in mind. Nothing may contrast more with that image than Bruce Jenner's groundbreaking gender transformation into Caitlyn Jenner. Her courage to be different only added to Jenner's status as one of the world's most recognizable Olympians.

The Kardashian-Jenner family has relied on their physical attributes just as much as any professional wrestling family ever has. Using their over-the-top reality personas as a launching pad, the Kardashian-Jenner family has collectively amassed a billion-dollar empire. While not quite the billions the Kardashian-Jenner family has amassed, the Anoa'i-Maivia family has held more than its fair share of big gold, collectively claiming an impressive fifteen world heavyweight titles. Their professional wrestling golden belts are symbolic of the very real fortune the legendary Samoan family possesses. The unbridled ambitions of these families have both of them potentially eyeing a role in the world of politics, possibly even the White House. It is hard to imagine that the footprints left by each of these prominent bloodlines will ever fade away.

HART / JACKSON

Overbearing patriarchs, large families full of captivating personalities, and some of the best talent in their respective fields are
some of the shared characteristics between these two famous
families. Michael Jackson is widely regarded as one of the best
performers the music industry has ever seen. In professional
wrestling, the same can be said for the Excellence of Execution,
Bret 'The Hitman' Hart. While at the top of their games both
of these megastars demonstrated incredible body control and
both were scrutinized for their off-stage actions. Jackson's iconic
dancing seemed almost alien, while Hart's in-ring proficiency is
still studied today. Michael Jackson's scandal plagued controver-
sies are some of the most discussed topics in pop music history.
Similarly, Bret Hart and the Montreal screw job incident is still
the most talked about moment in professional wrestling history.
At a certain moment in time, the Hitman and the King of Pop
were both poster children, not only for their families, but for
their respective industries.

These two families are both headed by stern patriarchs, men
who left many wondering if their hard nose parenting style crossed
the line into child abuse. Joe Jackson and Stu Hart both used a
strong hand to guide their children's careers, sternly teaching
them the ropes of their respective businesses. Both large sibling
groups are well known throughout their fields and each family's
sibling group has had two members reach that elusive level of
historical notoriety of their industry. Following in their families'
famous footsteps, the youngest sibling from each group would
be each family's second most famous member.

Despite living in the seemingly insurmountable shadows

of their megastar older siblings, Janet Jackson and Owen Hart each achieved an impressive level of individual success. Janet and Owen's careers stand on their own, winning Grammys and Slammys while enticing many fans to ultimately prefer their work over their older siblings. They both had an undeniably high level of talent, which silenced any nepotism criticisms. Each youngest sibling had memorable collaborations with their megastar older brother. In 1994, Bret versus Owen squared off at WrestleMania X in what many consider one of the greatest WrestleMania matches of all time. A year later Michael and Janet released "Scream" in what would be one of the King of Pop's final hit records. Like the Jacksons have done in the music industry, the Harts have cemented a legacy of excellence in the world of professional wrestling.

VON ERICH / KENNEDY

The Kennedys and the Von Erichs are two beloved iconic American families. These two good-looking All-American families share unbelievable levels of popularity and success. Tragically, they also share unimaginable sorrow with deep roots in Dallas, Texas.

During their heyday the Von Erichs weren't hot, they were scorching. The Dallas based professional wrestling family was undoubtedly one of the industry's most popular acts of the 1980s. Their good looks and charisma created a Beatles-esque following in any territory they wrestled in. Though their rockstar fame was most apparent in the boys' home territory of the Texas-based called World Class Championship Wrestling (WCCW). The Von Erichs filled arenas and stadiums as they participated in one of professional wrestling's most memorable feuds against the Freebirds. The battle between decency and filth dominated the professional wrestling headlines for years. Wherever they went a tornado of screaming fans packed venues and let everyone know that the Von Erichs were it.

If there ever was a politician as popular as the Von Erichs were in Texas, it was John F. Kennedy. The nation's first Catholic president garnered an average approval rating of seventy, the highest rating among any president since approval ratings became a thing. Kennedy's handsome appearance, charm, and inspiring speeches made him a favorite for Hollywood elite and common folks alike. The Kennedy family is full of congressmen, senators, ambassadors, and a host of other political titles held by various family members.

The professional wrestling lore told by many bards, most recently depicted in the 2023 *The Iron Claw* film, seem to agree that the Von Erichs and tragedy are synonymous. Well, the same can be said for the Kennedys, a family whom has suffered multiple untimely deaths. The Kennedys have endured so many calamities that have many, including their own, pondering if the fabled Kennedy curse is a real part of their reality. If one professional wrestling family can be said to be cursed, surely it's the Von Erichs. The Von Erichs have endured more loss than any family should, with five out of six of Fritz's boys all passing away before the age of thirty-five.

The Texas and Massachusetts based families have both had their familial history characterized by momentous success, tragic death, and public scandals. While seemingly living a luxurious life, our hearts break for the sorrow these families have endured. Yet despite it all, they have preserved. In 2024, Marshall and Ross Von Erich are working the independent scene looking to make a big splash in the professional wrestling scene, while Robert F.

Kennedy Jr. has launched an independent presidential campaign with the potential to have a huge impact on our next presidential election. Through triumph and tragedy both of these two iconic American families have left a lasting legacy on our world.

FLAIR / BUSH

The Flairs and the Bushes are home to two of the most influential parent-child duos in their respective fields. During the 1980s, these two families burst onto the national scene and strutted into living rooms across America. Since then, both have built influential legacies and maintained their household name status. In the 1980s, George H. W. Bush was serving as vice president of the United States while Ric Flair was racking up golden title belts across America.

During the decade of greed, Flair and Bush were both representing America on an international stage. While George H. W. Bush, a former fighter pilot, was using diplomacy to usher in an end of the Cold War, Ric Flair was battling the dastardly Russian villain, Nikita Koloff. These two industry leaders were in the upper echelons of their professions achieving worldwide fame and soaking in that rarified air that only "the man" can breathe.

Regardless of your politics, any family that has multiple members elected to America's highest office has attained a rare and impressive feat. In the 248 years of national sovereignty, George H.W. Bush and his son George W. Bush are only the second parent-child duo to have both members elected as the president of the United States. While many do not consider the Bushes two of the greatest presidents in American history, their family's continued service to the United States is indisputable.

They have led American forces against many foreign adversaries particularly those in the Middle East.

Ric Flair is widely regarded as one of, if not the, greatest professional wrestler to ever live. The sixteen- to twenty-five-time world champion (depending on whose counting) is a multitool player and everything a professional wrestler should be. His microphone skills have produced some of the most iconic professional wrestling moments and catch phrases in sports entertainment history. His in-ring work is both technically sound and theatrically entertaining. Naitch's compelling promos, five-star matches, and iconic eye-catching gimmick are what makes him one of the GOATs of professional wrestling. It's not surprising that he represented the very best of American wrestling everywhere he travels.

While Charlotte's in-ring story is still being told, many already consider her one of, if not the, greatest women professional wrestler of all time. Already a holder of fourteen women's titles, she has led the WWE women's division to new heights including her participation in the unprecedented WrestleMania 35 main event. Male or female, she is one of the most well rounded active professional wrestlers today.

Attempting to follow in their father's legacy, Reid and David Flair had short but unceremonious runs in the professional wrestling business. Similarly, Jeb Bush had his own unceremonious "low energy" presidential run. If only a frustrated Jeb pulled a David Flair and had publicly shaved George H. W. Bush's head. While these family member's legacies might not be as historic as their more famous kinfolk, they still left their marks on the world.

Whether you are hearing "Read my lips . . ." or "Wooooo!" these two families command attention and garner respect. When it comes to political parent-child duos, it's hard to surpass the esteem of a father and son whom have both sat inside the oval office as America's commander in chief. In the world of professional wrestling, it's hard to imagine that there will ever be a parent-child combo with more admiration and respect than Ric and Charlotte Flair. Their combined over thirty world titles are proof of that. Each of these decorated families have had multiple members sitting atop of their respective industry. We salute both of their contributions to the world. Wooooo!

RHODES / MANNING

These two legendary sports families are both headed by Hall-of-Fame patriarchs in Archie Manning and the 'American Dream' Dusty Rhodes. Both of these patriarchs fathered groups of children that include two men whose career accomplishments would rival or arguably even surpass their own.

These two southern families have a legacy of leadership in their respective athletic fields. The closest thing to a player/coach in the National Football League (NFL) is a team's quarterback. All three Manning men have been offensive architects on the gridiron excelling at the quarterback position. The trio set the tone for their locker rooms and created a winning philosophy. The Manning men (Archie, Peyton and Eli) combined for a total of thirty-nine NFL seasons, twenty Pro Bowl selections, and four Super Bowl titles. These on-the-field generals were proven winners and created lots of magic on the gridiron.

Similarly, the Rhodes family has lasting longevity in the athletic arena. Dusty debuted in the late 1960s, and his sons Dustin and Cody have been fighting opponents in the ring through at least 2024. The Rhodes family's in-ring accomplishments in the world of professional wrestling are common knowledge amongst fans. The three men have collectively won championships in virtually every major professional wrestling promotion. There is no doubt that all three men are ring generals capable of creating unforgettable matches. Their in-ring work is stellar, but perhaps their greatest collective contribution to the world of professional wrestling is as some of its backstage architects.

The closest thing to a player/coach in the professional wrestling world is the wrestler/booker. Dusty Rhodes was one of the most revered men when it came to wearing these two hats. Dusty was a celebrated booker, a mentor to many young wrestlers, and is credited with playing a crucial role in the development of many of today's top talents. The Rhodes patriarch is the namesake for the dusty finish, a match finish where the winner gets screwed out of a victory on a technicality. From WCW to WWE and NXT, Dusty has left his son of a plumber fingerprints on many well-known professional wrestlers' careers.

In 2019, Cody and his older brother Dustin carried on their father's influential tradition in All Elite Wrestling (AEW). Cody served as one of the company's executive vice presidents while also being one of the company's top babyfaces. Dustin also competes for AEW in the ring and serves as a coach, training the company's young talent. As AEW expanded their presence in the professional wrestling world, the Rhodes family proved fundamental in architecting the company's success. Cody expanded the family's footprint into reality television while Eli and Peyton are expanding their family's sports legacy into the broadcasting world with a Monday Night Football simulcast. In 2022, Cody once again swapped jerseys and return to the WWE where he is currently fighting to finish his story and cement his legacy as a true legend of the ring.

It's said that an average NFL career lasts three years and with the high degree of turnover an average major league professional wrestling career may be about the same. These two families have shattered those averages with exceptional, long-lasting careers. They are sports royalty, game architects, and creators of exceptionally entertaining athletic moments for those of us lucky enough to soak them in.

GUERRERO / WAYANS

Like an American wrestler pretending not to speak English so he could fully sell his heel foreigner gimmick, these two large families have become fully immersed in the entertainment industry. The Guerrero family boasts near double digit family members who have laced up the boots and stepped inside the squared circle. The Wayans family has eleven family members whom have made an impact in Hollywood. These two families both started out by developing a following with relatively small niche fan bases. Their collective talents grew their fame and elevated their surname to worldwide renowned status.

The Wayans family members often collaborated with each other in their comedic and film efforts. Many of their well-known projects like *In Living Color, Scary Movie,* and *White Chicks* involved multiple family members participating in the project's creation. Similarly, the Guerreros were seemingly almost always involved in the professional wrestling tag team scene with varied combinations of family members teaming up. Before Eddie and Chavo Guerrero Jr. ever teamed up and called themselves Los

Guerreros, the family had collectively amassed nine various tag team title reigns. Mando Guerrero, one of those Guerrero tag team champions, even helped train the women of the Gorgeous Ladies of Wrestling (GLOW), including future WWE superstar Ivory.

Keenen Ivory Wayans is the standout star among the various members of his large creative family. The family's most well-known film projects (previously listed) were all created by Keenen. When looking at the Wayans' contribution to the film industry Keenen's may be the greatest.

In the very talented Guerrero wrestling family, Eddie is their Keenan. Among today's professional wrestling fans, the most memorable Guerrero family wrestling moments revolve around Latino Heat himself, Eddie Guerrero. From his WCW Halloween Havoc match against Rey Mysterio to his shocking WWE championship victory over Brock Lesnar and his first major title defense against Kurt Angle at WrestleMania XX, Eddie was a pure professional wrestling genius.

The Guerrero and Wayans family contributed to all aspects of their respective entertainment genres. Whether it is Chavo Guerrero wearing a tiny Cowboy hat and galloping down to the ring on his toy horse or it is Marlon playing a dwarf posing as a baby, both families were willing to participate in rather silly premises all in the name of entertainment. No outfit is off limits either as demonstrated by Hector Guerrero's portrayal of the Gobbledy Gooker or Damon Wayans taking on the role of Homie the Clown. Whether in big or small roles, Los Guerreros and the Wayans are two large families whose legacy in their respective industry continues to grow. Only time will tell if the next generation can continue their families' widespread legacy in the business of show.

ORTON / COPPOLA

Two families with at least three generations of entertainment industry players. Francis Ford Coppola, Sofia Coppola, Nicholas Cage, and Jason Schwartzman are among the many acclaimed members of the storied Hollywood Coppola family. The Coppolas have collectively won nine Academy Awards and have been part of some of the most iconic films in cinematic history. The cinematic masterpieces of *The Godfather*, *Apocalypse Now*, and *Lost in Translation* have all been Coppola lead projects. Also, special shout out to Nick Cage for giving us *Face Off*, *Con Air*, and *Gone in 60 Seconds*. Also exceptional projects. A family full of excellence in the arts if there ever was one.

In the 1960s, the 'Big O' Bob Orton Sr., started off his family's venture into the national professional wrestling scene. The Missouri native traveled across America collecting championship gold in multiple territories. Following in the Big O's wrestling boots, during the 1970s 'Cowboy' Bob Orton Jr. broke into the industry. By the 1980s, Cowboy was a main event player who feuded with many of the business's top guys. Not many men can say they were part of the first ever WrestleMania main event, but Cowboy can.

For many years, among the numerous professional wrestling families the Orton family fell into the lesser talked about category. That was the case until Randy Orton burst onto the scene and quickly became the youngest WWE world champion of all time. Since then, Randy has built himself a legendary first ballot Hall-of-Fame career. Perhaps it was Good Ole JR who summed it up best when in 2021, while working for promotional competitor AEW, he was asked who was the best active professional wrestler in the business. His response was telling . . . Randy Orton. No matter what you give him (storyline or card placement) the Viper will deliver. Randy Orton maximizing his minutes is as dependable as it gets in professional wrestling. The Orton men combined for fourteen major heavyweight titles among the other belts and accolades they amassed during their careers. Yes, that is mostly Randy's doing but still, much like the Coppolas, the Ortons are a family full of well-respected industry players.

FUNK / SHEEN

These two famous families have provided the world countless hours of entertainment and too many jaw-dropping moments to count. Martin Sheen and Dory Funk serve as the patriarchs for these two prolific families. Martin has appeared in over one hundred film projects and has received critical acclaim for many of his performances. Dory Funk was a former professional wrestler who began managing Western State Sports in Amarillo, Texas. The West Texas based promotion produced many wrestling stars including Stan Hansen, Harley Race, Bruiser Brody and Funk's own sons Dory Funk Jr. and Terry Funk.

Each families' eldest sons, Dory Funk Jr. and Emilio Estevez, built upon their father's legacy. Emilio starred in memorable roles including his work in *The Outsiders, The Breakfast Club*, and *The Mighty Ducks*. Estevez's best work is found in the "The" section. While in 1969, Dory Funk Jr. became the National Wrestling Alliance (NWA) world heavyweight champion, carrying the prestigious belt for over four years. Dory Jr. would travel all over the globe having multiple "match of the year" caliber matches.

Terry and Charlie are both approximately three years younger than their older brothers. That's not all that the Hardcore Legend and the Warlock have in common, both men's bodies have been put through the ringer. Terry Funk has had too many bloody encounters to count, and Charlie has had enough booze and drugs to rival any of the hard partying boys in the locker room. Both men have had moments that have left the public wondering: How many screws have they lost? For Terry, middle aged and crazy was more than just words on a T-shirt. Who can forget Terry's insane promos, perpetual state of retirement, or wild Japanese death matches? The same can be said for tiger blood, epic rants, and interviews requiring mental gymnastics to comprehend.

Whether it is their performances in front of the camera or the drama behind it, these father and son trios have kept us entertained for decades. From epic feuds to all-time great sitcoms, these men have done it all. Whenever these two families set out to entertain us there is one thing we can be sure of: we are WINNING!

WINDAM-ROTUNDA / FONDA

These two famous families each have three generations of members whom have basked in that celebrity limelight and both have lost family members at far too young an age. The Fondas and Windam-Rotunda families have each had their share of controversy and run-ins with the law. The Fondas' stints with the law revolved around drugs and protest culture. Blackjack Mulligan and Kendall Windam each spent two years in federal prison for counterfeiting. Despite their personal tribulations, both families have left a lasting footprint on their respective industry.

The patriarchs of these two families, Henry Fonda and Robert Deroy Windam, aka Blackjack Mulligan, each have had noteworthy careers and acted in ways that led some to question their mental health. Henry Fonda was said to have loathed any displays of emotion and was described as "emotionally distant" with his children. Blackjack on the other hand, on multiple occasions, sucker punched André the Giant just to see what happened. Each time the two men fought, like a cartoon tornado on a rampage, they destroyed anything and everything in their path. On one famous occasion André dragged the big Texan out to the ocean and threatened to drown him. If picking a fight with André doesn't make others question your sanity, nothing will.

Henry Ford married Frances Ford Seymor and the couple had two children who became stars in their own rights, Peter and Jane Fonda. Blackjack married Julia Windham and they had three children named Barry, Stephanie, and Kendall Windam. Following in their father's footsteps both Peter and Jane Fonda became outspoken political advocates, which was reflected in some of their on-screen work. Similarly, Barry and Kendall Windam portrayed themself as the black hat cowboy character just as his father had.

While the Fonda family racked up ten Academy Award nominations, winning four of them, the Windam-Rotunda family has collectively amassed over double digit major professional wrestling championships. In 1991, worlds collided when Jane Fonda married WCW owner and boss to many a Windam-Rotunda family member, Ted Turner. In the late 1990s and under Turner's ownership, WCW became the first and only organization to legitimately contest the WWE's claim as the number one professional wrestling company in the world. In 2001, Turner ended his ties with both families, selling WCW then less than three months later divorcing Jane Fonda.

In 1984, professional wrestler Mike Rotunda, aka I.R.S.,

married Stephanie Windam and officially joined the Windam family. Rotunda was also a frequent tag team partner for Barry, and the duo captured the WWF tag team championships on multiple occasions. The couple, Mike and Stephanie that is, had three children together, including professional wrestlers Bray Wyatt and Bo Dallas.

While Peter and Jane Fonda were still in grade school, they lost their mother, Frances Ford Seymour. She was forty-two years old when she passed away. In 2023, the Windam-Rotunda family suffered a far-too-young passing when Bray Wyatt passed away at the age of thirty-six. Bray Wyatt brought innovative character work and a larger-than-life persona to the squared circle. The professional wrestling community still morns for the Eater of Worlds. R.I.P. Bray Wyatt.

CHAPTER 7

THE SLOBBER KNOCKER DRAFT

Like warm apple pie with a scoop of vanilla ice cream, nothing is more patriotic than two of our favorite pastimes: football and professional wrestling. We just love watching the meat smash as athletic men violently collide into each other. The athletic drama both enterprises display keeps fans coming back year after year.

In 2001, the World Wrestling Federation (WWF) and the National Broadcasting Company (NBC) entered into a joint venture creating the Xtreme Football League (XFL). The stakeholders were well aware of the overlapping fan bases between professional wrestling and football. While the new league struggled to find financial success, it revolutionized the use of sky cams, player microphones, and access to the players. Today one of professional wrestling's biggest stars in Dwayne 'The Rock' Johnson is spearheading the revitalization of spring football and a principal player in the new ownership of the United Football League (UFL), a league created following the merger of the United States Football League (USFL) and the revitalized XFL. Professional wrestling and football run on the same track and neither will stay out of the other's lane.

Over the years, so many future squared-circle superstars have strapped on their helmet and gone to battle on the gridiron. Every generation of professional wrestling talent is full of elite athletes, many of whom have put on the pads well before ever hitting the ring ropes. With so much physical talent out there the question arises: What decade would reign supreme in an all-wrestler football tournament?

To answer this question, we are creating four teams to represent the '80s, '90s, '00s, and the '10s. Given the longevity of many professional wrestler careers, there is going to be lots of overlap. Back in the day, we all loved arcade fighting games like *Street Fighter* and *Mortal Kombat*. The graphic violence, slick production, and over the top characters were dope. Sound familiar? Yet despite this dopeness, nothing was more annoying than when your friend picks the same fighter as you. It was just weak seeing two players locked on opposite sides of the screen throwing dueling fireballs at one another. We can't have that in this tournament. Our solution is simple: a fantasy football style draft.

Let's set some rules first. The teams will be comprised of limited football rosters, similar to your traditional fantasy football league. For the Slobber Knocker Draft our teams will need to select eligible professional wrestlers to fill these positions:

QB	QUARTERBACK
RB	RUNNING BACK
WR (2)	WIDE RECEIVER
TE	TIGHT END
LB	LINEBACKER
OL/DL (4)	OFFENSE/DEFENSE LINEMEN *(Playing both ways)*
K	KICKER

The draft will be conducted in a fantasy football snake style order, once a player is drafted, he is off the board. A team can only draft a wrestler who was an active competitor for at least four years during that team's respective decade. Once selected each wrestler plays as the best version of themselves as existed in the decade that drafted them. So, if a guy was a quality athlete in the past decade but barely managed to squeeze out four past his prime glory years in your decade, well, you get whatever it is that he has to offer while wrestling in your decade.

Like any good professional wrestling card, the Slobber Knocker draft has a spot for the tag team division to shine. Our line men will be selected in pairs. To be eligible, a tag team must have actively competed as a unit for at least two years in the decade that drafts them. On and off again partnerships or short-lived tag teams are out.

A wrestler can only be selected once. If a wrestler is selected as a singles competitor or as part of a tag team, he and any tag teams he was member of are off the board. That is unless that particular tag team invoked the Freebird rule, in that case the other two remaining members are still eligible.

Strategy will be paramount. Like Arn Anderson walking around an All Elite Wrestling (AEW) ring with a chicken and waffles menu, every decade is going to need a top-notch play caller.

THE HEAD COACHES

1980S ROCK 'N' JOCK MANIA
BOBBY 'THE BRAIN' HEENAN

Most considered him the greatest professional wrestling manager of all time. The Brain had a knack for selecting quality talent, making champions, and getting the best out of his men. Even the legendary André the Giant was elevated by his association with the Brain. Under Heenan's management, André competed in the most consequential match in professional wrestling history. The Brain's lightning quick wit was showcased during his legendary broadcast journalist career. Heenan brings intelligence and adaptability to his game plan. It'll be a tough road for whichever ham and egger goes against the family.

1990S END ZONE ERA
ERIC BISCHOFF

The New World Order (NWO) might have been the greatest collection of talent ever assembled under the roof of one stable. It was Easy E who served as the de facto general manager for their star-studded operation. Blackbelt Bischoff knows the business inside and out. If he can transfer his cunning backstage skills onto the gridiron, the End Zone Era might be just too sweet!

2000S RUTHLESS BLITZ
VICKIE GUERRERO

Never hesitating to insert herself into the action, Vickie Guerrero has influenced the outcome of many a wrestling match. As the only female coach/manager in the Slobber Knocker draft, Vickie may be vastly underestimated. Her neck-brace-sporting, wheel-chair-rolling, shrill-voice screeching self may be a part of that too. Any underestimation of her talents would be a mistake. The fiery cougar has proven her leadership and even frog splashed her way to victory at the grandest stage of them all: WrestleMania. Look for questionable calls to fall her team's way, as the refs will do anything to avoid hearing the Latina Karen screeching "Excuse me!" from the sidelines.

2010S TOUCHDOWN NETWORK
PAUL HEYMAN

In the '10s, it may seem like the professional wrestling managers had taken a back seat. Yet, even in this climate Heyman has been a stellar advocate for the Beast Incarnate Brock Lesnar, cutting killer promos that got the seemingly unstoppable juggernaut even more heat. Heyman inspires loyalty, ask any Extreme Championship Wrestling (ECW) guy and they will proudly tell you about diving off of various parts of the ECW arena under Paul's watch. Once Paul dons the baseball cap and headset, there is no doubt that the Touchdown Network will all become Paul Heyman guys.

We will need a commissioner to moderate the draft. The natural choice is Vince McMahon, but we need someone who is guaranteed to get that Roger Goodell at the NFL draft level of heat. Vinny Mac is a great heel, but if he is not trying to get booed, even in today's climate, it'll be tough to get a professional wrestling crowd to boo the man that basically created the modern industry. Let's go with Vince Russo here, he will definitely get that Goodell go-home heat.

Now let's set our pigskin classic's draft order. Following a brutal fatal four-way elimination match, Bobby 'The Brain' Heenan and the '80s Rock 'n' Jock Mania select first, followed by Vickie Guerrero and her '00s Ruthless Blitz. Eric Bischoff and the '90s End Zone Era draft third. Paul Heyman and his '10s Touchdown Network select fourth. Welcome to the Slobber Knocker Draft!

ROUND ONE

1980'S ROCK 'N' JOCK MANIA	1990'S END ZONE ERA	2000'S RUTHLESS BLITZ	2010'S TOUCHDOWN NETWORK
COACH/GM: BOBBY 'THE BRAIN' HEENAN	COACH/GM: ERIC BISCHOFF	COACH/GM: VICKIE GUERRERO	COACH/GM: PAUL HEYMAN
QB	QB	QB	QB
RB	RB	RB	RB
WR	WR	WR	WR
WR	WR	WR	WR
TE	TE	TE	TE
LB	LB	LB	LB
OL/DL	OL/DL	OL/DL	OL/DL
OL/DL	OL/DL	OL/DL	OL/DL
K	K	K	K

1. With the first pick in the draft, '80s Rock 'n' Jock Mania selects Doom. (Linemen)

Analysis: They don't call him the Brain for nothing. Bobby Heenan does it again, snatching up a pair of brutish football players with experience wearing NFL helmets. Ron Simmons and Butch Reed both played collegiate football and got a shot to continue playing at the highest level. Simmons, a Heisman Trophy finalist, was even selected to the College Football Hall-of-Fame. It is already shaping to be one hell of a line for the '80s.

2. With the second pick in the draft, the '00s Ruthless Blitz selects Brock Lesnar. (LB)

Analysis: No surprises here. The Beast Incarnate has all the physical tools to be an impact player on the field. Lesnar can do it all, he dominates professional wrestling, ultimate fighting, and even secured a tryout with the Minnesota Vikings. The invite was extended despite the fact that Lesnar had not played football since high school. Good pick up for the '00s. He had to be the top pick on the '10s board.

Side note: To those wondering if Lesnar had enough years in the '00s to be eligible. Yes, yes, he does. We are counting it. Pick stands.

3. With the third pick in the draft, the '90s End Zone Era selects 'Hacksaw' Jim Duggan. (LB)

Analysis: Duggan was a standout player at Southern Methodist University who was voted a team captain. He was drafted by the Atlanta Falcons and was trending to have a long NFL career, but then his knees had other plans. Hacksaw famously used a three-point stance clothesline to finish off his opponents in the ring. The love of the pigskin never left the inaugural Royal Rumble winner's heart. Solid pick.

4. With the fourth pick in the draft, the '10s Touchdown Network selects Randy Orton. (WR)

Analysis: Orton is a superior athlete; the Viper stands at 6'5" and possess a young sleek muscular build. A third-generation superstar, Randy has been part of professional wrestling's biggest promotion, World Wrestling Entertainment (WWE), for over two decades. With a lifetime of experience behind him, perhaps no one will have more inside information about any opposing team's roster than the Viper. If Randy can use the stealth quickness he relies on when hitting opponents with an RKO out of nowhere, he may be that breakout wide receiver the Touchdown Network needs to hit big plays.

5. With the fifth pick in the draft, the '10s Touchdown Network selects Ron 'The Truth' Killings. (WR)

Analysis: At 6'2" and possessing track star breakout speed, Truth has tons of upside with his big play potential. Killings was a star high school athlete in football and track and field. Anyone who saw Truth running around backstage with his 24/7 championship has witnessed that break neck speed. The Touchdown Network will have a tough task on their hands keeping Truth mentally focused. Big gamble betting on a man who at times has invisible friends, Heyman may have just drafted a huge liability, but if anyone can make it work it's the Wiseman.

6. With the sixth pick in the draft, the '90s End Zone Era selects Bill Goldberg. (TE)

Analysis: A former Georgia Bulldog standout, a former NFL draft pick, and a former World Bowl II champion, Goldberg has proven explosive speed and hard-hitting power on the football field. Goldberg would definitely be a better fit as a linebacker, but given that he has more athletic versatility than Duggan, the

End Zone Era has strategically moved him to the tight end spot. Hands might be a liability here. If that becomes the case, just run the ball behind a full speed blocking Goldberg and watch the yardage pile up.

7. With the seventh pick in the draft, the '00s Ruthless Blitz selects Dwayne 'The Rock' Johnson. (TE)

Analysis: A starting linebacker for the national championship winning U, the Rock will undoubtedly be laying the smackdown between the hashes. The *Ballers* star played linebacker for Miami earning him a tryout with the Canadian Football League's Calgary Stampeders. Johnson's size and quickness will allow him to smoothly transition to tight end. The Rock will need to keep raising and spitting on his hands as he gears up for some big catches up the middle.

8. With the eighth pick in the draft, '80s Rock 'n' Jock Mania selects Lex Luger. (LB)

Analysis: Another U alumnus, Luger was bringing his own brand of craziness to Miami well before the '80s Canes teams found their bad boy swagger. During his days at Miami, Luger was kicked off the team for trashing his hotel room. Despite his off the field issues, he was still able to land a tryout with the Green Bay Packers. Lex is a collegiate level linebacker with impressive athleticism, the total package.

ROUND TWO

1980'S ROCK 'N' JOCK MANIA	1990'S END ZONE ERA	2000'S RUTHLESS BLITZ	2010'S TOUCHDOWN NETWORK
COACH/GM: BOBBY 'THE BRAIN' HEENAN	COACH/GM: ERIC BISCHOFF	COACH/GM: VICKIE GUERRERO	COACH/GM: PAUL HEYMAN
QB	QB	QB	QB
RB	RB	RB	RB
WR	WR	WR	WR: RANDY ORTON (4)
WR	WR	WR	WR: RON 'TRUTH' KILLINGS (5)
TE	TE: BILL GOLDBERG (6)	TE: DWAYNE 'THE ROCK' JOHNSON (7)	TE
LB: LEX LUGER (8)	LB: 'HACKSAW' JIM DUGGAN (3)	LB: BROCK LESNAR (2)	LB
OL/DL: DOOM (1)	OL/DL	OL/DL	OL/DL
OL/DL	OL/DL	OL/DL	OL/DL
K	K	K	K

1. With the ninth pick in the draft, '80s Rock 'n' Jock Mania selects Tito Santana. (WR)

Analysis: Many years of flying forearms in the ring have Santana ready to make those diving catches on the gridiron. Santana is no stranger to the bright lights of football having played college ball for the West Texas State Buffalos. The collegiate tight end was talented enough to land a tryout with the Kansas City Chiefs. Santana's athleticism allows him to be a go to target all around the field.

2. With the tenth pick in the draft, '00s Ruthless Blitz selects Ted DiBiase Jr. (QB)

Analysis: When people think about the DiBiase family, they most remember their extravagant lifestyle rather than their athletic prowess. The physical ability is there though, 'Iron' Mike DiBiase and Ted DiBiase Sr. both played collegiate athletics. DiBiase Jr. was a starting high school quarterback in Mississippi, leading his team to a playoff appearance. He was talented enough to earn the starting quarterback spot for Mississippi College's football team. Looking like he just walked off the set of *Friday Night Lights*, DiBiase Jr. has the size and athletic pedigree to lead the Network.

3. With the eleventh pick in the draft, the '90s End Zone Era selects Mr. Perfect. (QB)

Analysis: Hit the music, wait for the symbols to clash, and roll the highlight reel. The perfect one has shown MLB Hall-of-Famer Wade Boggs a perfect hitting technique, former NBA Center Felton Spencer how to hoop, former NHL Allstar Mike Modano perfect goaltending, and most importantly former NFL All-Pro tight end Steve Jordan the perfect pass. Only Mr. Perfect can chuck the ball what seems like 80 yards up in the air, have it hang there, sprint down field, and make the catch himself. Perfect.

4. With the twelfth pick in the draft, the '10s Touchdown Network selects Lance Archer. (QB)

Analysis: Lance Archer grew up playing sports under the big Texas skies, the Murderhawk Monster is an outstanding pick for the Network. In college, Lance played quarterback for Texas State University. While that may not seem as prestigious as playing in a major collegiate football conference, when you look at the other potential quarterbacks in our pool of wrestlers, well it's like playing quarterback for the San Francisco 49ers during the 1980s. At 6'8", Archer will have no problem flinging the ball over any over-sized lineman standing in his way.

5. With the thirteenth pick in the draft, the '10s Touchdown Network selects Ricochet. (RB)

Analysis: Ricochet possess explosive speed and an uncanny ability to move around in eye popping ways. He is a master of the flippity flips but he's shown us much more. He's shown us total body control. Just imagine the hurdles the one and only can fly over. Can this gravity defying agility translate into that Barry Sanders type elusiveness on the field? All we know for sure, is that it will be fun to watch.

6. With the fourteenth pick in the draft, the '90s End Zone Era selects 'The Wildman' Marc Mero. (RB)

Analysis: Mero has been an outstanding athlete his entire life, participating in hockey, football, and boxing. Marc has had an acclaimed amateur boxing career, highlighted by his victory in the New York

Golden Gloves Tournament. The 6'1" high-flyer was ahead of his time, a talented professional wrestler who incorporated a variety of athletic techniques into his in-ring repertoire. Mero is a tough, all-around athlete who can move about faster than a man being stalked by a gigantic Nordic beast.

7. With the fifteenth pick in the draft, the '00s Ruthless Blitz selects Edge. (WR)

Analysis: With a lean 6'5" frame and explosive spearing speed, Edge is a solid pick up adding a tall and agile target for his QB. Edge is a fearless athlete. If he's willing to fly across the field like he's flown off of gigantic ladders he'll be a consistent target. The Rated 'R' Superstar can keep the chains moving for the decade that made him a Hall-of-Famer. Can Vickie get the most out of him? Ruthless Blitz better hope their tumultuous relationship can coexist for four quarters.

8. With the sixteenth pick in the draft, the '80s Rock 'n' Jock Mania selects Flyin' Brian Pillman. (TE)

Analysis: Flyin' Brian Pillman possesses an immense amount of football experience. Pillman played for the Buffalo Bills, the Calgary Stampeders, and most notably the Cincinnati Bengals. The former defensive tackle has exceptional agility. Just like professional wrestling's favorite tight end, George Kittle, Pillman will be a solid blocker with dual threat potential for racking up yards after catch. Let's just hope he sticks to the game plan and doesn't go into business for himself; that or show up with a 9 mm, you never know with the loose cannon.

ROUND THREE

1980S ROCK 'N' JOCK MANIA	1990S END ZONE ERA	2000S RUTHLESS BLITZ	2010S TOUCHDOWN NETWORK
COACH/GM: BOBBY 'THE BRAIN' HEENAN	COACH/GM: ERIC BISCHOFF	COACH/GM: VICKIE GUERRERO	COACH/GM: PAUL HEYMAN
QB	QB: MR. PERFECT (11)	QB: TED DIBIASE JR. (10)	QB: LANCE ARCHER (12)
RB	RB: MARC MERO (14)	RB	RB: RICOCHET (13)
WR: TITO SANTANA (9)	WR	WR: EDGE (15)	WR: RANDY ORTON (4)
WR	WR	WR	WR: RON 'TRUTH' KILLINGS (5)
TE: FLYIN' BRIAN PILLMAN (16)	TE: BILL GOLDBERG (6)	TE: DWAYNE 'THE ROCK' JOHNSON (7)	TE
LB: LEX LUGER (8)	LB: 'HACKSAW' JIM DUGGAN (3)	LB: BROCK LESNAR (2)	LB
OL/DL: DOOM (1)	OL/DL	OL/DL	OL/DL
OL/DL	OL/DL	OL/DL	OL/DL
K	K	K	K

1. With the seventeenth pick in the draft, the '80s Rock 'n' Jock Mania selects Ricky 'The Dragon' Steamboat. (RB)

Analysis: Steamboat is a solid pick for running the ball with legs powerful enough to execute multiple leapfrogs in a single sequence and hands toughened from years of karate chopping. He's got that low center of gravity, quickness, and undoubtable athletic agility required to carry the ball out of the backfield. Flair and Savage can attest that the Dragon's athleticism and timing are second to none. Running behind that stacked NFL alumni filled offensive line will surely let the Dragon soar.

2. With the eighteenth pick in the draft, the '00s Ruthless Blitz selects Shelton Benjamin. (RB)

Analysis: A National Junior College 100-meter champion, a National Junior College National Wrestling champion, and a NCAA All-American. What more can you ask for? Shelton has the right combination of power, speed, and toughness to make him an all-star in the backfield. Also reuniting him with his former University of Minnesota training partner, Brock Lesnar, should be a building block for solid team chemistry.

3. With the nineteenth pick in the draft, the '90s End Zone Era selects Booker T. (WR)

Analysis: At 6'3" Booker T is street tough, in-ring tested, and a two-time WWE Hall-of-Famer who played football and basketball in high school. Booker T is a natural fit at wide receiver with that Playmaker, T.O., Ocho Cinco, insert wide receiver diva here, top star personality. Although, End Zone Era better get a handle on making sure Booker's animated face doesn't telegraph every single ball thrown his way. If he does score, there is no better touchdown celebration out there than the Spinaroonie!

4. With the twentieth pick in the draft, the '10s Touchdown Network selects Roman Reigns. (LB)

Analysis: Before he was sitting at the head of the table, the big dog was mowing down ball carriers for the Georgia Tech Yellow Jackets. A three-year starter and eventual team captain, Reigns lived up to his hard-hitting bloodline legacy. Roman was released by the Minnesota Vikings after the team physically diagnosed him with leukemia. His early exit from football leaves Reigns with a lot left to prove on the field. The Tribal Chief will leave it all out there and let everyone know whose yard it is.

5. With the twenty-first pick in the draft, the '10s Touchdown Network selects Baron Corbin. (TE)

Analysis: Corbin played offense at the collegiate level and was good enough to get a tryout with a couple of NFL teams. The big man with constantly rotating gimmicks will protect his quarterback like they are a check writing McMahon. He will also be able to lay out some serious blocks for his running back. Will Baron have the speed and agility to get open and make catches down the field? That's a bigger question than if Corbin will ever settle on a gimmick.

6. With the twenty-second pick in the draft, the '90s End Zone Era selects Rob Van Dam. (WR)

Analysis: He's got the hops. He's got the explosiveness. He's got the look. At 6'1", Rob Van Dam possesses some of the greatest agility ever witnessed inside the squared circle. A disciplined martial artist and kickboxer, Van Dam has the stamina to close the game out down the stretch. Every defensive back better watch out cause RVD just might leave them in a daze of smoke.

7. With the twenty-third pick in the draft, the '00s Ruthless Blitz selects Christian. (WR)

Analysis: For Ruthless Blitz building, a La Familia type atmosphere seems like a top priority. The Patriarch will add stern leadership to the Blitz locker room. Not only is Christian a tall slender athlete with the toughness of a Canadian hockey player, but he is also a lifelong best friend to his most memorable tag team partner, Edge. Whether it is running cross routes or blocking defenders to free each other up, the duo will be a difficult offensive tandem for opponents to overcome.

8. With the twenty-fourth pick in the draft, the '80s Rock 'n' Jock Mania selects the 'Macho Man' Randy Savage. (WR)

Analysis: Macho Man is a superior athlete who had a four-season minor-league baseball career. He might not be the fastest receiver drafted but he's got the hands. We don't know whether that hand strength comes from his baseball career or years of snapping countless Slim Jims. We do know that Savage's athletic prowess and mostly controlled craziness will serve him well on the football field.

ROUND FOUR

1980S ROCK 'N' JOCK MANIA	1990S END ZONE ERA	2000S RUTHLESS BLITZ	2010S TOUCHDOWN NETWORK
COACH/GM: BOBBY 'THE BRAIN' HEENAN	COACH/GM: ERIC BISCHOFF	COACH/GM: VICKIE GUERRERO	COACH/GM: PAUL HEYMAN
QB	QB: MR. PERFECT (11)	QB: TED DIBIASE JR. (10)	QB: LANCE ARCHER (12)
RB: RICKY 'THE DRAGON' STEAMBOAT (17)	RB: MARC MERO (14)	RB: SHELTON BENJAMIN (18)	RB: RICOCHET (13)
WR: TITO SANTANA (9)	WR: BOOKER T (19)	WR: EDGE (15)	WR: RANDY ORTON (4)
WR: 'MACHO MAN' RANDY SAVAGE (24)	WR: ROB VAN DAM (22)	WR: CHRISTIAN (23)	WR: RON 'TRUTH' KILLINGS (5)
TE: FLYIN' BRIAN PILLMAN (16)	TE: BILL GOLDBERG (6)	TE: DWAYNE 'THE ROCK' JOHNSON (7)	TE: BARON CORBIN (21)
LB: LEX LUGER (8)	LB: 'HACKSAW' JIM DUGGAN (3)	LB: BROCK LESNAR (2)	LB: ROMAN REIGNS (20)
OL/DL: DOOM (1)	OL/DL	OL/DL	OL/DL
OL/DL	OL/DL	OL/DL	OL/DL
K	K	K	K

1. With the twenty-fifth pick in the draft, the '80s Rock 'n' Jock Mania selects the Road Warriors. (OL/DL)

Analysis: Adding this intimidating jacked pair of former bouncers to the line fits nicely for Mania. Hawk and Animal had a reputation for genuinely being some of the toughest guys around. It's not surprising that Animal's son James Laurinaitis had an eight-year NFL career after his all-American days at Ohio State. Their legendary face paint is absolutely required. The spikes do have to come off the pads though. Sorry.

2. With the twenty-sixth pick in the draft, the '00s Ruthless Blitz selects the Brothers of Destruction. (OL/DL)

Analysis: Taker and Kane both played high school football and basketball. Kane went on to play both sports at the collegiate level, while Taker contemplated playing professional basketball overseas before pursuing a career in professional wrestling. The tallest linemen drafted the Deadman, and the Big Red Machine should be able to knock down lots of passes headed in their direction. These two giants will give Blitz solid locker room leadership.

3. With the twenty-seventh pick in the draft, the '90s End Zone Era selects the Faces of Fear. (OL/DL)

Analysis: A pair of imposing Tongan heavy hitters are coming off the board. They are big strong, tough, mean men, whom in Meng's cases are known to bite body parts off of anyone who pisses him off. Urban legend states that Meng was the only man formidable enough to intimidate André the Giant. Given his reputation as one of professional wrestling's toughest dudes, I 100 percent believe it. And let's not forget the Barbarian at 6'2" and 300 lbs. of pure South Pacific muscle. This pair of former sumo stars have more than enough tools to match up with anyone inside the lines.

4. With the twenty-eighth pick in the draft, the '10s Touchdown Network selects the Prime Time Players. (OL/DL)

Analysis: These two men may not have had the storied professional wrestling careers of some of the other draftees, but they are experienced football players with all the athletic tools. Titus O'Neil was a University of Florida defensive end racking up forty-four games of on the field SEC football experience. He also spent four years playing arena football around the county. As if entering the Greatest Royal Rumble, Titus Worldwide can gracefully slide all over the field. Young also played collegiate football albeit at a much lesser-known university. These two add another layer of experience to an already gridiron tested Network team.

5. With the twenty-ninth pick in the draft, the '10s Touchdown Network selects the Authors of Pain. (OL/DL)

Analysis: With so much size on the line already drafted this is a nice addition for the Network. Add a couple of tough, athletic, 6 foot plus, 300 pounders to the line and you can't go wrong. It also helps that Rezar has been studying combat sports since he was four years old and Akam is a three-time Canadian freestyle wrestling champion. These boys can go toe to toe with Road Warriors, the Faces of Fear, or pretty much any tough guys out there on gridiron.

6. With the thirtieth pick in the draft, the '90s End Zone Era selects the Steiner Brothers. (OL/DL)

Analysis: These Wolverine lettermen bring that Michigan blue chipper tenacity to the game. Scott has the size and the bite and Rick well he's got the headgear and the bark. You have to wonder whether the dog faced gremlin can hang with the size most teams have accumulated. We know that shouldn't be an issue for Big Poppa Pump, fortunately for him, and, well, a lot of boys, the Slobber Knocker draft has a pretty lax steroid testing policy.

7. With the thirty-first pick in the draft, the '00s Ruthless Blitz selects Three Minute Warning. (OL/DL)

Analysis: Yes, one of them was known as Rosey but these 300 lbs. plus Samoan brutes do have that knock you on your butt power level. In high school Rosey, Roman Reign's older brother, blocked for Emmitt Smith. He went on to play college football at the University of Hawaii. And Umaga, well, he can finally make amends with the world for depriving us of seeing Donald Trump's head shaved at WrestleMania 23.

8. With the thirty-second pick in the draft, the '80s Rock 'n' Jock Mania selects Tully Blanchard. (QB)

Analysis: Perhaps the game changing pick of the draft. The Brain's extensive management career pays off when he selects this former Brain Buster who actually played quarterback at the collegiate level. Blanchard quarterbacked West Texas State University on the same team as Tito Santana. For whatever reason it seems like half of West Texas State University football roster found its way into a professional wrestling locker-room. Despite this late selection, Tully might very well be the most valuable pick.

Side note: Blanchard was only eligible to be drafted by the '80s team, so, yeah, that's why he fell so far in the draft.

ROUND FIVE

1980S ROCK 'N' JOCK MANIA	1990S END ZONE ERA	2000S RUTHLESS BLITZ	2010S TOUCHDOWN NETWORK
COACH/GM: BOBBY 'THE BRAIN' HEENAN	COACH/GM: ERIC BISCHOFF	COACH/GM: VICKIE GUERRERO	COACH/GM: PAUL HEYMAN
QB: TULLY BLANCHARD (32)	QB: MR. PERFECT (11)	QB: TED DIBIASE JR. (10)	QB: LANCE ARCHER (12)
RB: RICKY 'THE DRAGON' STEAMBOAT (17)	RB: MARC MERO (14)	RB: SHELTON BENJAMIN (18)	RB: RICOCHET (13)
WR: TITO SANTANA (9)	WR: BOOKER T (19)	WR: EDGE (15)	WR: RANDY ORTON (4)
WR: 'MACHO MAN' RANDY SAVAGE (24)	WR: ROB VAN DAM (22)	WR: CHRISTIAN (23)	WR: RON 'TRUTH' KILLINGS (5)
TE: FLYIN' BRIAN PILLMAN (16)	TE: BILL GOLDBERG (6)	TE: DWAYNE 'THE ROCK' JOHNSON (7)	TE: BARON CORBIN (21)
LB: LEX LUGER (8)	LB: 'HACKSAW' JIM DUGGAN (3)	LB: BROCK LESNAR (2)	LB: ROMAN REIGNS (20)
OL/DL: DOOM (1)	OL/DL: FACES OF FEAR (27)	OL/DL: BROTHERS OF DESTRUCTION (26)	OL/DL: PRIME TIME PLAYERS (28)
OL/DL: ROAD WARRIORS (25)	OL/DL: STEINER BROTHERS (30)	OL/DL: THREE MINUTE WARNING (31)	OL/DL: AUTHORS OF PAIN (29)
K	K	K	K

And now the kickers . . .

1. With the thirty-third pick in the draft, the '80s Rock 'n' Jock Mania selects Shawn Michaels. (K)

Analysis: Sweet. Chin. Music.

2. With the thirty-fourth pick in the draft, the '00s Ruthless Blitz selects X-Pac. (K)

Analysis: The kid's karate kicks were his best offensive weapons, maybe his only one. He's got the educated feet and looks the part.

3. With the thirty-fifth pick in the draft, the '90s End Zone Era selects Glacier. (K)

Analysis: In WCW, Glacier pulled off one tall task. He somehow managed to make one of the coolest video game characters of all time in Subzero seem lame. Despite his characters overall wackness, he was still a karate champion capable of pulling off a variety of kicks.

4. With the thirty-sixth pick in the draft, the '10s Touchdown Network selects Bryan Danielson. (K)

Analysis: YES! YES! YES! The YES kicks say it all.

FINAL SLOBBER KNOCKER DRAFT RESULTS

1980S ROCK 'N' JOCK MANIA	1990S END ZONE ERA	2000S RUTHLESS BLITZ	2010S TOUCHDOWN NETWORK
COACH/GM: BOBBY 'THE BRAIN' HEENAN	COACH/GM: ERIC BISCHOFF	COACH/GM: VICKIE GUERRERO	COACH/GM: PAUL HEYMAN
QB: TULLY BLANCHARD (32)	QB: MR. PERFECT (11)	QB: TED DIBIASE JR. (10)	QB: LANCE ARCHER (12)
RB: RICKY 'THE DRAGON' STEAMBOAT (17)	RB: MARC MERO (14)	RB: SHELTON BENJAMIN (18)	RB: RICOCHET (13)
WR: TITO SANTANA (9)	WR: BOOKER T (19)	WR: EDGE (15)	WR: RANDY ORTON (4)
WR: 'MACHO MAN' RANDY SAVAGE (24)	WR: ROB VAN DAM (22)	WR: CHRISTIAN (23)	WR: RON 'TRUTH' KILLINGS (5)
TE: FLYIN' BRIAN PILLMAN (16)	TE: BILL GOLDBERG (6)	TE: DWAYNE 'THE ROCK' JOHNSON (7)	TE: BARON CORBIN (21)
LB: LEX LUGER (8)	LB: 'HACKSAW' JIM DUGGAN (3)	LB: BROCK LESNAR (2)	LB: ROMAN REIGNS (20)
OL/DL: DOOM (1)	OL/DL: FACES OF FEAR (27)	OL/DL: BROTHERS OF DESTRUCTION (26)	OL/DL: PRIME TIME PLAYERS (28)
OL/DL: ROAD WARRIORS (25)	OL/DL: STEINER BROTHERS (30)	OL/DL: THREE MINUTE WARNING (31)	OL/DL: AUTHORS OF PAIN (29)
K: SHAWN MICHAELS (33)	K: GLACIER (35)	K: X-PAC (34)	K: BRYAN DANIELSON (36)

CHAPTER 8
MULTI-MAN MATCH MADNESS

When you're putting on three or more weekly shows year-round, you're going to need a few reliable gimmick matches to keep your audience entertained. Royal Rumble, Elimination Chamber, War Games, and Money in the Bank are just a few of the multi-man gimmick matches that have earned a place in the hearts of professional wrestling fans. This love has earned the matches a center stage at annual pay-per-view events. These extravagant matches keep things fresh and set the stage for a hopeful grappler to achieve that breakthrough performance. Would Seth Rollins be Seth 'Freaking' Rollins without his Money in the Bank victory and historic WrestleMania cash in?

Not every gimmick match is worthy of those proverbial "this-is-awesome" chants, many multi-man gimmick matches are overly contrived dumpster fires. World Championship Wrestling's (WCW) World War 3 was a match where sixty-men are spread out across three connected rings, in an over-the-top rope battle royal. While in theory it sounds like non-stop action, in reality watching that much action at once makes one end up watching nothing. It's a sensory overload that really leaves you appreciating the well-paced structure of World Wrestling Entertainment's (WWE) Royal Rumble.

Speaking of the Royal Rumble, if you ever wanted to gamble on professional wrestling, without one of those advertised companies, the Royal Rumble is about the only legit way to do it. The Royal Rumble draw can be played with anywhere from two to thirty friends. If you have less than thirty players just make sure the numbers are evenly divided. Set your entry fee, if there is an extra number just charge someone a little more to keep it all level.

Now let's assume you have thirty people, place the names in one hat and the numbers one through thirty in another. Draw a name and a number. If the wrestler who enters at your number wins, then you win the pot. The payout can be structured, winner takes all, top two get paid, top four get paid etc. In the event of a screwy finish, split the pot among the final two or four players.

Now, World War 3 is not alone the horribly planned and/or executed multi-man matches category. WWE's 2008 Championship scramble was so particularly unsatisfying it was scrapped after one pay-per-view appearance. Here is the premise. Once a competitor gained a pin or submission, they were the interim champion. From then on whoever had the most recent pin or submission against any of the other competitors was champion. This game of professional wrestling hot potato continued until the clock ran out. It's no surprise that the only match where Brian Kendrick was even momentarily awarded the WWE championship is seemingly modeled after a children's playground game.

When the COVID-19 global pandemic hit, everything shut down, everything, that is, except professional wrestling. Professional wrestling carried on without the electric energy that a live crowd brings. The creative people in the back were constantly trying to bring something new and entertaining to the fans. Graveyards, football stadiums, and giant pools of mimosas all had their moment during the pandemic era of professional wrestling television programing. Each elaborate match hoped to be panned as groundbreaking creative work while avoiding being slapped with the "Well, this is just ridiculously stupid" label.

Thankfully, things gradually got back to normal and live crowds once again packed arenas across the world. Creatively it's difficult to develop elaborate multi-man matches that can simultaneously be enjoyed by the live crowds and those watching at home. If you've ever been on the far side of a caged double ring, glaring over steel and space to see the action, you know what I mean. To that end we offer the following ideas and if they all fall on their face, well, it won't be our money funding the ridiculousness.

CAPTURE THE FLAG

Premise: A professional wrestling take on the traditional game where two teams compete to capture the opposing team's flag and return it back to their team's home base.

Setup: Two teams consisting of four or more wrestlers compete in three successive rings with the goal of capturing the opposing team's flag and retuning it to their home base. The three rings will be set up with each team having their base ring on opposing ends and one neutral ring in the center. Think a bigger basketball court with two rings serving as the hoops and one as center court. In each team's base ring, a pole holding their flag will be placed at that ring's furthest ring post.

The rings can be spaced out with as much or little space in between them as desired. Though, at least half a ring length in between each ring would facilitate out of the ring action. Capture the flag can be conducted with or without weapons provided to the wrestlers or with obstacles, like steel cages, placed throughout the match area.

Rules: To win a team must grab their opponent's flag, cross the neutral ring, and hang the flag on their team's home base post. Once a wrestler grabs the opposing team's flag, they can take it themselves or pass it off to a teammate. At all times wrestlers are free to fight, including when a wrestler has control of the opposing team's flag.

If a team has had their flag removed, they will need to use brute force to stop the opposing flag holder by physically removing the flag from their possession. If a wrestler loses control of a flag or it hits the ground for any reason, a referee will retrieve the flag, and rehang it on that team's pole. Once rehung by the referee, the flag is immediately back in play.

Each team can disperse their team members throughout the match area as they see fit. Everyone can go after the opposing team's flag, some can stay back to defend their own flag, or some can be strategically placed in the neutral territory. If at any time a wrestler is pinned, submitted, or otherwise deemed unable to compete, that wrestler is out of the match. The fallen wrestler's team will have to continue on at a handicapped disadvantage with the rest of their remaining members. At least three referees, one near each ring, will be needed to count pin falls, tap outs, and rehang flags.

Potential for Greatness: This elaborate match offers plenty of opportunity for both faces and heels to thrive. With the possibility of a team having a numerical advantage, the faces could easily be facing seemingly insurmountable odds. The rule requiring a reacquired flag to be rehung by a referee will provide ample opportunity for heelish foul play or unnecessary delays to occur.

Pitfalls: Setting up three successive rings for a live crowd could be very problematic, if not impossible. A match like this would be well suited for a stadium venue. If the match must occur in an arena or smaller venue the middle ring could be scrapped or the entire match area could be scaled down to as small as one ring. The match can also be produced in a studio with little to no crowd.

ULTIMATE LADDER MATCH

Premise: A multi-level multi-man ladder match taking place in an elevated ring at a predetermined height above the ground.

Setup: A ring and surrounding floor area with an encasing barrier is constructed in the air. The elevated ring is supported by a center column and four columns with one placed at each ring corner. Each of the four corner columns has climbing ladder rungs attached to it. The ground level is covered by crash pad mats, the thick kind, like the ones used in *American Gladiators*. Numerous ladders and other weapons are placed around and underneath the ring. Kendo sticks or other weapons can be attached to the center column on the ground level. As in any ladder match the belt, briefcase, or other match ending item will be suspended high above the ring.

Any weapons that can cause serious harm if dropped on a wrestler should be avoided. Probably not a good idea to let wrestlers throw any weapons from the top level at all. Now throwing each other from the elevated level onto tables placed around the ground level, that would certainly garner that sought after "Holy Sh*t!" chant. If done right it just might be enough to put a smile on Mick Foley's toothless face.

Rules: The match starts with four or more wrestlers placed in various locations on the ground level. Everyone for themselves rules apply. There are no friends. The first wrestler to retrieve the match ending item hung above the elevated ring wins.

Potential for Greatness: The wrestlers start the battle on the ground as the melee ensues wrestlers eventually climb their way up to the elevated ring. Once the wrestlers climb into the elevated ring, they can toss each other over the barricade and back down to the ground level. The possibility of a fall from atop a ladder to the ground level would be worth the price of admission alone.

Pitfalls: Given the elaborate setup of this match it would be nearly impossible to set it up in some random arena. Creating an elevated ring would have to be constructed well in advance and would require more time than any intermission can provide. It's safe to assume that constructing an elevated ring would need to be done at least a day in advance. That could be problematic on the road as arenas are shared with concerts, basketball games, hockey games etc.

This match would almost certainly have to be done as an in-studio production. A live audience could still be incorporated much like a sitcom or late-night show uses. Just as Roman citizens watched death matches in a pit below them, the crowd may have to watch from some type of elevated seating area. As with any match involving elevated falls, the risk for injuries is readily apparent.

ESCAPE FROM THE THUNDERDOME

Premise: Two teams of wrestlers, each with a designated runner, are pitted against each other in a race to escape the arena.

Setup: The standard ring is set up with some extra barriers put in place. The entry ramp and walkway are divided by horizontally placed steel guardrails splitting the isle into two equal sides. At the top of the walkway two war games style holding cells are set up. A vertically placed guardrail is set up where the isle meets the surrounding ring area.

An exit area inside the arena, most likely at an arena's loading dock area, is selected. In this exit area another two holding cells are positioned one to the left and one to the right of the clearly marked exit door.

Outside of the exit area is a semi-circular blocked off parking lot area. Two trailers are positioned across from each other. In the middle facing directly across from the exit and past the trailers is the finish line consisting of a podium containing a giant buzzer or bell. If desired, various weapons can be placed throughout the race area. Fans can also be positioned around each of the fighting areas for extra excitement.

Rules: Two teams of four or more wrestlers are selected. Each team will designate one wrestler as their runner. The other three wrestlers are tasked with blocking the opposing team's runner. One blocker from each team will be locked inside of the holding cells placed on the entry ramp—let's call this wrestler the isle blocker. Another set of opposing blockers are locked inside the pods by the exit area—let's call them the exit blockers. The final set of blockers are each locked inside of their respective trailers and will be known as the outside blockers.

The two runners start off inside the ring, there they must battle it out for a designated time period, ten minutes should be good, before they can enter the walkway area. During the first ten minutes of the match, the two wrestlers fight each other, hoping to do enough damage to their opponent to slow them down before the start of the race. Legs will be targeted.

Once the clock counts down, the barrier separating the isle from the ring and the pods containing the isle blockers are simultaneously opened. Each runner's goal at this point is to make it through the opposing team's side and go past the curtain on the entrance ramp. The isle blockers are, in theory at least, limited to the area from the entrance to the end of the walkway barrier. The blocker's job is to incapacitate the opposing team's runner and prevent them from getting to the back. If a wrestler makes it past the entrance, the opposing team's isle blocker is technically out of the match. This is professional wrestling though, so rest assured the rules will be loosely enforced.

After a runner escapes the isle area, the opposing team's exit blocker's cell will open as the runner makes their way to the exit area. The exit blocker has one goal: do not let the runner make it outside. If the runner makes it outside then the opposing team's exit blocker is technically out of the match—again, "technically."

Once the trailing runner makes it through the entrance ramp, the remaining exit blocker will be released. If both exit area blockers are released and "in play," it's a free for all. At this point both teams have the same goal of getting their team's runner to exit the arena and keeping the opposing team's runner inside.

After a wrestler fights his way out of the arena, the opposing team's trailer will be unlocked, and the final blocker will be released. This is an ideal spot for a promoter to use whatever monsters are on their roster. Now, the runner's goal is simple, make it up to the podium and hit the match ending apparatus. If both runners make it to the outside before the match is over, it is a free for all between the wrestlers still "in play." Once one of the runners hits the designated device the match is over and their team wins.

Potential for Greatness: We finally have a match that can be set up without a ton of extra ring set up preparation time. Given the "who is legal?" nature of this premise the heels will have ample opportunity to engage in unsportsmanlike tactics. Lots of potential for live crowd satisfying action throughout an arena. The victorious runner may get a boost of credibility for picking up the strenuous win and working their way through the gauntlet of blockers.

Pitfalls: The rules are a lot to digest. A detailed explanatory video package going over all stages of the match, when is wrestler legal, how a team wins, etc., will definitely be needed. That package should be shown on television at least seven times before this match occurs. If the WWE is putting on this match that should take about a week.

CONDEMNED ISLAND

Premise: Inspired by 'Stone Cold' Steve Austin's action-packed leading man theatrical film debut we bring you: Condemned Island. Six or more wrestlers are scattered throughout an "island." Each wrestler is eliminated by being locked inside various "caves" placed throughout the island. The last wrestler on the island to elude captivity wins.

Setup: This one is going to require quite a bit of space, probably a football field sized space, maybe two. The "island" is the designated match area. It can be decked out as a tropical island, oozing volcano, haunted mountain, or really whatever theme the promoter desires. Throughout the island "caves" (decorated holding cells) are scattered about. The number of caves should be at least double the number of participants. The cave doors are all open and will only lock after a wrestler pulls a trigger and starts a five second countdown clock. After the countdown ends the cave door will lock and anyone trapped inside is eliminated. This tropical island set could include sand traps, pools of waters, trees, vines, mud pits, rocks, hills, or whatever other "natural" elements that can be incorporated into the action.

While in other elaborate multi-man matches hardcore weapons are optional, for this match they are required. If you were ever going to try and use timed C4 explosives in a match, the Condemned Island is the one.

Rules: No holds barred. It's every wrestler for themselves. Eliminations occur when a wrestler is locked inside a cave. The last surviving wrestler wins.

Potential for Greatness: The cave's five second clock will allow the match to build suspense. Wrestlers can escape or others can intervene, allowing for last second tosses into the cage. The environment will provide fodder for many antics, i.e. sand in the eye, falling in the mud, thrown in water, etc. Also, the elimination style will protect wrestlers as no one needs to be pinned or submitted here. Despite this match's earthy nature, no one has to be buried. Furthermore, if a promoter is crazy enough to use explosives, the wow factor is high. This unique studio produced match works well with younger or lesser-known talent looking to gain exposure.

Pitfalls: This one is a logistical nightmare and virtually impossible to pull off in front of a live crowd. This match has to be a made for TV special. The match runs a high risk of coming across as some low budget B movie, yet it's probably also the most expensive match to pull off. If any promoter is crazy enough to use explosives and they actually work, the risk of injury is high. If the explosives don't work well, it may look as lame as All Elite Wresting's (AEW) 2021 exploding barbed wire death match.

SCRAP TO THE SUMMIT

Premise: A battle royal number of wrestlers fight it out in three-rings with a rock-climbing structure in the center.

Setup: Three rings are situated around a triangular 3D mountain structure complete with rock climbing footholds and handholds. Think WCW's World War 3's ring setup but where the rings meet there is a large mountainous rock climbing structure with a flat platform at the top. Hanging directly atop the platform will be the match ending apparatus. AEW's Casino Battle Royal has a poker chip, the scrap to the summit has the hiker's backpack. A special bag that contains the prized contract, title, or whatever stipulated prize a promoter desires. As in any match ladders, tables, and other weapons can be incorporated.

Rules: Wrestlers enter the match in groups at predetermined intervals. Once all wrestlers are in the match, the hiker's back-pack comes into play. When a wrestler solely stands on the top of the mountain, a predetermined countdown clock begins. Ten seconds feels right. Once the clock ends the backpack is lowered until it sits about five feet above the flat platform. If another wrestler reaches the mountain top or the wrestler who started the countdown clock is knocked off the peak, the backpack is raised again. This process is repeated until a wrestler takes possession of the hiker's backpack and wins the match.

Potential for Greatness: This match is ideal for numerous high spots. The mass of humanity and sheer size of the structure offers ample opportunity for high flyers to showcase their talents. This match is ripe for action and might be best served by multiple camera angles broadcasting simultaneously via a split screen setup. Spears, moonsaults, and flying cross bodies off the top of the mountain are all recommended.

Pitfalls: Due to the height of the rock-climbing structure, there is ample potential for injury. The larger competitors may have a difficult time scaling the rock-climbing structure making it virtually impossible for them to win. The size of this structure makes it difficult for this match to go down in a traditional arena packed with fans. The structure can be downscaled to a two-ring setup. Think of the two ringed wargames setup with a rock-climbing structure in the middle. However, even with the scaled down structure setting up this structure on a card with other regular matches is going to be a headache.

THE GLADIATOR GAMES

Premise: Four of more wrestlers compete in a best of five series of *American Gladiators* style games. The games include joust, human cannonball, powerball, pyramid, and breakthrough and conquer.

Setup: Each of the games are set up as the *American Gladiators* television show portrayed them. Four or more wrestlers from a promotion's roster will be selected as the competitors. Other wrestlers from the promotion's roster will be selected to serve as the game's gladiators. Joust can be set up on the entrance ramp and played in front of the live studio audience. All other games will have to be produced in a studio setting. The *American Gladiators* games can be modified as needed, for example the competitors may joust with each other instead of the game's gladiators.

Rules: The games will be modified to allow the wrestlers to be ranked from first through fourth place. For instance, in human cannonball should multiple wrestlers knock off the gladiator, overtime play will determine the rankings. Points will be awarded based off of a wrestler's ranking in each respective game. At the end of the games, the top two competitors will face off in an eliminator obstacle course to determine the games champion. The competitor with the number one ranking will get an advantage similar to the final event of the *American Gladiators* television show. The competitor to finish the eliminator obstacle course first will win the games and whatever prize, belt, or trophy the promotion wants to award them.

Potential for Greatness: The gladiator games can be presented as an event rather than as a single match. Any excess or lower card talent who has nothing going on can participate. The event can take place and aired over an extended period of time. Months of content can be created in a single taping. One event can be aired over the course of a show or multiple shows. The games will provide a short but entertaining break from the monotony of the wrestling match after wrestling match after wrestling match format. The finale can be aired on a promotion's upcoming big show. The games can be presented as a legitimate competition or as a comedy bit. If you're going with comedy, make sure to have a creepy Elvis impersonator on standby.

Pitfalls: As was the case in the original *American Gladiators* show, the potential for injury is high. If the games are predetermined this may reduce the injury concern. The promotion wanting to run these games will most likely have to work out some type of licensing deal with the owners of *American Gladiators*. The hokiness of these games may alienate many of the professional wrestling hardcore faithful.

CHAPTER 9

THE WHEEL OF REALITY

Professional wrestling has a lengthy history of closely guarding the secrets and personas that live behind the curtain. There was a time when the mere insinuation that a heel and babyface could legitimately like each other was enough to spin fans into an uproar. In 1987, most fans weren't upset that 'Hacksaw' Jim Duggan was arrested for alcohol and drug possession, at the time that kind of behavior was pretty much expected from professional wrestlers. However, the fans were furious that Jim Duggan was riding around town with the dastardly Iron Sheik. Back in those days, if the script called for it, professional wrestlers pretended to not speak English, sold storyline injuries to the point where they kept fake casts on inside their own homes, and, even if related, publicly stayed away from opposing wrestlers. In the name of kayfabe, many accepted this seemingly bizarre culture as the way.

As time passed and the professional wrestling industry evolved, the business began shedding its kayfabe traditions. In the 1990s reality television hit the airwaves and the public's desire for more genuine programing hit with it. Professional wrestling took note and gradually started shifting programing from the cartoon superhero-esque programming of the HulkaMania era to more reality-based programing. Then the age of social media shot steroids into this reality-based programing and created an atmosphere where fans demand more access to their favorite personalities than ever before.

As the professional wrestling industry progressed, the curtain was pulled back and fans were given a window into a different side of the fascinating world of suplexes, spandex, and table dives. On July 28, 2013, *Total Divas* debuted on the E! network and introduced fans to the "reality" of being a World Wrestling Entertainment (WWE) Diva. In *Total Divas* fans got a backstage pass and were shown sincere moments depicting the personal struggles, relationships, career highs and lows, and the fun of being a female competitor in the world of professional wrestling. But as is the case with most reality television, much of the show's content felt very much manufactured.

Many of the life events depicted in the series such as serious injuries, untimely deaths, or genuine romantic relationships seem 100 percent legit. However, oftentimes the forced group pairings or fish out of water outings seem way too improbable for anyone to believe that they aren't at least partially staged. In this respect, reality TV borrows a page from the world of professional wrestling: we all know it's planned but some of this stuff has to be real, right?

In filming an entire season of reality television, a producer is going to need some go-to tropes to keep the camera's rolling. The same is true with actual professional wrestling, whose creative directors are consistently relying on classic gimmicks, familiar storylines, and battle tested specialty matches to keep the ball moving forward. When it comes to reality television, instrumental pop techno background music and stock picturesque scenery footage is just the start. To that end we present the "Wheel of Reality."

Naturally, some of these tropes may be easier to stage than others. It would be pretty tasteless to stage a wedding or legitimate injury for the sake of a television show, but they are reoccurring themes on professional wrestling reality television so they've earned a spot on the wheel. Besides, when has the world of professional wrestling ever shied away from faking an injury or throwing a shame wedding?

To avoid any confusion about the professional wrestler's involved we will refer to them by the moniker they used at the time: Divas. Struggling to fill a season? Just use one of these tropes to fill in a segment or episode. Spin the wheel and make the deal!

1. The Wedding—Whether it is a match made in heaven or a match made in hell professional wrestling fans have always loved a good wedding. Who can forget Jake's infamous snake in a box gift at Randy and Elizabeth Savage's wedding or watching Jesse 'The Body' Ventura dive face first into Uncle Elmer's wedding cake. Being a major life event, a wedding is the perfect event for a season or mid-season finale. Broadcasting that very special day will give instant reality credibility to the entire season.

Throughout the season the wedding planning can easily be a television producer's go to workhorse. It's a theme very capable of carrying an entire season. The drama over the choosing of the dresses, the cake, the bridesmaids, and the overall wedding theme will entice female viewers to tune in. The Diva-bride will also be able to argue with her soon to be husband over the costs, the venue, particular décor, or guest list for the wedding. More likely than not, by the time the wedding comes around the groom will inevitably acquiesce to his bride's wishes, as many husbands have done before him, but the build to that decision provides plenty of episode cliffhangers.

Emotions run high during a wedding, anxiety can reach crazy levels, so much so that the drama will flow as smoothly as those must-have chocolate fountains. Ultimately, the elegant wedding will prove to be a joyous film worthy event. Fans will be invested as they feel like a part of the professional wrestling family getting a front row seat to witness this momentous occasion in the happy couple's life.

2. The Vacation—The producers must find a location that provides ample opportunity for the Divas to gallivant around in their bikinis. As with all of professional wrestling, the fans' deep admiration of the human body will be fully exploited. The audience should be provided with a plausible reason for this sun-kissed gathering of the Divas. A bachelorette party works well, but a birthday or a simple girls' trip will suffice. The Divas must stay in the same luxurious resort home, close quarters ensure fiery bickering. Just pour out some alcohol and watch as the feistiness over the assignment of the rooms or some other mundane reason ensues. The alcohol and drama will simultaneously flow throughout the trip. The potential for some type of physical altercation is high. There is a 50/50 shot someone's drink will fly in another's face. Just plan a few excursions, throw in a cultural event for that end of episode self-reflection/appreciation of the sisterhood inspirational ending, and you're all set.

3. The Catfight—Professional wrestlers having backstage heat with each other is as old as the business itself. This is nothing new or exclusive to the Divas division. If any two Divas are having backstage drama throw some alcohol on the fire and zoom in on the action. It won't take much fuel to ignite a bonfire of rage between two inebriated claws out divas. All you need is for a Diva to hint about another Diva's lesser position in the company, create some type of backstage gossip, or simply talk to another Diva's man without permission.

Throwing drinks at each other, getting into physical altercations, and making cutting remarks about each other's lives won't leave the long-lasting riffs in the women's locker room that one might think. By the next week it seems that all is forgiven. Could this be the exaggerated nature of a worked shoot? Who knows? But if reality tv has taught us anything, the bigger the fight the bigger the ratings.

4. The Lame Date—A Diva's partner will plan an out of the ordinary date. The Diva will give a confessional-esque promo about how lame she thinks her partner's plans are. She will reluctantly go on the date, comedically fumbling through the planned tasks while complaining about how her partner doesn't understand her at all. Her partner's enthusiasm will turn into frustration as his, once thought fun and original plans, go over like a lead balloon.

Inevitably, the Diva will realize that her partner is making an effort for the couple to enjoy a unique experience during their "time off." She will come to appreciate the activity for what it is and express regret for having a negative attitude throughout the date. The two will express their love for each other and sweet cheerful music will play them off.

5. The Wacky Celebration—The wacky celebration will take place at one of the Diva's homes. The Diva will agonize over planning a party that meets her colleagues' standards. This event is an easy way to work in a cameo or two. The host will agonize over the décor, the actual home, or the food preparation. For some inexplicable reason, caterers, party planners, or other event professionals are barred from being hired.

Due to poor planning, the Diva will feel her house has been disrespected whether by property damage, pets being let out, or drink and food spillage. The Diva will eventually realize that the fellowship of the party is much more important than food, decorations, or mess. An obligatory "while it was not perfect it was still fun and thank you for coming" toast will cap off the group festivities.

6. The Relationship Drama—Relationship drama, whether serious or trivial, legitimate or staged, scandalous or innocent, is the essence of all reality television. Given that these reality shows are designed to provide fans with new insights into their favorite superstars' personal lives, this one is a vital trope.

When beautiful people surround each other for extended periods of time it's only natural that they start pairing up. The pairings are even more likely when you work in a busy travel schedule that makes it difficult to spend a significant amount of time in any one place. This is the case in the world of professional wrestling as countless superstars have found a romantic partner backstage.

The professional wrestling power couple will give audiences multiple perspectives into the reality of the industry. The Divas will also be able to advise, speculate, and meddle in each other's romantic endeavors. Perhaps nothing makes for better television than these real moments of happiness or sorrow. Whether the relationship recovers or ends, watching a Diva's journey to find a fulfilling human connection will undoubtedly be satisfying. After all, at the end of the day, all you need is love.

7. The Medical Situation—In any athletic endeavor dealing with injury is just a part of the game. The one true sport of professional wrestling is no exception. One of the most upsetting parts of following a professional wrestler's career is watching its abrupt end. It's an all too real struggle, one that adds legitimacy to any reality show. Medical doctors are not going to change their opinion because the cameras are rolling. Well, we hope not anyway. Aside from the in-memoriam programming, a professional wrestler's forced retirement speech is the most emotionally trying segment on professional wrestling television. Watching a professional wrestler process the possible ending of their career can elicit empathy from even the most obnoxious fans.

The body is a wonderland, and its resiliency can surprise even the most optimistic of us. Wrestling fans have always popped for that big return, even more so when it's an injury that caused the departure. We are all a sucker for that Sylvester Stallone Rocky-esque comeback story. Reality programing can show the audience just how hard and emotionally taxing the road back to the ring can be. Showcasing a wrestler's passion and dedication for the business is about as big a push as anyone can ask for.

People say absence makes the heart grow fonder. When the fans see how important it is for a wrestler to get back into that ring, like the Grinch at Christmas or André refusing his acromegaly medication, their hearts will grow bigger.

8. The Reinvention—Well before national television cameras started rolling, becoming a stale act was a top concern for professional wrestlers. The prevailing industry thought has been that in order to be successful you have to show the people something they haven't seen before. In an industry with decades worth of thousands of professional wrestlers, bringing something new to the table can be a tall task.

The Divas, like all professional wrestlers, want to change up their act whenever they feel like things aren't going as well as they could for them. They will, without "permission" of their employer of course, change their hair, ring attire, or gimmick altogether. The changes are done in the hopes of giving their career a boost. The transforming Diva will inevitably freak out over her "unapproved" change and "worry" that she will be fired. Management will give her the "We love your creativity and initiative but we need to be in on the process" speech before forgiving her unapproved actions. Either that or she will be wished well on her future endeavors as her gear is handed to her in a garbage bag. Serious acting is needed for this one. It's very hard to believe that any substantial character changes at a major league professional wrestling organization would happen without prior approval.

9. The Training/Ringwork—A professional wrestler honing their craft through training and practice is pretty much required for any professional wrestling reality show. Any NASCAR fan can appreciate the "why we can't turn away from watching a rookie bump around" mentality. That will they crash and burn feeling is readily apparent. Even watching some of the more seasoned wrestlers preparing for their first time participating in whatever type of dangerous gimmick match is on deck can be captivating. For whatever reason, maybe it's our primal tendencies, watching someone put their body on the line for our amusement is time tested entertainment.

Total Divas has documented many significant moments in the revolution of the women's division. We have seen the division go from being the first matches cut if needed to becoming a vital part of many major pay-per-views or premium live events. Through this evolution the emphasis on ring work has moved to the forefront. From watching the rookies learn the basics to seeing veterans offer mentorship while honing their craft, fans have a front row seat in the never-ending quest to improve the quality of the ring work.

10. The Big Match—If a professional wrestling company is investing big money into a major event, it makes sense that the promotion would find as many ways to make money off of that event as possible. This includes having the event serve as fodder for reality television cameras. The fanfare and usual end of storyline matches can serve as a mid-season or season ending finale.

Not only does your reality show have instant content, but that content also serves a dual role in promoting your product. In the *Total Divas* WrestleMania episodes, from showing the international fans to the surrounding events, the producers gave us a look at the grander of the big event. While WrestleMania is the most highly anticipated event of the year, any premium live event will do. The Divas will nervously agonize over their performance, hoping to live up to the fans big match expectations. This is the perfect time to work in some "state of career" reflection confessional segments.

11. The Family Drama—For many professional wrestlers, whether it be through blood and marriage, the ties to the world of professional wrestling run deep. If a Diva is tied to a professional wrestling family there is instantly that much more interest in her personal life. Many fans will get a kick from that nostalgic feel of seeing one of their childhood heroes make an appearance, even if they are just doing fairly ordinary things. If a Diva comes from a family outside of the business, there's a good chance drama will ensue when she introduces her family to her "crazy" professional wrestling romantic partner. If none of that works there is always mom. The surprise water works inducing mom "look at how far we have come" segment is always good for a cheap pop.

Sibling fights whether big or small are always entertaining to watch. The Bella twins' constant snarky verbal jabs and overstepping of personal boundaries is pure reality television gold. Their beauty, charm, and feisty personalities have kept them in the lime light well after *Total Divas* went off air. Try not to laugh after one of the twins' remarks "I'm not one to interfere in my sister's life, but . . ." for the umpteenth time. The family quarrel and resulting threat that one of the most important relationships in a person's life may be drastically changed forever is great for building the drama. Inevitably, the family will make amends and profess that while it's not always easy to get along, family really does come first.

12. The New Girl—Any particular professional wrestling card only has so much room on it. The intense fight for space is even more apparent in the women's division. For years they have been given significantly less match time than their male counterparts. Professional wrestling shows can only last for so long. We saw this at WrestleMania 35, when the show ran past midnight causing fatigued fans to head for the exits before the historic women's division main event match went on. With so much real competition for time, it's understandable why some newcomers aren't welcome with open arms.

But professional wrestling is an ever-changing business, one with a perpetually changing cast of characters. New talent is always needed. Yet when a new girl comes onto the scene, there will be a certain degree of anxious hostility and hazing from the established roster. The rookies' willingness to adapt to the written and unwritten professional wrestling locker room rules provides for instant drama. In a business that heavily emphasizes respect, the new girl's acceptance of her spot on the pecking order will serve as perfect interview fodder. Her young girl status will also provide an excuse, though one is never really needed, for some good old fashioned professional wrestling ribbing. Watching a newcomer enter the, oftentimes bizarre, world of major professional wrestling will deliver backstage entertainment for both the hardcore faithful and the casual professional wrestling observer.

CHAPTER 10

THE SQUARED CIRCLE PRESIDENTS: PART TWO

During the 2000s, the cult of personality was never more apparent. As technology advances the world moves at a seemingly ever-increasing lightning-fast pace. To keep the public's attention in this climate requires dynamic personalities, those capable of grabbing attention, and standing out in an overcrowded space. In the social media age, where the world is viewed through filters, quick videos, and short statements, almost everyone has a gimmick. When all have a voice, those who are the loudest hold the greatest clout. In the 21st century, two recent presidents have captured that, pretty much now required, professional wrestling swag: Barack Obama and Donald J. Trump.

Obama is akin to that naturally charismatic wrestler, the one who can deliver some of the most moving promos we have ever heard. Trump is akin to that professional wrestler who just looks like he doesn't belong, yet for whatever reason the fans just can't get enough of him. Love them or hate them, it's undeniable that both are incredibly over with their respective basis.

President Donald J. Trump sat front row (and remained

there for the entire show) at WrestleMania IV. The Trump Plaza hosted the event, and as the Donald put it in *The True Story of WrestleMania,* "I never sold tickets to anything so easily as I have to this." The venue also hosted the following years WrestleMania. It seems like somewhere along the way a lightbulb went off and Trump realized that larger than life personas win people over in record numbers.

In 2007, the battle for the "You're fired!" slogan came full circle at WrestleMania 23rd's battle of the billionaires. In a cornerman hair versus hair match, Donald J. Trump was in the corner of real-life United States Army veteran Bobby Lashley, while Vincent K. McMahon choose the Samoan bulldozer Umaga as his champion. Bobby Lashley with the assistance of special guest referee 'Stone Cold' Steve Austin emerged victorious over Umaga. Then, right there in the middle of the ring, future President Donald J. Trump shaved Vincent K. McMahon's head. No one in their right mind would have predicted that a future President of the United States/World Wrestling Entertainment (WWE) Hall-of-Famer would fall victim to the devastating Stone Cold Stunner? But yes, that really happened.

The 21st century is a crazy world in politics, professional wrestling, and beyond. Let's see what the next century of squared circle elections brings.

PRESIDENTIAL ELECTION FOR 2004

The professional wrestling world was coming off a high bigger than any buzz post-match booze and pills cocktail provided. When you come down from that monumental high, the fog clears and things start to look different. On March 26, 2001, World Championship Wrestling (WCW) aired the final broadcast of its flagship *Monday Night Nitro* show. The once dominant southern professional wrestling company was struggling financially and sold off to the WWE. Shortly thereafter in April of 2001, Extreme Championship Wrestling (ECW) facing similar financial strain, officially closed up shop. WWE bought out what was left of its competition and was left with a virtual monopoly on the industry.

The professional wrestling world was also dealing with the in-ring retirements of two of its biggest stars. 'Stone Cold' Steve Austin and Dwayne 'The Rock' Johnson both departed the ring and cut their active competitor wrestling careers short. Austin left because of legitimate medical issues, while the Rock went on to pursue more lucrative pastures in Hollywood. With two top superstars gone and only one major American professional wrestling company left, the world of professional wrestling would have to adapt to this new era. In this chaotic time, the search for new leadership was pivotal in preserving the traditions of the squared circle while ushering in a new generation. During this search one familiar face and another fresh one would emerge. Our candidates are . . .

BROCK LESNAR V. TRIPLE H

CAMPAIGN FOR BROCK LESNAR

Anyone who takes one look at Brock Lesnar should realize the man is a physical specimen and chances are he is going to be pure money. Lesnar could deadlift 720 lbs., squat 695 lbs., and bench 475 lbs. well before ever signing a professional wrestling contract. From the moment he stepped into the spotlight, Brock looked like an unstoppable juggernaut; he was a Norse Viking who anyone would believe was being heavily recruited by Charles Xavier.

In 2003, Lesnar won the Royal Rumble match by last eliminating the legendary Undertaker. A few months later, he closed the show on a WrestleMania card that included HBK versus Y2J, Hulk Hogan versus Vince McMahon, and The Rock versus Stone Cold. In September of 2003, Lesnar attempted to quiet the concerns any critics had regarding his in-ring work rate. On *Smackdown*, Lesnar and Kurt Angle put on a *Professional Wrestling Illustrated* match-of-the-year, award-winning sixty-minute ironman match. The big man proved he could go the distance with the best of them.

By the 2003 Survivor Series, Lesnar had headlined five out of twelve of WWE's pay-per-views for the year, and those included many brand split pay-per-view cards that he wasn't even booked on. In November of 2003, Brock was already a two-time world champion and currently carrying the WWE championship. If you were ever going to elect a young head turning rookie to lead the world of professional wrestling, perhaps no one is more suited for the part than the 'Beast Incarnate' Brock Lesnar.

CAMPAIGN FOR TRIPLE H

Triple H might not have as intimidating a physical presence as the Cowboy Viking does, but he is definitely chiseled from the same block of granite. A big difference is that Hunter's statute contains a cerebral mind known for its creative innovation inside the world of professional wrestling. The Cerebral Assassin has the ring psychology and knowledge of the business that Lesnar lacks.

In 2000, Dave Meltzer's *Wrestling Observer Newsletter* named Triple H the wrestler of year. When professional wrestling icon Chris Jericho released his self-determined star ratings for his matches, three of his elusive five-star rated matches were against Triple H. Triple H is a talent that can build a story inside the ring, through riveting promos, or in low budget goofball comedy on-location shoots. Trained by Killer Kowalski, the Game has the wrestling pedigree to lead the locker room.

By November of 2003, Triple H has close to fourteen years of experience in the professional wrestling business. Around ten of those years were spent within a major wrestling promotion. For at least five of those years Trips would be considered a "top guy." Hunter battled every major player in the business and is a five-time WWE champion. The Game may just have the playbook the professional wrestling world needs.

THE PROJECTED WINNER IS . . .

Lesnar has all the physical tools to lead the business but he lacks the passion. He doesn't have that unbridled love of professional wrestling like so many other legends do. You can feel it. In November of 2003, Lesnar had about four years in the professional wrestling business under his buckle, two of which were spent in the WWE developmental system called Ohio Valley Wrestling. Yes, he is an imposing beast, but he doesn't have the mind or mouth to be the president of wrestling. If you want to be president, you're going to need to cut way better promos than any of the one's Lesnar has delivered to date.

On the other hand, Triple H has spent much of his career forming strategic alliances. By fall of 2003, Hunter had led two memorable on-screen factions in D-Generation X and Evolution. The locker room power of his offscreen faction, the Kliq, is well known. If he wasn't a big enough electoral favorite already, the Game pulled of the ultimate fall surprise. On October 25, 2003, Paul Michael Levesque, aka Triple H, married the billionaire princess, real-life daughter of Vincent K. McMahon, Stephanie McMahon. The Cerebral Assassin's chess moves are just too much for the Beast Incarnate to overpower.

Triple H wins.

PRESIDENTIAL ELECTION FOR 2008

Heading into the election of 2008, the professional wrestling world was once again coping with scandal and tragedy. Chris Benoit committed the most gruesome crime ever associated with professional wrestling when he perpetrated the heinous act of murdering his wife and son. Immediately after committing these unthinkable acts, Benoit took his own life. Once again, the world of professional wrestling would be subjected to mainstream media scrutiny. After steroids were found at the crime scene, speculation that "roid rage" caused Benoit's behavior was the prevailing thought in the media.

There was also a lack of varied programming and competition in the space. The void left by WCW and ECW's departures was eventually filled by the Dixie Carter ran Total Nonstop Action (TNA) wrestling and its *Impact!* television programming. In this new professional wrestling landscape, the industry would search for a leader to once again make the world of body slams, clotheslines, and suplexes palatable to the mainstream audience. In this search two household names emerged and both sought professional wrestling's highest office. Our candidates are . . .

JOHN CENA V. THE UNDERTAKER

CAMPAIGN FOR JOHN CENA

In 2007, John Cena main evented WrestleMania and ended the night in an action-packed match against Mr. WrestleMania himself Shawn Michaels. After an excellent match, Cena submitted HBK cleanly in the middle of the ring. If there was any question about which young star Vince was banking on, WrestleMania 23 sure answered it.

The following Summer Slam was headlined by John Cena versus Randy Orton in another exceptional match, this one kicked off one of WWE's all-time epic feuds. Building political momentum, Cena was coming off back-to-back wins of the prestigious *Pro Wrestling Illustrated* wrestler of the year award and was also ranked number one in the publication's "PWI 500" list for 2006 and 2007. In 2007, Cena gained more acclaim by winning the *Wrestling Observer Newsletter* wrestler of the year award. The proponent of the hustle, loyalty, respect mantra was on top and receiving Roadwarrior-esque pops. Already a three-time WWE champion and consistent headliner, Cena wasn't lying when he rapped "it's the franchise boy my time is now" in his somewhat annoying, but undeniably catchy, theme song.

CAMPAIGN FOR THE UNDERTAKER

Since his WWF debut at the 1990 Survivor Series, the Undertaker has always been a main event player. At the following year's Survivor Series, Taker would defeat the immortal Hulk Hogan and win his first WWF championship. The Deadman rose up the card faster than his eyes ever rolled to the back of his head. While many major players would come and go, spending time with various promotions, Taker remained loyal, relevant, and next level over with the WWE universe.

His character was so well received that the WWF decided to attempt the rarely seen spin off gimmick and created Taker's demonic "brother" Kane. Now, this has all the makings of a very wonky professional wrestling storyline, but with the talented Glen Jacobs playing the role of the Devil's Favorite Demon, it all somehow clicked. It is a testament to the Undertaker's level of overness that a spinoff character was created and actually worked!

At the time, Taker was a twenty-year veteran and a four-time WWE champion who was still achieving new feats. In 2007, he won his first Royal Rumble and followed it up by capturing the big gold belt at the subsequent WrestleMania. At the time, the

Undertaker's WrestleMania's win-loss record, otherwise known as the streak, was sitting at an unheard of 15-0. In 2007, Undertaker was the locker room leader, the judge of wrestler's court, and hands down one of the most respected men that ever laced up a pair of wrestling boots.

THE PROJECTED WINNER IS . . .

Even against a legendary opponent like the Undertaker, Cena was heavily leading in the polls. John had been the longest reigning WWE champion in nearly two decades. Then in October of 2007, the unpredictable nature of professional wrestling once again surfaced. In a match against Mr. Kennedy on *Raw,* Cena suffered a legitimate torn pectoral muscle and was subsequently stripped of his title. The promotion reported that the Doctor of Thuganomics would be out of action for six months to a year.

A month prior to Cena's injury, the Undertaker made his own return to the ring after suffering a torn bicep. He was quickly thrust into the main event picture feuding with Batista for the big gold belt. The risk of having a president who has to potentially sit out 25 percent of his term is just too much for Cena to overcome. In politics, professional wrestling, and life timing is everything.

The Undertaker wins.

PRESIDENTIAL ELECTION FOR 2012

In 2011, the constant creative teetering between the reality-based storylines written for the more mature fan and the PG rated presentation targeting the younger audience was in full swing. Reality based animosity between competitors was surrounded with celebrity guest appearances, all in an attempt to widen the audience. Whether you laughed at the Muppets-guest-hosting *Raw* or rejoiced when the whole show seemed to go off script, the world of professional wrestling was doing what it has always tried to do: produce entertainment with mass appeal. It doesn't take an economics degree to realize that the company increasing their fanbase would ultimately increase their bottom line. Amongst this struggle, two professional wrestlers emerged to give the world of professional wrestling two qualified and starkly different choices to lead them in the years to come.

JOHN CENA V. CM PUNK

CAMPAIGN FOR JOHN CENA

Armed with extra motivation after his 2008 presidential election was derailed by serious injury, the Champ seemed hellbent on claiming his spot atop of the professional wrestling world. In January of 2008, John Cena gave fans the WWE's most shocking Royal Rumble surprise return when that spinner inspired riff hit and the Champ emerged from the tunnel. The crowd roared with excitement and the sentiments of fans happy to see their mainstream babyface back and ready to lead the world of professional wrestling were felt across the universe.

At that year's WrestleMania, Cena battled for the WWE

championship. At the following year's WrestleMania, Cena battled for the world heavyweight championship. The year after that's WrestleMania, Cena once again battled for the WWE championship. And the year after that's WrestleMania, yes, you guessed it, Cena battled for the WWE championship. It's no surprise that Cena won the *Wrestling Observer Newsletter* wrestler of the year award in 2010.

In the years leading up to this election, Cena faced the top guys in the business and helped create new stars when feuding with the young upstart Nexus faction. For anyone watching the action, there was no doubt, Cena's time was now.

CAMPAIGN FOR CM PUNK

In 2011, CM Punk cemented his legacy as one of the best talkers in the business. When Punk sat down, we all stood up. The acclaimed Pipe Bomb speech, where CM Punk ripped apart the WWE's way of doing business and seemingly bit the hand who fed him, had lasting ramifications felt throughout the world of professional wrestling. It was a moment that breathed reality into a product that many felt had drifted too far into the cartoony waters of WWE's past.

CM Punk showed leadership amongst professional wrestlers and was booked as the front man for the Straight Edge Society faction. While the faction was short lived, lasting less than a year, it created many memorable moments and elevated the careers of those involved. Following his faction's breakup, CM Punk went on to feud with the authority figures and presented a new breed of anti-hero. It was a change fans, who were growing tired of the clean-cut role model babyfaces pushed into the stratosphere by management, were clamoring for. That year Punk won the *Pro*

Wrestling Illustrated wrestler of the year award. John Cena finished second. CM Punk also won the *Wrestling Observer Newsletter* best on interviews award. Still questions remained if Punk and his critically acclaimed run were enough to take over the top spot.

THE PROJECTED WINNER IS . . .

As with many presidential elections before it, the 2012 election puts two superstars who represented different spectrums of the professional wrestling universe against one another.

In one corner we have John Cena, the say your prayers and take your vitamins type of babyface with major crossover appeal. In the other corner we have CM Punk, a professional wrestler's professional wrestler, an indy darling who honed his craft and seemingly wanted nothing more than to carry on the tradition of in-ring excellence. John Cena represented the poster boy athlete who could thrive with the star-making ability of the WWE strongly behind him. CM Punk represented the independent wrestler who struggled to prove that he was just as good or better than any professional wrestler the Connecticut corporate machine could manufacture. Cena looks like a superhuman bodybuilder. Punk, with his lean toned physique, looks like a more relatable athlete.

It's the difference between those who found professional wrestling and those whom professional wrestling found. There is a sort of majestic beauty that can happen when these two spectrums of professional wrestling collide. In 2011, we witnessed that majesty at WWE's Money in the Bank. At the pay-per-view, Cena and Punk tore the house down and received the Meltzer five-star stamp of approval. The match also accomplished that rare feat of winning both the *Pro Wrestling Illustrated* and the *Wrestling Observer*

Newsletter match of the year awards. It was Punk's second five-star rated match and Cena's first.

In November of 2011, Survivor Series demonstrated just how close this election is. Punk would successfully defend his WWE championship. But it was Cena who got the ultimate last-minute endorsement when he tagged with the Rock to close out the show. Like the Mega Powers before them, this pairing left no doubt as to which active professional wrestler was ready to take command.

John Cena wins.

PRESIDENTIAL ELECTION FOR 2016

As quickly as any professional wrestling promotion can build new stars, injuries can just as quickly shelve them. By November of 2015, many of professional wrestling's stars slid into the injured column. Randy Orton, Daniel Bryan, Jeff Hardy, and Tyson Kidd were all among those lost to injury.

Professional wrestling's longest lasting weekly program *Raw* saw its ratings hit an all-time low. While TNA wrestling saw its television programming move from Spike to the more obscure Destination America network. Eventually the minor cable network would cancel TNA's programming, striking a serious blow to any professional wrestling fans searching for a WWE alternative. Lucha Underground emerged and brought a fresh combination of drama and wrestling, creating an entirely different kind of professional wrestling show. Developed by well-known Hollywood creators Mark Burnett and Robert Rodriguez, Lucha Underground took cinematic vignettes to a whole new level.

Out of this new landscape a leader was sought and the professional wrestling universe selected the 2013 *Pro Wrestling Illustrated* tag team of the year to face off against one another for the highest prize in the land.

SETH ROLLINS V. ROMAN REIGNS

CAMPAIGN FOR SETH ROLLINS

By election day, Seth Rollins had spent more than a decade honing the craft that is professional wrestling. He worked his way up through the independent circuit, Ring of Honor (ROH), and eventually to the WWE main event roster. During his time in ROH, Rollins captured the promotion's world championship.

WrestleMania 31 was a breakout moment for Rollins. Early on in the big night, Seth wrestled and lost to Randy Orton, leaving everyone thinking the Architect's night was done. During the main event match between Roman Reigns and Brock Lesnar, Rollins cashed in his Money in the Bank and shocked the world. Rollins's cash in worked and by the end of the night it was the Architect holding WWE major gold. The shocking moment was dubbed the heist of the century and became a jaw-dropping, instantly classic moment within the world of professional wrestling.

In September of 2015, Seth Rollins defeated Sting at WWE's Night of Champions. The 'Icon' Sting described Seth as the most talented professional wrestler whom he has ever seen or worked with. It was high praise from a former presidential candidate and one of professional wrestling's non-WWE based iconic legends. Most of the professional wrestling world shared Sting's assessment of Rollins being a highly talented in-ring performer.

In 2015, Seth took home the prestigious *Pro Wrestling Illustrated* wrestler of the year award. He was also thriving as a heel winning the magazine's most hated wrestler award that year. The previous year Rollins won *Pro Wrestling Illustrated* feud of the year with former running buddy Dean Ambrose. Young, talented, and acclaimed Seth Rollins just might be the new hope the professional wrestling universe is searching for.

CAMPAIGN FOR ROMAN REIGNS

The WWE, always in a perpetual state of rebuilding, was pushing Roman Reigns hard. He was clearly the next chosen one to become the face of the billion-dollar company. Roman won the 2015 Royal Rumble, but lost the night when he was subsequently booed out of the building. The boo birds were carrying a direct message to the folks sitting in gorilla. To top it all off, this went down while standing next to the Rock, a man who hadn't heard such an unforgiving reaction inside the squared circle since the infamous "Die Rocky Die!" chants.

Despite this reception, the powers that be remained undeterred and Roman Reigns faced Brock Lesnar at WrestleMania 31. Though he lost the title match, Reigns was quickly becoming one of the major faces of professional wrestling. At this point in his career many pundits criticized his push, claiming he was greener than the Incredible Hulk and the Wicked Witch of the West's love child. Roman was coming into the business from a football background and had not spent any time in the independents as his Shield stablemates had.

When Roman first arrived on the scene, standing at 6'3" and spending most of his life shaping his physique for the gridiron, he had the build of a professional wrestling superstar. Roman had one more card up his sleeve: his name. No, not Reigns. Anoa'i, the surname of the legendary professional wrestling Samoan dynasty. Bound by blood and blood oath to numerous well known professional wrestlers, it feels like Roman was sent by the elders of the isle of Samoa to carry on his storied family's legacy.

THE PROJECTED WINNER IS . . .

The Shield was one of the most impactful factions of their day. All members were inserted into the main event picture and never left. The group feuded with the top names in the business. Yet all their accomplishments don't do much to sway this election, as both candidates were equally important members.

An entertainment business that intertwines reality with fiction is by its very nature unpredictable. The election of 2016 would be no exception, and on November 4, 2015, during a match against Kane, Seth Rollins tore his ACL, MCL, and medial meniscus in his knee. Rollins required surgery, and doctors estimated he would be out of action for six to nine months.

With the neck and neck rising of prominence for both men, this election is one of the closest in professional wrestling presidential history. It's Roman's pedigree, build, and athleticism versus Rollin's experience, charisma, and in-ring proficiency. In a match this close, Rollin's injury is too much to overcome. Besides, Vince likes bigger guys anyway.

Roman Reigns wins.

PRESIDENTIAL ELECTION FOR 2020

In April of 2019, a once unimaginable booking occurred, a women's match headlined professional wrestling's biggest show: Wrestle-Mania. On the shoulders of this success for the first time ever, women have entered the candidate pool for the presidency of professional wrestling. Becky Lynch, Charlotte Flair, and Sasha Banks all have their names floating around. Among the WWE men's roster Seth Rollins, AJ Styles, Randy Orton, Kofi Kingston, and Roman Reigns are up for consideration. Among the non-WWE associated talent Chris Jericho, Cody Rhodes, Jon Moxley, and Kenny Omega are all established talent vying to make it out of the primaries.

In the fall of 2019, a new age of professional wrestling was upon us. On October 2, 2019, All Elite Wrestling's (AEW) *Dynamite* aired on the TNT network. It was the first non-WWE live weekly professional wrestling programming to air on a major television network since WCW's heyday. Two days later WWE's *Smackdown* aired its 20th anniversary show on FOX. It was the first time in years that professional wrestling aired on one of the major four over the air networks. It was a glorious time to be a professional wrestling fan.

The two wrestlers vying to leads us into the next decade are both truly revolutionary figures . . .

KENNY OMEGA V. BECKY LYNCH

CAMPAIGN FOR KENNY OMEGA

In 2017, former presidential powerhouse 'Stone Cold' Steve Austin had some high praise for Mr. Omega. The Texas Rattlesnake opined, "I think he could be the next big thing in the United States, I think he could be THE guy." Those listening to Austin's comments on Omega were unsurprised by the high praise. If basketball power forward legends Tim Duncan and Charles Barkley morphed together and turned into a professional wrestler, the end product would be the technically sound and full of charisma Kenny Omega.

Kenny possesses a Hall-of-Fame level knowledge of the fundamentals of the game and a charismatic personality that captures audiences' attention. Watching Kenny deliver his snap dragon suplex, one has to wonder if any professional wrestler has ever executed a move as flawlessly as the Cleaner does. Omega is a leader among his fellow professional wrestlers. He was trusted enough for the Bullet Club faction to dismiss the acclaimed and presidential contender in his own right AJ Styles and back the Cleaner as their leader.

In 2018, Kenny Omega was ranked number one in the *Pro Wrestling Illustrated* 500 and finished second in the magazine's wrestler of the year award. *Sports Illustrated* named him wrestler of the year in 2017 and the *Wrestling Observer Newsletter* crowned him as the wrestler of the year in 2018. His New Japan matches against Okada are so compelling they became must-watch television for even the most resistant to Japanese professional wrestling fans out there. The Cleaner is the corecipient of the highest star rating (seven stars) professional wrestling journalist Dave Meltzer has ever given out. Omega's previous encounters with Okada also garnered critical acclaim with Meltzer giving each of them a six plus star rating. He is also the only non-Japanese wrestler to win the prestigious New Japan Pro Wrestling's G1 Climax.

During AEW's formation in 2019, Omega was called upon to headline Double or Nothing, the promotions' inaugural pay-per-view event, against the biggest mainstream name the promotion had signed, Chris Jericho. Backstage Omega served as one of the executive vice presidents of the young company. In the fall of 2019, it is clear that AEW is all-in on Kenny but is the rest of the professional wrestling world ready to follow a Wrestling God?

CAMPAIGN FOR BECKY LYNCH

Some may think that Becky is a relative newcomer to the ring, but the truth is that the Irish Lass Kicker has been bumping around since 2002. Since signing with WWE in 2013, Becky honed her craft in NXT before her eventual call up to the main roster. When Stephanie McMahon called for a revolution in the WWE's divas division, she called up three talented women capable of being main event players: Charlotte Flair, Sasha Banks, and Becky Lynch.

Even early on in Becky's main roster run there were indications that she could be a headliner. At Summer Slam 2015, Lynch led her team to victory by pinning the more established superstar, Brie Bella. On WWE's second biggest card of the year, this was the only match to feature women and it ended with Becky's arm raised. At the following year's WrestleMania, Lynch was in the newly renamed women's title match. While she did not win the title, she established herself as a perennial championship player.

In 2016, Lynch outlasted six other challengers to capture the inaugural WWE *Smackdown* women's championship. In 2018, a repacked Becky Lynch went on a winning streak and earned herself a title match. She lost but was turned heel, and a new Becky Lynch emerged. The WWE universe largely rejected the new heel Becky, cheering for her more than ever before. The new anti-hero Becky 'The Man' Lynch had officially arrived. The Man would regain major gold and further cement her new tough chick persona by sustaining a legitimate broken nose at the hands of the dominating Nia Jax.

In 2019, Lynch would win the women's Royal Rumble match leading to her eventual participation in the main event of WrestleMania 35. Becky Two Belts now had tons of momentum heading into the fall of 2019.

THE PROJECTED WINNER IS . . .

During unprecedented times, we have the most unprecedented election in professional wrestling presidential history. On the one hand you have an established critically acclaimed wrestler backed by a brand-new promotion, on the other hand, you have a very talented female wrestler striving to shatter the proverbial glass ceiling.

When Stone Cold gave his comments on Omega, he did add that to be the guy, Omega would need a green-light push with all systems go. With AEW launching their flagship show less than two months ago, whether they can deliver that push is a huge question mark. The biggest unknown with Becky is her reliability. In 2006,

Becky suffered a severe head injury and stepped away from the ring for many years. Can the professional wrestling world take a chance that she will be there to lead for the next four years?

At the end of the day when it comes to developing worldwide stars no one in the business has a better track record than Vinny Mac. While it is true that Mr. McMahon was on the latter end of his revolutionary career, he was still the leader of the most prominent professional wrestling promotion in the world. Despite all the buzz the exciting new promotion known as AEW is generating, there are just too many unknowns with a less than a year-old promotion. The Man has WWE backing her and that makes all the difference in this election.

Becky Lynch wins.

PRESIDENTIAL ELECTION FOR 2024

Coming into this election it is undeniable that professional wrestling is on a huge upswing. Event attendance, television ratings, merchandise sales, social media/Youtube presence are all trending up. In 2020, professional wrestling biggest event grew even bigger when WrestleMania expanded to two nights. In 2023, a relatively young promotion AEW packed eighty thousand fans at the historic Wimbley Stadium. Both of these companies plan to keep packing stadiums as often as they can. With today's vast number of high-quality professional wrestling talent, it's no surprise that so many are willing to pay the ever-increasing ticket prices.

Outside of what the professional wrestling promotions

directly control there are many indications that business is booming. Not a week goes by where professional wrestling isn't at some point in time the number one trending topic worldwide. Several of Hollywood's current leading men use to spend their days slamming jabronis all over the mat. Mainstream music has allowed professional wrestling to license its songs at a once unheard-of rate. *Busted Open* is now the most popular program in SiriusXM's sports department and there are several other (too many to list) quality professional wrestling podcasts that have amassed significant followings. The professional wrestling industry has never been hotter. Now in a packed field we look to find a leader to keep pushing the industry to unprecedented heights. Our candidates are . . .

ROMAN REIGNS V. CODY RHODES

CAMPAIGN FOR ROMAN REIGNS

Roman has come a long way from his last presidential reign. He went from being the less-than-loved Big Dog to the loudly-acknowledged Tribal Chief. At WWE Payback in 2020, Roman defeated 'The Fiend' Bray Wyatt and Braun Strowman to capture the universal championship and never looked back. Micheal Cole has said it over a hundred times by now: Roman Reigns has been your WWE Universal champion for 1,219 days and your WWE champion for 638 days (as of January 1, 2024). He is currently ranked as the fourth longest reigning world champion in WWE history.

Reigns is the lead player in what many consider to be one of, if not the, greatest storylines professional wrestling has ever produced with the Bloodline. The Tribal Chief is the front man for the Samoan bound by blood faction that has elevated the public interest in the product. Many consider the Bloodline to already be one of the greatest factions of all time. Under his tribal leadership Jimmy and Jey Uso became the longest reigning tag team champions in WWE history. Solo Sikoa went from another NXT guy to a crucial player within WWE's main roster. Sami Zayn was elevated from a mid-card heel to a main event babyface. Even Paul Heyman was given a new breath of relevancy when switched from a beastly advocate to the special counsel to the Tribal Chief.

During this historic run Roman has defeated almost every major player on WWE's main roster. Sure, the four-time WWE champion cheated to beat most of them, but when the smoke cleared it was his hand that was raised. When the real big shows go down it is Roman Reigns who shows up on the late-night shows or ESPN or any other national media to promote them. Despite his brash attitude it's hard to imagine that the professional wrestling industry won't acknowledge him as their next president.

CAMPAIGN FOR CODY RHODES

If anyone can go up against the Samoan dynasty's current Tribal Chief it's the from undesirable to undeniable second-generation superstar Cody Rhodes. The Rhodes family has a long legacy of putting professional wrestling shows together, developing talent, and being a creative force in the industry. The years 2020-2024 were monumental for the legacy of the 'American Nightmare' Cody Rhodes. He served as an executive vice president for AEW, headlined WrestleMania, became a father, and got a very questionable neck tattoo.

In 2017, professional wrestling journalist Dave Meltzer opined that no company outside of the WWE could sell 10,000 tickets to a professional wrestling event in America. Cody accepted that challenge and was pivotal in putting on the historic independent event known as All-In. The event drew over 11,000 fans and directly led to the creation of AEW. During his time in AEW, Cody helped develop young rookies at the Nightmare Factory and coached up the locker room talent. Former AEW world champion Maxwell Jacob Friedman credits Cody with playing a huge part in his career development.

In the ring, Cody had a hard-hitting dog collar match against the late great Brodie Lee, knocked Shaquille O'Neal through a table, and delivered a must-watch Cody cutter to Sammy Guevara during an epic ladder match. In 2019, Cody earned more critical acclaim when his match against his brother, Dustin Rhodes, won the *Pro Wrestling Illustrated* match of the year award.

When Rhodes's contract was up, the American Nightmare jumped ship to WWE. At WWE, Cody continued to pad his resume. Rhodes defeated Seth Rollins three times in an epic trilogy of matches that included a Hell in the Cell match where he wrestled with a very visible legitimately-torn pectoral muscle. The purple pit of perdition match earned Cody Rhodes his second *Pro Wrestling Illustrated* match of the year award. After watching a horrendously bruised Rhodes compete through that wince-inducing match, no one could question his old school toughness.

After returning to in-ring action, Rhodes won the Royal Rumble, main evented WrestleMania, and gave Roman one of his closest matches to date. After suffering that heartbreaking WrestleMania

39 loss, Cody went on to best the 'Beast Incarnate' Brock Lesnar winning two out of three matches and earned his overbearing opponent's respect. With his storied family legacy and current status as one of professional wrestling's top babyfaces, Cody may just be the man to dethrone the Roman empire.

THE PROJECTED WINNER IS . . .

Roman and Rhodes each have played a pivotal role with the current success of the professional wrestling industry. Each have told intriguing stories, elevated those around them, and both have gotten way over with the fans. Both men have learned a lot from 'the American Dream' Dusty Rhodes. In 2022, *Pro Wrestling Illustrated* named Roman Reigns as the wrestler of the year while Cody finished third. Maybe it was Roman's far superior tattoo game. Both candidates are extremely well qualified, but we must acknowledge the historic title reign the Tribal Chief is on.

Roman Reigns wins.

THE SQUARED CIRCLE MOUNT RUSHMORE

Virtually every professional wrestler, pundit, journalist, commenter, podcast host, and fan have their Mount Rushmore of professional wrestling. This book is no exception. The folks who have held the office of President of the Squared Circle are a legendary group. All of those who have been nominated in these elections have had Hall of Fame careers and have unquestionably left their mark on the business. From this star-studded field, we carve out our Mount Rushmore. Here are our four faces:

Ric Flair—The man is the epitome of what a professional wrestler should be. He was an incredible professional wrestler and even better sports entertainer. The sixteen- to twenty-five-time (depending on who is counting) world champion captivated worldwide audiences with his superb matches and must-see promos. He is everything a professional wrestler should be.

Hulk Hogan—Hulk is the single most important professional wrestler when it comes to the professional wrestling industry becoming the pop culture phenomena that it currently is. He was an eighties megastar babyface, a nineties groundbreaking heel, and played both roles to perfection. Hogan took part in what many consider the most iconic moment in professional wrestling history when he slammed André the Giant and forever changed the business.

'Stone Cold' Steve Austin—No one may have been hotter than Austin was during his heyday. The beer-drinking, mud-hole-stomping, trash-talking Texas Rattlesnake gave us so many great moments in a relatively short career. His continued television presence is indicative of his lasting star power that still shines bright today. Austin made professional wrestling cool, and for that we will crack open some stone-cold Steveweisers.

The Undertaker—No other professional wrestler has been a main event player for as long as Taker was. His famous WrestleMania streak includes entrances that are among the most memorable and matches that are among professional wrestling's greatest. Spending decades in the position, the Deadman is perhaps the most respected locker room leader of all time.

CHAPTER 11

SHATTERING GLASS: WOMEN IN WRESTLING

Not since the first WrestleMania was produced has there been a more transforming moment for the world of professional wrestling than the women's revolution. In the golden days of professional wrestling, women were considered a novelty act akin to midget wrestlers or the wrestling bears that inhabited the carnivalesque professional wrestling landscape. The promoters of the day paid the women substantially less than their male counterparts and most took illicit advantage of their place in the power structure, perpetrating sexual harassment on the women. One promoter, Billy Wolfe, was notorious for sleeping with many of the women who wrestled for him. The lack of job opportunities and the negative ramifications of being blackballed led to many women acquiesce to Wolfe's advances.

Compounding the exploitation problem, women were faced with the fact that many states in America would not even permit them to wrestle. The amoral good ole boy system in American and professional wrestling politics facilitated the sexual abuse of many women wrestlers. This sexual mistreatment ranged from be paraded around in scantily clad outfits, to prostitution, or even, in the most egregious cases, rape. For women in the world of professional wrestling, the road to equality would be long and bumpy.

I was too young to witness the 1984 rock 'n' wrestling event called The Brawl to End it All. I missed seeing the Fabulous Moolah defend her World Wrestling Federation (WWF) women's championship against Wendi Richter during the main event. The build involved Cyndi Lauper lending her celebrity status to elevate women's wrestling and let the girls finally have some fun. The pop culture crossover show was revolutionary for the incorporation of mainstream celebrities into the world of professional wrestling. Yet, despite this and the fact that the 1984 event would earn the highest ratings in the history of Music Television (MTV), it didn't alter the course that the sputtering women's division was on. It was a long time before we would witness women headlining any major professional wrestling shows again.

My first real memory of women in professional wrestling was watching the lovely Miss Elizabeth cheer on the seemingly unbeatable tag team of Hulk Hogan and the 'Macho Man' Randy Savage collectively known as the Mega Powers. For a long time, my appreciation for women in wrestling was limited to watching Miss Elizabeth's dismayed face—you'd think she would have built up a tolerance to the violence after all her years around the business, but that wouldn't be very ladylike. Maybe she was suffering from battered woman syndrome due to years of abuse at the hands of Savage. It was either watching Miss Liz or seeing the dastardly 'Sensational' Sherrie take off her heels and try to spike someone on the head. It was like this for a while: women in wrestling were valets, managers, and arm candy used to accentuate the male talent.

During the early 1990s, women's wrestling was suffering from a lack of emphasis on their matches and struggled to find a place on major television programing. Despite being led by the talented Alundra Blayze; WWF's women's division was soon scraped from the show entirely. Frustrated, Blayze jumped ship to World Championship Wrestling (WCW) and infamously dropped the WWF's women's title in the trash. There it was on national television, a talented performer left without a stage, now looking for a controversial restart. A restart not only for her career, but for the entirety of a woman's place in professional wrestling. Ironically, the trash can incident helped usher in a new era, one that would not be so nurturing for serious women's wrestling.

The attitude era hit at just the right time for me, my teenage mentality began thinking that the superhero wrestler was too childish to be cool. The reality-based wrestling approach was the product the major promotions were pushing and I was sold. The timing was perfect as my raging hormones were also transforming my interests to more titillating content, in and out of the world of professional wrestling. As cliché as it is, it's still a universal truth: sex sells. My love for professional wrestling started at a young age and amounted to much more than just catching the weekly shows on television. I had the bed sheets, some of the classic Hasbro '90s wrestling action-figures, played the video games, and most importantly for my thirteen-year-old self, read the magazines.

In those days when you bought an independent professional wrestling magazine there was usually an advertisement section hidden way in the back. It had small black and white pictures advertising what pretty much amounted to scantily clad women wrestling each other and men in a soft-core porn fashion. I didn't know it then, but it was called apartment wrestling. It was quite the added bonus for a hormonal teenage professional wrestling fan. Best of all, because the covers and vast majority of the magazine covered mainstream professional wrestling, no one was the wiser.

One day, I was at the grocery store with my mom when I saw it. It was glorious, and I had to have it, but working up the nerve to even try and buy it, especially in front of my mom, was quite the task. It was the 1996 WWF *Raw* magazine with Sunny scantily clad in dark green lingerie and teasing the exposure of her secrets. This was different from any professional wrestling magazine I had ever bought. That was clearly evident by the cover having for the "mature" fan stamped on it. Pamela Anderson, Carmen Electra, and Jenny McCarthy all excelled at being the hottest sex symbols of the day, but if I had my pick, Sunny was it.

It took every ounce of moxie that I had but as my mom finished loading the groceries onto the conveyor belt, I reached for the check-out lane divider. I pulled out my allowance and plopped Sunny down on the belt. My mom glared at me; "What kind of magazine is that?" she asked with a glare mixed with sadness of my growth and disgust at my teenage "perversion." It's a wrestling magazine I frantically said, pointing to the WWF logo. She gave a look of disapproval with both myself and professional wrestling, but didn't stop the transaction. It was all mine!

Miss Elizabeth and 'Sensational' Sherri were memorable enough, but for me Sunny was different. She was not the parsley on a professional wrestling plate, she was the sizzling steak. I don't know if she had ever wrestled a single match, but in the modern era she was one of the first female performers who could truly stand on her own. Sunny would outshine whatever tag team they had her managing, and this is while she managed some good to great teams. In 1996, America Online (AOL) named her the most downloaded celebrity on the internet. Her success, even though it heavily relied on sex appeal, paved the way for countless female superstars to follow. In many respects she proved that women in professional wrestling could be more than just a prop used to bolster a male wrestler's box office appeal. Sunny showed that the women themselves could be the box office draw. She had star power and that in and of itself in the world of professional wrestling was progress.

In the late 1990s and early 2000s, women in professional wrestling were used primarily to titillate the highly desired slightly mature male audience. Got to hit those key demographic markets. Sable arrived on the scene and it wasn't long before her sexuality was on full display. On WWF's *Raw*, Sable's *Playboy* cover unveiling received about as much fanfare as if she had won a major wrestling championship. Since then, several other women in professional wrestling have barred it all for the adult magazine's storied pages. The WWF was quick to promote the risqué spreads every time. The worldwide leader in sports entertainment was all in on this new use of female talent and even aired a few "accidental" wardrobe malfunctions resulting in bare breasts being broadcast over their pay-per-view programing.

Mirroring Sunny's success, Sable's star power soon outshined her real-life husband and professional wrestler who she managed, Marc Mero. Some in the locker room took offense that a blonde, busty, chest painted bombshell was getting a bigger reaction than their hard hitting in-ring action. Sable's reaction grew so big that she became the first female to have her image appear on a WrestleMania promotional poster. These wrestling's pinups were resented for reaching the fame and glory that professional wrestling has to offer without making physical sacrifices inside the ring. For some odd reason, having a no bump clause in a professional wrestling contract wasn't well received in the locker room.

In 1997, a very unique and revolutionary woman named Chyna emerged on the scene. She was a different breed of femininity; she possessed a muscular build that was on par with her male counterparts. Chyna didn't rely on sex appeal and welcomed bumping and competing against the entire roster, men and women included. She achieved in-ring success, participating in the Royal Rumble match and winning WWF's prestigious intercontinental title. Chyna's appropriate billing as the 9th wonder of the world (André was the 8th) was indicative of just how rare it was for any female professional wrestler to be viewed as a serious physical threat inside the ring.

In the late 1990s, Stephanie McMahon made her on-screen debut in the world of professional wrestling. Her character expanded the range of roles a woman could play on the vast stage that is professional wrestling. The billionaire prince notably added the authority figure role to the list. In typical McMahon fashion, she didn't ask anyone to do anything she wouldn't do herself. Stephanie didn't shy away from marketing her sexuality or subjecting herself to humiliating slurs and deeds. Sure, she never pranced around on WWF television in a thong, as virtually all the women with the company at the time did at some point, but she did take a stink face from a thong-wearing Rikishi. That's not nothing. Her unfettered devotion to the business would be rewarded as she eventually served as World Wrestling Entertainment (WWE, formerly known as WWF) co-CEO. Her tenure lasted seven months.

Around the time of Stephanie McMahon's on-screen debut, the WWF started using women's professional wrestling pioneers

Mae Young and the Fabulous Moolah in their television programming. In retrospect how these iconic talents were used is telling. Instead of playing off of the women's storied professional wrestling legacies, where they could serve in a coach or mentor role, the WWF powers that be used them in an, on par for the nineties, shock jock type comedic skit's role. Decades had passed since their heyday but as was the case then, Mae and Moolah's sexuality was up for exploitation. Yet it's hard to be sympathetic to Moolah, who according to professional wrestling lore, had a decades old history of doing her own exploitation, including indentured servitude, forcing prostitution, and taking an unfair portion of her women wrestler's money as her booking fee. During the attitude era, the new exploitation, although far less severe than what was done by Moolah herself, took the form of mocking their golden years sexual appetite.

It's fair to question the tastelessness of how Mae and Moolah were utilized as talents, but for the women themselves during this twilight stage of their careers they were just happy to be utilized at all. Mae Young was so into her final run that she persistently insisted that the heavyweight hardcore legends known as the Dudley Boyz slam her through a table just as hard as they would any of the boys in the back. When Bubba Ray Dudley obliged the professional wrestling world got one of the most jaw dropping moments. The 6'3" powerhouse lifted Mae over his head, jumped off the entrance ramp, and slammed the seventy-seven-year-old woman through a table placed on the floor. Holy sh*t! For Mae Young equal treatment was earned the hard way.

In the early 2000s, two female wrestlers emerged with a fresh combination of sexuality and athleticism: Lita and Trish Stratus. Their in-ring work vastly exceeded anything seen from women's wrestling during the attitude era. The foundation of a true women's division was finally beginning to set. Though that one double-edged, time-tested, universal truth, sex sells, would hinder the women's divisions' legitimacy while simultaneously ensuring them a place on the card for years to come.

During the early 2000's the women of wrestling were all too often involved in questionable hypersexualized storylines and bits. These segments and angles ranged from bad taste to straight up sexual assault. From having male professional wrestlers' barge into the women's locker room while they dressed, to pretty much every type of Jerry Springer-esque love affair storyline possible. In one of the most cringe worthy moments in professional wrestling television history, Trish Stratus was made to strip down to her underwear and bark like a dog in a twisted demonstration of loyalty orchestrated on screen by Vince McMahon himself. Oh, the foreshadowing.

At the time, a women's place in professional wrestling revolved around titillation. The sheer number of women who, for whatever reason, found themselves at one time or another strutting around the ring in only a bra and thong was vast. Anyone playing a Jerry Lawler says puppies drinking game wouldn't make it through the first hour of any primetime wrestling show.

For women in the world of professional wrestling, outside of WWE things were not much better. The most noteworthy moments in non-WWE women's professional wrestling came to us via Total Non-Stop Action (TNA), a wrestling promotion whose double entendre name sought to cash in on the sexualization of the business and the women involved in it. On March 12, 2003, two important moments for TNA's women's division unfolded. First, the National Wrestling Alliance (NWA) women's championship was won by Leilani Kai in a dark match and second, Lollipop, a wrestler whose gimmick revolved around sucking on a lollipop, had her shirt ripped off in a planned wardrobe malfunction. Due to Leilani feeling that TNA did not treat the women's championship with proper respect, she intentionally missed shows and was subsequently stripped of the title. History would underscore her claim as years passed before TNA really established a legitimate women's division.

As the 2000s rolled on, the WWE continued to set a low standard for women in professional wrestling. In 2004, the WWE ran a pay-per-view aptly titled Taboo Tuesday. The women's portion of the card featured a schoolgirl outfit battle royal, with no over the top rope elimination rule, and a lingerie pillow fight. In the following year's Taboo Tuesday, the pillow fight was dropped and only the battle royal, this time in lingerie, was featured. No matter what they were wearing, women were struggling to get any television time.

On December 6, 2004, Trish and Lita's hard work was finally paying off and the two of them were presented as the main event for *Raw*. It was the first time in a long time that women headlined any major professional wrestling television event. It was a watershed moment that proved pivotal for the growth of women's wrestling.

WrestleMania is unquestionably the largest and most prestigious annual event in the world of professional wrestling. What happens at Mania has lasting implications for the world of professional wrestling both in and outside of the WWE. In 2006, WrestleMania 22 brought us a monumental moment for the women's revolution. The women of the WWE had two very different types of matches on the main card. One was the women's champion Trish Stratus pitted against Mickie James. The two women started the build to the match as allies; ultimately, Mickie, who was playing an obsessed fangirl heel gimmick, turned on Trish after she rebuffed her kisses. The match was set, Trish and Mickie delivered and put on what was perhaps the best women's match seen to date. Mickie, with her lower butt cheeks hanging out, did such great ring work with Trish that the fans did their own turn and were cheering on the heelish Mickie James by the end of the match.

The other match on the card was a *Playboy* pillow fight between Torrie Wilson and Candice Michelle. This match was a stark contrast to any serious wrestling, with a bed decked out with *Playboy* apparel placed right in the middle of the ring. Most of the action consisted of Torrie and Candice stripping each other down to their bra and panties while they tussled around the bed. The match was nearing its finish when the crowd revolted. A "This is bullsh*t!" chant gained momentum, but was drowned out by Torrie's music hitting as she picked up the victory. For anyone observing the night's action the message was clear, the crowd was yearning for actual in-ring wrestling to take precedence over cheap titillation.

Despite the stellar ring work of Trish, Lita, and other proficient female in-ring competitors, for the rest of 2006 women were mostly used for sexual titillation. At the time bra and panties were as much a staple of professional wrestling as the proverbial steel chair shot. When Lita had her "last match" in that year's Survivor Series, the whole segment was capped off by her bra and panties tastelessly being sold off to the crowd. JBL even asked if he could sniff them before making an offer. This trend of the professional wrestling industry putting women's sexuality before their talent continued for many years to come.

In 2007, the main women's match featured at WrestleMania was between *Playboy* cover girl and WWE diva Ashley Massaro and Melina, a diva who entered the ring by doing a split on the apron to bring even more attention to her assets. By this point the WWE rebranded its female competitors as divas. The match was about as bad as you're thinking it was. Later in 2007 at the Great American Bash, Melina showcased her in-ring ability and took on WWE women's champion Candice Michelle. The women wore wrestling gear that was pretty much the equivalent of what you would see today and had a respectable in-ring outing.

For anyone thinking that the WWE would finally be focusing on in-ring ability over sex appeal, the match was immediately followed up with a segment where Candice Michell poured bottles of water over her sweaty body. This lustful segment was set to the tune of late-night soft-core porn music and went down while her male counterparts enthusiastically looked on. Someone must have written a memo because shockingly a month later at a beach themed Summer Slam event none of the WWE's divas appeared in bikinis.

At WrestleMania 24, the WWE once again sent a message to their women's division. Sex appeal is a sure-fire way to get TV time. BunnyMania featured the champ Beth Phoenix and veteran Melina in a lumber-jill tag team match pitted against *Playboy* cover girls/WWE divas Maria Kanellis and Ashley Massaro. Perhaps nothing says we value our female talent and their wrestling ability like having them walk out next to giant inflatable *Playboy* bunny symbols.

Following WrestleMania 24 there was progress on the non-sex focused ring work of women's wrestling. The 'Glamazon' Beth Phoenix, Mickie James, Melina, and others put on matches that looked like well actual major league professional wrestling. Beth Phoenix and Melina even had a pay-per-view women's "I quit" gimmick match. For perhaps for the first time in WWE history, a women's gimmick match was put on and did not revolve around sexual titillation.

Months later at the Great American Bash the WWE introduced the divas title to the world. The inaugural title match took place between Michelle McCool and Natalya Neidhart. While vying for the not-so-subtle, vulva-esque divas butterfly belt, the two women put on a solid in-ring match. You'll have to excuse the commentary of professional wrestling legend Jim Ross who seemed astonished that two divas could rely on varied submission moves throughout a match.

Despite the patronizing nature of the labeling of the freshly pressed divas championship belt, the addition of a second championship to the women's division was a substantial moment. While one can argue that the title's design was belittling, at least it was never treated with such disrespect as to be cut in half for two competitors to share. Yes, that happened. (See Laycool.) It finally appeared that the female professional wrestlers were able to showcase their wrestling ability without blatantly selling sex. The addition of a second belt also may have signaled that the back office finally recognized that just maybe the women deserved more time on professional wrestling's stage.

During this time period, the WWE sought to increase the interactiveness with its devoted fan base (labeled the WWE Universe by the company) and allowed them to live out their booking fantasies by voting for a variety of matchmaking possibilities. For the women the WWE Universe was asked to vote in an old-fashioned Slut-O-Ween costume contest. Throughout the show, segments showcasing the diva's roster, in entertainingly varied, yet still mostly sexy Halloween outfits bumpered the action provided by the men's division. The universe surprised everyone when it didn't vote for the blonde with the skimpiest outfit and instead choose Mickie James, and her comparatively modest Lara Croft's *Tomb Raider* outfit as the winner. It was a progressive victory, just ignore the presumably fake pistols Mickie James waived around to the crowd.

At WrestleMania 25, the women's division was slated for a twenty-five woman battle royal and the depth of a true women's division was really beginning to show. Santino Marella, a male wrestler in drag, would comedically win the contest. Once again, the lack of any sincerity in the WWE's incorporation of a true women's division into their product was readily apparent.

Throughout 2009, the women's division seemed to be progressing toward equality with their male counterparts. Then as the year was coming to an end, the WWE placed Michelle McCool and Mickie James into a very distasteful body shaming storyline. The angle was Michelle bullying Mickie by insulting her looks and referring to her as "Piggie James." The audience watched a very fit Mickie tear up over her body image issues. The story lasted for months and once again the WWE let the world know that for them the emphasis was on their female competitors' physical appearance. This was especially apparent when the two ladies clashed in the feud's big payoff match at the Royal Rumble. It lasted twenty seconds. From another perspective one can argue that women talent were finally being treated similarly to the men, whom have also had repeated involvement in tasteless storylines with little to no payoff. (See "Race and the Ring.")

In 2010 at WrestleMania 26, the women of the WWE were

once again placed in another popcorn match. The women's division's sole match on this card was sandwiched between two major men's title bouts, The whole thing was over in under four minutes. This time the women's division was showcased in a five-on-five match that primarily centered on professional wrestling personality Vickie Guerrero. While Vickie pointing to the sky and then hitting her opponent with a frog splash (if that's what you want to call the move she performed) was a feel-good moment, it certainly did not epitomize the in-ring prowess of the women's division. Despite being an emotionally satisfying moment for a woman whose looks were constantly ridiculed on television, it was a forgettable affair and over before fans had time to ask for extra butter.

At WrestleMania 27, four women competed at the showcase of the immortals. They were lumped into a mixed tag match that featured reality show star Snooki and Trish Stratus against LayCool. The match was another forgettable outing, this one lasting 3 minutes and 16 seconds. Oh, hell no! That following Summer Slam, eight women were featured on the show, Kelly Kelly and Beth Phoenix actually wrestled, and yes, it was the shortest match of those promoted for the card, but at this point that was expected. The Bella Twins, Rosa Mendes, and Alicia Fox also appeared as background dancers for musical guest CeeLo Green who performed his unintentionally aptly titled song "Forget you" (radio edit).

This trend of massive underuse continued into 2012 as WrestleMania 28 lumped the women's division into another celebrity infused multi-person match. This time Maria Menounos would be called upon for that alleged celebrity eyeball expanding bump. The match, which practically had just as many booty centered moments as wrestling moves, lasted six minutes and twenty-two seconds so . . . progress?

For these women trying to make an impact in the world of professional wrestling, the television time was short and the road was long. In April of 2013, the WWE held its twenty-ninth annual WrestleMania. The event was headlined by Dwayne 'The Rock' Johnson versus John Cena and set a new record as the highest grossing live event in WWE history. For the Connecticut corporation it was a smashing success, but for the women's division it was a very upsetting night. The only match featuring women, a mixed tag with Brie and Nikki Bella, collectively known as the Bella Twins, teaming with Cody Rhodes and Damien Sandow against Naomi and Cameron teaming with Brodus Clay and Tensai, was cancelled due to time constraints. To those watching it was clear that the women's locker room was an entirely expendable commodity.

On July 28, 2013, the women of the world of professional wrestling finally got some serious screen time albeit in a very unorthodox way. The WWE debuted a new reality show aptly titled *Total Divas* on the E! television network. Seven women including the Bella Twins, Natalya Neidhart, and Naomi gave us a view into their personal lives and professional wrestling careers. While filming a team of women bicker with each other, discuss their personal relationships, and party it up might not seem like a pivotal part of any feminist movement, the reality show would undoubtably play a vital role in paving the way for many glass shattering moments to come. The screen time did exactly what professional wrestling screen time is designed to do: get fans to care.

During the 2014 Survivor Series, AJ Lee was set to face Nikki

Bella for the diva's championship. The pay-per-view title match involved a girl-on-girl kiss and lasted less than five minutes. Months of storytelling to get the fans to actually care about the match all went down the drain way too quickly. Squash matches are a part of the professional wrestling business. They serve to highlight one performer's dominance, to stun the crowd, or to cover up an aging or injured wrestler's diminished ability. None of these squash reasons applied to the women competing on that night. They were simply told to keep it short and sweet.

The women's division was finally growing, combining the mainstream notoriety that the divas brought with in-ring technical proficiency fans were enjoying from the likes of Paige and AJ Lee, amongst others. Once the fans started to notice the amount of match time the women were given, it didn't take long for them to realize that for the bookers women were simply filler, an afterthought to the men's matches, an entire division whose time could easily be cut as needed.

On February 23, 2015, the world of women's professional wrestling was drastically changed. On an episode of *Raw* the Bella Twins took on Paige and Emma in a tag team match. The women, frustrated by repeated time cuts in their matches, sent a message to everyone backstage and put on a thirty second match. The Bella's finisher was the only move performed. The faux match sent angered fans rushing to Twitter. #GiveDivasAChance trended to the point where even Vince McMahon himself had to address the changing desires of the WWE universe.

A month later at WrestleMania 31, AJ Lee and Paige faced off against the Bella Twins in a tag team match. Despite the tweets the match was still the shortest on the card. Ronda Rousey made a cameo appearance at the event foreshadowing the Ultimate Fight

Championship (UFC) champion's future involvement with the world of professional wrestling. Following WrestleMania, on July 13, 2015, major changes were implemented into WWE programming with Stephanie McMahon calling for a revolution and introducing new talent to the expanding women's roster.

Enter the Four Horsewomen, Charlotte Flair, Becky Lynch, Sasha Banks, and Bayley, who along with other notable female superstars would propel women's wrestling to unprecedented heights. The developmental mingling of these four athletes elevated all of their respective careers into future Hall-of-Famer status. The joint training sessions, competitive environment, and desire to elevate the in-ring work benefitted each woman and eventually transformed the business. Charlotte, Becky, and Sasha were moved to the WWE's women's main roster raising it's in-ring work rate, while Bayley would hold the NXT women's championship for nearly a year before her eventual call up.

At the following year's WrestleMania, thirteen members of the women's roster were featured. The women received a combined match time of over twenty-seven minutes. A triple threat match between Charlotte, Becky, and Sasha took up the majority of that time. A year later in 2017, twelve women competed and received similar match time. WWE's female talent were active participants in four different WrestleMania matches, a new high point for their level of participation in professional wrestling's grandest event.

The inclusion of women in the world of professional wrestling continued its progression at WrestleMania 34. This WrestleMania card included a twenty-woman battle royal and two women's single match. It was another sign the tide was turning as for the first time in twelve years a WrestleMania card made room for women's singles matches.

Later that year, an unprecedented event occurred in the world of professional wrestling. WWE held its first ever all women's event called Evolution. It was the first, and to date the only, all women pay-per-view or premium live event put on by a major professional wrestling promotion. The packed card, full of Hall-of-Famers and legends in the making, featured two championship matches that underscored the progress of the women's division. One match featured Becky Lynch and Charlotte Flair battling it out in a "last woman standing" match. The in-ring ability, hardcore action, and wrestling psychology on display was at expert level. The other match featured Ronda Rousey versus Nikki Bella and highlighted the mainstream celebrity status that many female professional wrestlers had achieved.

While many dubbed WWE's Evolution as the storybook crowning achievement for women's equality in the world of professional wrestling, the reality was not as ideal. WWE has not held an all-women's show since, and according to Mickie James a WWE official told her that the premium live event was the lowest rated in WWE history. Reports also stated that fan engagement via YouTube were lower than those typically received by *Raw* or *Smackdown*. These statements, if taken as true, indicate that separate women's programming may not lead to the equality that many are hoping for.

In 2019, the world of women's professional wrestling reached once unimaginable heights: main eventing WrestleMania. Three women, Becky Lynch, Ronda Rousey, and Charlotte Flair collided in a triple threat match. On a show that featured ninety-plus world class professional wrestlers, these three superstars were given the honor of closing out the show of shows. Despite having a screwy ending and having to work in front of heavily fatigued fans, some of whom left, most critics were satisfied with the quality of the match that the trio put on.

A couple of years later in 2021, the women's division had another groundbreaking moment. Sixteen women participated in the now two-night mega event. With the pivotal moment being Bianca Belair and Sasha Banks competing in night one of WrestleMania's main-event. It was a match that many considered one of the best of the year and won an ESPY as ESPN's "Best WWE Moment."

WrestleMania 37 cemented the new status of women in current professional wrestling, it showed that women headlining WrestleMania was not a one-time occurrence. The depth of quality female professional wrestlers has never been greater than it is today. Nowadays, seemingly every well-known professional wrestling company invests, through placement on the cards, television time, and character development, in a women's division. It's the right move as women wrestlers have proven that they can be just as big a draw as their male counterparts.

The importance of women in the world of professional wrestling outside of WWE has never been stronger as well. This was evident in 2021 when Thunder Rosa and Dr. Britt Baker, DMD had a *Pro Wrestling Illustrated* award winning "Unsanctioned lights out" match of the year. The physical toughness of professional wrestling's female performers has, arguably, never been stronger than the current era's stars. Many considered the hard-hitting match put on between Rhea Ripley and Charlotte Flair to be among the very best of the 2023 WrestleMania weekend.

While long overdue, women's involvement in the world of professional wrestling has never been more vital to the success of any professional wrestling promotion than it is today. Nowadays, gender seems to be less relevant when it comes to a professional wrestler getting over with the fans. If you have the talent and personality, the highest levels of popularity are now within reach. Charlotte Flair, Becky Lynch, Jade Cargill, Rhea Ripley, Asuka, Mercedes Moné, Bayley, and Dr. Britt Baker, DMD, among others, have become some of the biggest names in all of professional wrestling. Women in the world of professional wrestling have become as plentiful, diverse, and as important as they are in our society, and we are all that much better for it.

CHAPTER 12

TOURNAMENT DE JERICHO

Chris Jericho is one of the most dynamic professional wrestlers of all time. His travels throughout the world have given him the in-ring experience to hang with the best of them. His charisma and wit have helped him craft so many memorable moments and entertaining promos. In so many ways he is a trailblazer, including creating the current trend of professional wrestling sing-a-longs. There are many who embraced the trend, but only Jericho can actually sing his own song. His smash hit "Judas" peaked at number five on the Billboard mainstream rock chart and has over sixty-six million YouTube views. The passionate hard-rocking tune is a far better song than any of the ones belted out by a professional wrestler before it. Jericho is a future first ballot Hall-of-Famer who has achieved professional wrestling innovative legend status.

On any given show odds are that Jericho will deliver one of the most entertaining promos or matches of the night. León D'Oro, Corazón de León, Lionheart, Y2J, the Alpha, the Painmaker—Le Champion, the Demo God, the Wizard, the Learning Tree, the names may change but with Jericho the results stay the same. If you're watching Chris Jericho, you will be entertained.

Reinvention in professional wrestling is a difficult thing to pull off. It can be a risky endeavor. Once a professional wrestler finds a gimmick that works, they generally tend to stay with it. The examples are far reaching. Charles Wright went through several characters, including an evil Visio priest and supreme fighting machine until he found his career defining gimmick. Once the Godfather's train left the station, the character and person would become practically synonymous. The majority of well-known professional wrestlers are primarily known by their one career defining gimmick. Bret is the Hitman, Charlotte is the Queen, and Jake is the Snake.

When a successful reinvention occurs for any given professional wrestler, it usually happens only once or twice. Terry Bollea is either known as the real American hero Hulk Hogan or as the black stubble bearded air guitar playing leader of the New World Order (NWO), Hollywood Hogan. Mark Callaway is either known as the grave digger undertaker or the American badass biker. For most, once you find a persona that gets over you may tweak it here or there but you're pretty much set. Making any major changes can backfire, but if you pull it off, your range as a performer will be shown and your legend will grow.

When it comes to reinvention, Chris Jericho is quite the anomaly. Perhaps no one in the history of professional wrestling has had as many successful looks, entrance songs, persona variants, and even finishing moves as Chris Jericho. For a while there it seemed like Chris would change his nickname every month just to mess with us. Every time we puzzled, "He's calling himself what now?" Chris would do his thing, and by the end of the night we'd be cheering on the Canadian chameleon.

Jericho has penned five books, hosted a long running podcast, spent plenty of time in the commentator's booth, and has appeared in a multitude of other creative projects. The man has provided fans with a plethora of firsthand insight into the business and his own legendary career. The charismatic master of reinvention is the perfect man for the ultimate test of if a professional wrestler can find their best professional wrestling self.

The Tournament de Jericho pits eight different Christopher Keith Irving's against each other. The eight Jericho's have been carefully selected and seeded to find the absolute best ever version of Jericho. Ya dig!

Our contestants appearing in chronological order:

1. Chris Jericho 'Man of 1004 holds'—March 30, 1998, (Reading of the list of holds)
2. Chris Jericho 'Y2J'—August 9, 1999, (World Wrestling Entertainment (WWE) debut)
3. Chris Jericho 'The Undisputed Champion'—December 9, 2001, (Dual WWE champion)
4. Chris Jericho 'The Code Breaker'—October 5, 2008, (No Mercy ladder match v. Shawn Michaels)
5. Chris Jericho 'Best in the world'—April 1, 2012, (WrestleMania match v. CM Punk)
6. Chris Jericho 'The One with the Lists'—February 13, 2017, (Festival of Friendship)
7. Chris Jericho 'The Alpha'—January 4, 2018, (5 Star Match v. Omega at Tokyo Dome)
8. Chris Jericho 'Le Champion'—August 31, 2019, (All Elite Wrestling (AEW) world championship win at All-Out)

TOURNAMENT DE JERICHO

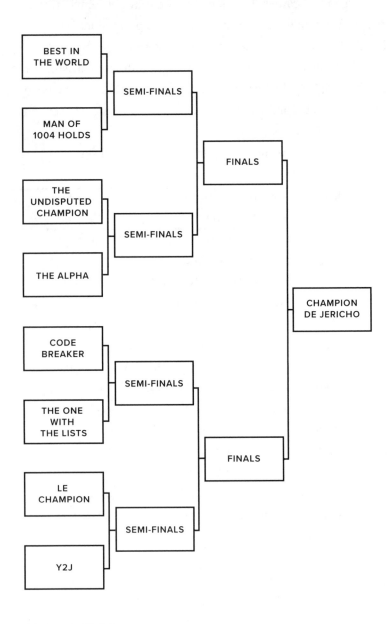

ROUND ONE MATCHUP: BEST IN THE WORLD V. MAN OF 1004 HOLDS

TALE OF THE TAPE	BEST IN THE WORLD	MAN OF 1004 HOLDS
AGE	41	27
SLOGAN OF THE TIME	"I'M THE BEST IN THE WORLD AT WHAT I DO!"	"WELCOME TO MONDAY NIGHT JERICHO!"
NOTABLE PHYSICAL FEATURES	LIGHTBULB INFUSED SPARKLY JACKET	LONG BLONDE HAIR
PRO WRESTLING ILLUSTRATED "TOP 500" ANNUAL RANKING	29	10
PRIOR 20 MATCH WIN/LOSE RECORD	17-3	14-6
MOST SIGNIFICANT WIN IN PRIOR 20 MATCH RUN	KOFI KINGSTON	EDDIE GUERRERO

When he was an afterthought with the professional wrestling powers that be Jericho took it upon himself to stand out. During his memorable feud with Dean 'The Man of a 1000 Holds' Malenko, Jericho hysterically claimed that he was 'The Man of a 1004 Holds' and recited his never-ending list of arm bar variations as proof. In World Championship Wrestling (WCW), Jericho made an impact despite whatever little effort creative put into his spot on the card.

By 2012, Jericho was an accomplished ring veteran. He had proven himself in and out of the ring. Chris was coming off one, if not the, best feuds of his career against CM Punk. The feud was a brilliant blend of reality storyline and solid in-ring work. This match was over before it started.

Winner: Best in the World

ROUND ONE MATCHUP: THE UNDISPUTED CHAMPION V. THE ALPHA

TALE OF THE TAPE	UNDISPUTED CHAMPION	THE ALPHA
AGE	31	47
SLOGAN OF THE TIME	"LISTEN UP, JUNIOR!"	"I'M THE ALPHA!"
NOTABLE PHYSICAL FEATURES	TWO OF THE MOST ICONIC WORLD CHAMPIONSHIP BELTS IN PROFESSIONAL WRESTLING HISTORY	THE ALPHA (BULLET CLUBESQUE) T-SHIRT
PRO WRESTLING ILLUSTRATED "TOP 500" ANNUAL RANKING	9	N/A
PRIOR 20 MATCH WIN/LOSE RECORD	8-11-1	12-7-1
MOST SIGNIFICANT WIN IN PRIOR 20 MATCH RUN	DWAYNE 'THE ROCK' JOHNSON 'STONE COLD' STEVE AUSTIN	KEVIN OWENS

Who can say that they beat 'Stone Cold' Steve Austin and Dwayne 'The Rock' Johnson on the same night? Chris Jericho can and when he did it, he captured both of WWE's major gold straps, becoming the undisputed champion. On this night, the most unlikely winner of those in the matches fought for his place among the squared circle greats.

The Alpha persona gave Jericho that big fight feel around his matches. His reduced schedule and select opponents added that can't miss mystique to the storied superstar. Matched against a stellar in-ring opponent in Kenny Omega, Jericho showed the world that he was still able to command the action inside of the ring. Jericho had already proven that he was one of the greatest sports entertainers of all time but now he was operating on a level that was on par with any five-star professional wrestler.

The Undisputed Champion got a win over two of the greatest men to ever lace them up, problem was it felt cheap. Maybe it was the use of classic heel tactics or maybe it's because out of the four men competing for the title that night, Kurt Angle being the fourth, Jericho felt like the least deserving winner from the group. It was an unsatisfyingly shocking moment. If you watch Jericho's Tokyo Dome match against Omega and aren't satisfied, you just need to stop watching professional wrestling. Satisfying the masses wins the day.

Winner: The Alpha

ROUND ONE MATCHUP: THE CODE BREAKER V. THE ONE WITH THE LISTS

TALE OF THE TAPE	THE CODE BREAKER	THE ONE WITH THE LISTS
AGE	37	46
SLOGAN OF THE TIME	"SAVE US Y2J!"	"YOU JUST MADE THE LIST!"
NOTABLE PHYSICAL FEATURES	SHORT HAIR	FASHIONABLE SCARFS
PRO WRESTLING ILLUSTRATED "TOP 500" ANNUAL RANKING	29	22
PRIOR 20 MATCH WIN/LOSE RECORD	9-11	3-17
MOST SIGNIFICANT WIN IN PRIOR 20 MATCH RUN	CM PUNK	SAMI ZAYN

In 2008, Chris was thrown into one of the greatest feuds of his career when he squared off against the greatest in-ring performer in professional wrestling history: 'The Heartbreak Kid' Shawn Michaels. Unsurprisingly, Jericho won WWE's superstar of the year award that year.

In 2017, Chris was paired with Kevin Owens and the duo soon became best friends. When Jericho wanted to show his appreciation for the prize fighter he threw a Festival of Friendship celebration, in typical professional wrestling fashion things took a predictably goofy turn. Despite the segment being well received, the feud didn't culminate with the big payoff we would expect from these two. According to Jericho, Vince McMahon once called it "the worst match in WrestleMania history."

Going into this match the Code Breaker was being booked as

a top guy while the list maker dwindled in mid-card player purgatory. These two Jerichos were giving us captivating storytelling in and outside of the ring. The difference being one felt like he was way more appreciated than the other. An employee, sorry an independent contractor, no matter how professional they are, can be coached up into giving their best performance. In this match it is the coaching and booking that puts the Code Breaker over.

Winner: The Code Breaker

ROUND ONE MATCHUP: LE CHAMPION V. Y2J

TALE OF THE TAPE	BEST IN THE WORLD	MAN OF 1004 HOLDS
AGE	48	28
SLOGAN OF THE TIME	"A LITTLE BIT OF THE BUBBLY!"	"WELCOME TO RAW IS JERICHO!"
NOTABLE PHYSICAL FEATURES	LE CHAMPION NECK BANDANAS	VARIETY OF PONY TAILS
PRO WRESTLING ILLUSTRATED "TOP 500" ANNUAL RANKING	N/A	29
PRIOR 20 MATCH WIN/LOSE RECORD	9-10-1	5-15
MOST SIGNIFICANT WIN IN PRIOR 20 MATCH RUN	KENNY OMEGA	PERRY SATURN

We have two versions of Jericho that arose out of his journey into new professional wrestling companies matched up here. One was his debut with the largest professional wrestling company the world has ever seen in the WWE and the other was his surprising decision to work for an up-start new exciting promotion called AEW. Whenever a familiar wrestler debuts with a new promotion, the professional wrestling community buzzes about all the new exciting booking possibilities. The potential for new feuds, storylines, and, in Jericho's case, new personas stirs up exhilarating anticipation amongst the fans.

In 1999, Jericho reached the pinnacle of major league professional wrestling the WWE. Hailed as one of the best debuts of all-time, Jericho entered the stage by interrupting Dwayne 'The Rock' Johnson during one of his unforgettable promos. Fans were elated as the two verbally sparred and Jericho was instantly established as a main event player.

In 2019, there was no doubt that Jericho was a well-established main event player, the experienced superstar headlined the upstart AEW's All-Out event against 'Hangman' Adam Page. The two battled over who would be the company's inaugural world champion and when it was all said and done, Chris was reborn as Le Champion. It's French for the champion.

In combat sports, when you pit two experienced fighters against each other and one is twenty years older than the other, the smart money is on the youth. But this is professional wrestling, a spectacle unlike any other, and anything can happen when the twenty-nine-year-old Y2J faces off against the forty-nine-year-old Le Champion. At forty-nine years old, it was Chris Jericho who was called upon to lead this new professional wrestling promotion. Why? Because he has all the tools to do it. Y2J has all the talent in the world, but at this point he needs to add more tools in his professional wrestling box to get the win over his twenty-year senior.

Winner: Le Champion

TOURNAMENT DE JERICHO

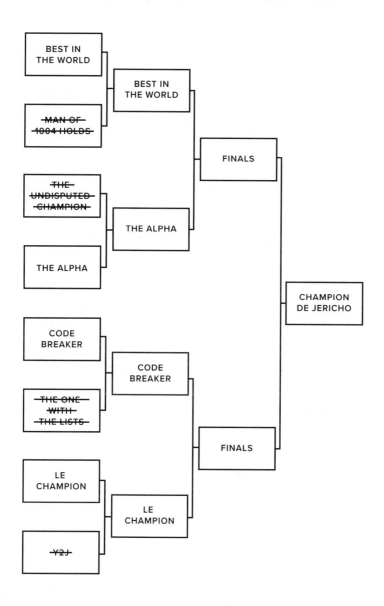

SEMI-FINALS:
BEST IN THE WORLD V. THE ALPHA

It's the sparsely-wrestling, part-time ring schedule veteran versus the week-in-week-out company work horse. It's hard to top a guy that keeps the crowd entertained and invested each and every week. Even with the rarified mystique that the late in his career Chris Jericho in Japan has, he can't beat the man who is elevating the WWE champion CM Punk every time the two of them share the stage.

Winner: Best in the World

SEMI-FINALS:
CODE BREAKER V. LE CHAMPION

By 2008, Chris had been wrestling professionally for nearly twenty years. If my math is correct, by 2019 he had been wrestling professionally for over thirty years. In that over a decade of professional wrestling, there were undoubtedly many lessons learned. But with twenty years in the business, Code Breaker Jericho already possessed a plethora of knowledge and ten years less of wear and tear on his body. During this run Chris was feuding with Shawn Michaels. They say iron sharpens iron. Who better to sharpen your skills against than the man many consider the greatest in-ring performer of all-time, the Heartbreak Kid?

Winner: Code Breaker

TOURNAMENT DE JERICHO

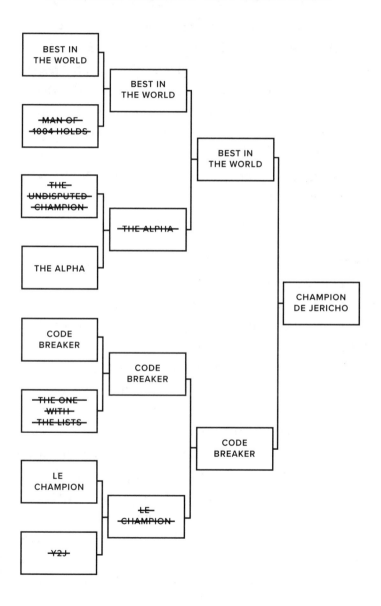

FINALS: BEST IN THE WORLD V. CODE BREAKER

There are two main things that make a professional wrestler great. One is their skills on the microphone or their ability to cut a promo. It's these talking segments that are often responsible for getting the audience invested in the matches. Hell, at times these promotional segments are the most entertaining thing on a show. This is crucial, as an entertained and invested audience keeps coming back for more.

The other is a professional wrestler's technical prowess or in-ring ability. Even the most compelling storylines may be quickly forgotten if a match doesn't deliver the in-ring goods. A solid match will have fans begging for more. This can lead to a rematch and extend the fans investment in the product.

These two versions of Jericho are only four years apart. Given that, there isn't a lot noticeable difference in terms of in-ring ability, microphone work, or knowledge of the business. Both of these Jerichos were coming off epic feuds with exceptional in-ring workers who could be, well, let's just say difficult to work with. It's a battle of the diva opponents if you will. Both of these feuds involved captivating reality driven storylines.

The Best in the World was coming off a fresh return from a nearly two-year absence. The Code Breaker had been steadily wrestling for over a year after another two-yearish absence. Typically, the fresher the return, the more excitement there is for whatever storyline creative has lined up for you. That's usually the case, but working with Shawn Michaels is not usual. Countless legends have attested that Shawn will bring the best out of you. Chris Jericho is no exception. The Code Breaker wins.

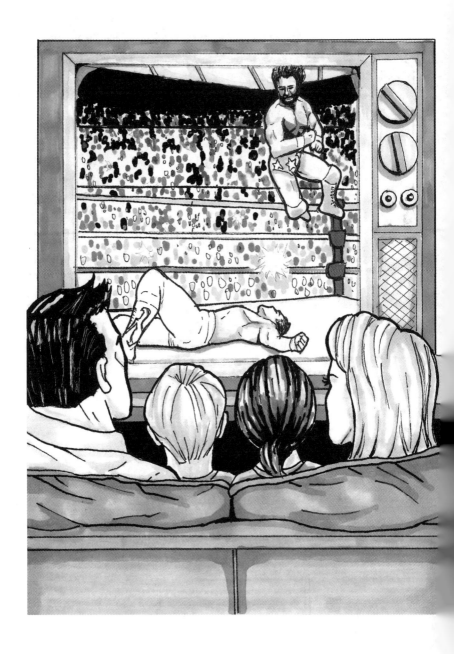

CHAPTER 13

PROFESSIONAL WRESTLING MATCH HALL OF FAME

It is almost too cliché to include a hall-of-fame chapter in a book about professional wrestling. The professional wrestling world is full of halls, including promotional, national, regional, and journalist driven ones. The most well-known hall of fame, the World Wrestling Entertainment (WWE) Hall of Fame was founded in 1994. Its sole entrant was the legendary André the Giant. The following year the WWE inducted seven legendary professional wrestling figures into the hall, ever since the induction ceremony became a mostly annual tradition that continues to this day.

Professional wrestlers, managers, broadcasters, and even celebrities have all found their way into the storied hall. Yet where are the structural beams that lay the foundation for the skyscraper that is professional wrestling? In other words, where are the actual wrestling matches? The matches are the main course in the dinner that is a professional wrestling card. They deserve the recognition that induction into a hall of fame carries. That's where we come in.

To enter the hall, a match's quality, innovativeness, and overall importance to the world of professional wrestling are judged. A Hall-of-Fame match will have its build, bell-to-bell performance, and legacy assessed. The work done in the match, during the build, and throughout the participants' entire careers will be considered. For our inaugural class only, one-on-one singles matches will receive consideration. Out of the millions and millions of professional wrestling matches that have gone down over the years, eight will be chosen to enter the Professional Wrestling Match Hall of Fame.

Ladies and Gentlemen, we present the Professional Wrestling Match Hall of Fame. In chronological order, here is our inaugural class:

RICKY 'THE DRAGON' STEAMBOAT V. 'THE MACHO MAN' RANDY SAVAGE (WWF INTERCONTINENTAL CHAMPION)

THE MATCH DATA

EVENT: WrestleMania III

DATE: March 29, 1987

VENUE: Pontiac Silverdome, Pontiac, MI, USA

CROWD: 93,173 (disputed)

PROMOTION:
World Wrestling Federation (WWF)

PROMOTER: Vince McMahon Jr.

STAKES: WWF International Championship

CORNER PEOPLE:
George 'The Animal' Steele (Steamboat)
Miss Elizabeth (Savage)

REFEREE: Dave Hebner

COMMENTARY TEAM:
Gorilla Monsoon and
Jesse 'The Body' Ventura

RING ANNOUNCER: Howard Finkel

MATCH TIME: 14:35

THE BUILD

It took a six-month-long feud, where Randy 'Macho Man' Savage injured the larynx of Ricky 'The Dragon' Steamboat, to get to this match. On November 22, 1986, during a match on WWF *Superstars of Wrestling* the Macho Man and his devastating double axe handle from the top rope, along with a flying ring bell, sent the Dragon to the hospital. In a miraculous fashion and after intense speech therapy, Steamboat was able to recover from the attack. Perhaps it's because he possessed the best medicine out there . . . tremendous heart.

The Dragon would extract his revenge by doing the one thing that would undoubtedly drive Randy crazy: messing with Miss Elizabeth. Granted, he messed with her in the most innocent way possible by aligning with the dull wild man known as George 'The Animal' Steele, a furry man-beast who was crushing hard on the lovely Elizabeth. But if you even looked at Liz with a hint of doted infatuation in your eyes, Savage was ready to rip your throat out and then proceed to berate Liz for allowing anyone to yearn for her. These two masters of the ring were set to square off one more time, and this time it was "personal."

THE MATCH

Macho enters the ring first, and despite Savage playing the heel, the fans cheer on their appreciation for the madness. The Macho One's charisma is undeniable. A karate-themed Ricky 'The Dragon' Steamboat hits the ring to a typical babyface ovation.

The two lock up and begin teasing the technical pureness that a match between these two squared circle technicians is capable of. They start the dance, and then Savage notices Elizabeth is standing a little too close to George 'the Animal' Steele. Macho quickly relocates her to a neutral corner. The fans are torn as they love Macho as a professional wrestler but as Liz's man, well, he's kind of a huge jerk.

Savage returns to the ring and the action hits a feverish pace. The two men display high impact moves, classic wrestling holds, and the essence of face/heel ring psychology to the crowd. Speed, athleticism, and world class wrestling are already on full display.

Savage gains the upper hand, hitting Steamboat with a hard clothesline that knocks him out of the ring. Randy stalks him and soars at the Dragon with a high knee to the back. Ricky spills over the guardrail onto the cold unforgiving concrete. The Animal carries him back into the ring only for Macho to toss him out at the other end. Savage is relentless and quickly hits Steamboat with a double axe handle off the top rope onto the floor. It's the same move that injured Ricky and forced him to relearn how to pronounce the letter E. Savage rolls Steamboat back into the ring and hits him with another one.

The action continues and the crowd rallies behind Steamboat. Ricky hits a desperation back body drop that propels Savage over the ring ropes, all while the announcers try to establish, explain, and justify the inconsistent rules of professional wrestling. The Dragon quickly brings Savage back into the ring. Steamboat hits the top turnbuckle and glides over the referee, hitting Savage with a flying karate chop. Steamboat unleashes his hybrid wrestling/karate offensive moves, which basically consists of your standard wrestling moves with a few emphatic karate chops thrown in, onto Savage.

Savage regains control by using a handful of tights to propel Steamboat into the steel ring post. The referee gets caught up in the fast-paced action and is inadvertently knocked out. Instead of turning to standard heelish tactics, Savage climbs the ring ropes and hits his signature flying elbow on Ricky. He has the pin but with no one there to count, it doesn't matter.

Savage's denial of the unspoken rules of heelishdom does not go unpunished. Quickly returning to the dark side Savage grabs the ring bell. The same kind of blue bell that hospitalized Ricky before. Randy climbs the ropes, attempting to smash Steamboat with the bell, but this time he is pushed off the rope by an interfering Animal. Savage rises to his feet and picks Steamboat up for a scoop slam. Steamboat reverses into a small cradle, the referee counts one, two, three! A new intercontinental champion is crowned.

THE LEGACY

This battle over the intercontinental gold is still regarded as one of, if not *the*, greatest matches of all time. On a card headlined by André the Giant versus Hulk Hogan, many professional wrestling pundits opined that it was this match that stole the show. Their argument is a testament to the in-ring excellence displayed by these two wrestling greats. Randy's meticulous work mapping out the match move by move paid off. It wasn't long after when WWF, on its quest for new stars, put the world title on Randy Savage. The Macho One enjoyed an extended run as the company's main champion. While a few years later, Ricky 'The Dragon' Steamboat won the NWA world heavyweight championship. For those smaller wrestlers watching, this match was truly inspirational. To those who don't shop at the big and tall store, the message was clear: you don't have to look like an overgrown character ripped from the pages of a comic book to deliver a show-stealing match.

ANDRÉ THE GIANT V. 'THE IMMORTAL' HULK HOGAN (WWF CHAMPION)

THE MATCH DATA

EVENT: WrestleMania III

DATE: March 29, 1987

VENUE: Pontiac Silverdome, Pontiac, MI, USA

CROWD: 93,173 (disputed)

PROMOTION:
World Wrestling Federation (WWF)

PROMOTER: Vince McMahon Jr.

STAKES:
WWF Championship/
fifteen-year "undefeated" streak

CORNER PEOPLE:
Bobby 'The Brain' Heenan (André) / None (Hogan)

REFEREE: Joey Marella

COMMENTARY TEAM:
Gorilla Monsoon and
Jesse 'The Body' Ventura

RING ANNOUNCER: Bob Uecker

MATCH TIME: 12:01

THE BUILD

On February 7, 1987, many a child's jaw dropped when the Giant appeared on "Piper's Pit" alongside his new manager Bobby 'The Brain' Heenan. With fingers so big you could push a hard-boiled egg through any one of his rings, an angry Giant ripped the crucifix and signature shirt off of Hulk Hogan's chest. It was such a simple but impactful gesture that left Hogan bloody. A true testament to the 7'4" Giant's raw power. André, upset that he was being upstaged, challenged Hulk to a championship title match at WrestleMania. A week later Hogan would respond to André's challenge with an emphatic YES!, sending the crowd and professional wrestling world into an uproar. The epic showdown was set.

THE MATCH

No music was needed to accentuate the larger-than-life André the Giant. As the big man and Heenan ride down the aisle in a motorized miniature wrestling ring, the boos of the crowd say it all. The hated heels are unfazed by the trashed hurled at them. They are ready for the moment. Hogan pumps up the crowd as he enters the ring to his now iconic "Real American" entrance music.

The bell rings. Hogan quickly goes for the slam but collapses under André's massive weight. As swiftly as André chugging a beer, Hogan is nearly pinned. The Giant toys with his victim, hitting him with punishing slams. Hogan uses his quickness (compared to André, he's the Flash) to mount a comeback. André sticks out his size 24 boot to end the champ's offensive flurry. The Giant methodically puts the squeeze on Hogan, showcasing one of his signature moves the bear hug. At the time, André may have had a limited offensive move set, but he could still squeeze the life out of you.

Hogan draws power from his HulkaManiacs and like Bruce Banner turning green, Hogan Hulks up. The indestructible force rocks the Giant with a barrage of hits. The immovable object withstands Hulk's power and sends him to the outside. Neither of these men appear mortal. Hogan gains the upper hand and believing himself a real-life superhero attempts to pile drive the near 500 lb. monster. The laws of physics do apply and Hogan doesn't pull off the move. Mercifully, the action returns to the ring. Hulk hits André with a clothesline knocking him onto the mat. The shockwaves from the impact seem to electrify Hogan and once again he surges with power. Then it happens. The immortal moment. The slam heard around the world. Hogan scoops up André and slams him down to the mat. Hulk follows it up with his signature leg drop. The ref counts, albeit slightly fast, one, two, three. It's all over. Hit the music and wait for the pose down.

THE LEGACY

The showdown in the Silverdome has the most lasting legacy of any individual professional wrestling match. It's the first moment depicted in WWE's opening television sequence shown. Hulk Hogan's "body slam heard around the world" and his subsequent victory took the Venice Beach muscle man's career to unprecedented heights. When Hogan did the unthinkable and slayed the Giant, to all the little HulkaManiacs out there he was the closest thing to a real-life superhero there was. André, with his body declining and on the back nine of his in-ring career, honored the professional wrestling gods and passed the torch. WrestleMania III broke pay-per-view and attendance records. What better way to showcase the power of Vince McMahon's relatively new nationwide promotion? The match ushered in a new era and did more for professional wrestling than any match, before or after, has ever done.

'THE NATURE BOY' RIC FLAIR
V. RICKY 'THE DRAGON' STEAMBOAT
(NWA WORLD CHAMPION)

THE MATCH DATA

EVENT: Clash of Champions VI: Ragin' Cagun

DATE: April 2, 1989

VENUE:
Louisiana Superdome, New Orleans, LA, USA

CROWD: 5,300

PROMOTION:
National Wrestling Alliance (NWA)/
World Championship Wrestling (WCW)

PROMOTER: Ted Turner

STAKES: NWA World Championship

CORNER PEOPLE:
None (Flair) / None (Accompanied to the
ring by his wife and young son) (Steamboat)

REFEREE: Tommy Young

COMMENTARY TEAM: Jim Ross and Terry Funk

RING ANNOUNCER: Gary Cappetta

MATCH TIME: 55:32

THE BUILD

The Ric Flair-led Four Horsemen had spent the better part of a month tormenting babyface Eddie Gilbert. Gilbert was fed up and challenged them to a tag team match on WTBS *Saturday Night*. Enter mystery partner Ricky 'the Dragon' Steamboat. Steamboat pinned the NWA world champion and a historic feud was ignited. In February of 1989, at the Chi-town rumble Steamboat pulled off the upset and captured his first NWA heavyweight title. The rematch was set but off camera an even bigger storyline was brewing.

In a futile attempt to stem the momentum that the then WWF had gained, the NWA did the now unthinkable act of running a major professional wrestling event opposite of WrestleMania. Clash of the Champions VI: Ragin' Cajun was broadcast on free TV in a blatant attempt to hurt WrestleMania V's pay-per-view ratings. This wasn't the first-time rival promotions put on competing events against each other. The tactic of hosting a competing event was one the WWF was all too familiar with.

In 1987, the WWF held the inaugural Survivor Series pay-per-view the same day as the NWA's highly promoted Starrcade. McMahon also threatened to withhold the broadcasting rights to WrestleMania against any cable companies that dared to broadcast his competitors pay-per-view. Following this trend, in 1988 the WWF broadcast the inaugural Royal Rumble event on the USA network; the date was chosen in a direct effort to undermine the NWA's Bunkhouse Stampede pay-per-view. In response Jim Crockett put together, an airing on free TV, the Clash of the Champions event to compete directly against the WWF's WrestleMania VI. The cut throat anti "rising tide raises all ships" mindset came to a head in April of 1989.

The main events of both professional wrestling shows had some similarities. WrestleMania V featured a main event of Hulk Hogan versus Randy 'Macho Man' Savage with a brilliantly crafted storyline consisting of the former tag team partners the Mega Powers exploding. Clash of the Champions featured a two out of three falls match for the NWA world title between Ric Flair and Ricky Steamboat with a storyline built mainly around competition. Both headlining bouts featured a technically proficient professional wrestling superstar facing off against the most popular wrestler their promotion had.

While the WWF had the advantage in terms of star power, the NWA had the advantage of overall excellent in-ring work from its combatants. The math is simple: Hogan and Savage combined star power was far greater than the NWA's duo, but Flair and Steamboat's combined wrestling ability far outweighed any duo containing Hulk Hogan. The final battle between gritty in-ring rasslin' and slickly-produced character and storyline driven sports entertainment was underway.

THE MATCH

Naitch donning his famous black butterfly robe struts down to the ring surrounded by a bevy of beauties. In stark contrast to his opponent's playboy lifestyle, the Dragon, in his karate attire, makes his way to the ring accompanied by his wife, wearing a wedding gown (there was no wedding) and infant son wearing a dragon costume (it was not Halloween).

The bell rings and the two grapplers begin feeling each other out as they lock up. Steamboat backs Flair into the corner and lays a disrespectful slap across his face. Flair keeps his composure, and the two men take to the mat in an exchange of amateur wrestling maneuvers. Steamboat wrestles Naitch into the corner, the two men rise, and Steamboat delivers another thunderous slap across Flair's face.

They lock up again and exchange locks and holds, fluctuating between rapid paced off the ropes action and rest holds. Hard hitting chest chops are thrown into the mix. After all, you can't have a match between the Nature Boy and a black belt without a healthy number of chops.

Steamboat hits Flair with a high back body drop, the move seemingly sends him up into the rafters. Ricky follows it up with a crisp dropkick and a stunned Flair falls to his knees begging for mercy as only Ric can. Steamboat relents and Flair seizes the opportunity with a kick to the midsection. The action is back on. The two rain blows on each other until Flair walks out of the corner and collapses face first to the mat.

The pace quickens with Steamboat getting in the majority of offense causing Flair to retreat to the outside. Flair stalls then reenters the fight. They lock up and this time Flair gains the advantage but Ricky brawls back. Neither man has been able to sustain an offensive attack against the other, a testament to just how evenly matched they really are. Flair goes for the figure-four leglock, Steamboat reverses it into a small package pinning combination, Flair flips it and pins Ricky for the three count. The first fall goes to the Nature Boy.

Flair's confidence grows as he struts around the ring. Round two is on and Steamboat attacks, flying around the ring hitting Flair from all angles. Steamboat slows the pace and wears Flair down with classic wrestling holds. They battle back and forth.

Steamboat drops upwards of ten elbow drops on Flair's knee. Not one really hits Flair's knee but Steamboat delivers them with such vigor we all wince in sympathy. The Dragon slaps on Flair's patented figure-four leglock, but the ropes save Flair. Steamboat slams Naitch toward the middle of the ring and slaps on a Boston crab. The ropes save Flair again. Flair chops back but Ricky out wrestles him and Ric retreats to the outside.

Steamboat is dragged to the outside and violently whipped against the steel guardrails. They return to the ring. Flair collects double-digit near falls with Steamboat kicking out every single time. Flair climbs the ring ropes. Steamboat recovers and catches him with a superplex off the middle rope. Steamboat beats at Flair's back and puts him in a double arm chicken wing lock. Flair writhes in pain and submits. They are tied at one fall a piece.

After the customary one-minute commercial break, the exhausted ring veterans go at it once again. The third and final round is on. The two weary men trade blows each delivering chops and high impact wrestling maneuvers. Flair momentarily gains the advantage and puts Ricky in the figure-four leglock. The Dragon quickly finds the ropes and gets back to his feet. He chops away at Flair and whips him into the corner turnbuckle. Flair flips back first over the turnbuckle and stammers down the ring apron where he is met with another smacking chop. Naitch begs for mercy but craftily uses the momentary hesitation to regain control and attempts to pin the Dragon with his foot resting on the ring rope for added leverage. It's hard to be a heel when you are this loved, but Slick Ric will be damned if he doesn't try every dirty play in the book.

Flair's now in control, he punishes Steamboat focusing in on his knee. He twists and jerks it every which way until he slaps on the figure-four leglock, this time smack dab in the middle of the ring. Steamboat will not give up; he squirms in pain until he rolls the two interlocked men into the ropes. The ref breaks the hold. The fatigued combatants exchange blows until Steamboat once again whips Flair into the corner. Flair hits his flip and runs the apron again, but this time he climbs the ropes and hits the Dragon with a flying cross body. It's not enough, Steamboat battles back with speed and high impact offense. Flair withstands the attack and the two exhausted men fight on until Steamboat hits a swinging neck breaker. Each high impact wrestling move looks a little less crisp than the one before, in a moment of reality we can feel the exhaustion setting in.

Flair catches Ricky in a sleeper hold. The Dragon's arm falls down twice, the ref positions himself to call for the bell, but Steamboats pops back to life. Steamboat charges the corner and perfectly bounces Flair's head off the turnbuckle, breaking the hold. The two men have now wrestled for fifty minutes. As Jim Ross puts it this isn't walking out to music and posing, this is wrestling.

The clock winds down and the two exasperated men trade blow for blow, each angling for that decisive moment when they can be crowned the winner. Flair climbs the ropes hoping the high-risk move will finally put an end to the Dragon. Steamboat counters and body slams Flair off the top rope. He ties Flair up in the double arm chicken wing lock. The weary warriors can't hold the lock and they collapse. The ref counts one, two, three. Both men's shoulders are pinned and both have one foot positioned under the rope. The crowd hangs in suspense and the ref declares Steamboat the winner.

Once again, a lack of instant replay has cheated the professional wrestling community out of a decisive winner. For the sake of all involved just ignore Steamboat's post-match interview, it was about as bad as this match was great.

THE LEGACY

Many professional wrestling pundits state that the 1989 Ric Flair versus Ricky Steamboat trilogy of matches were the greatest series of matches in the history of professional wrestling. There is ample proof to back this claim. Sadly, though, less than 10 percent of the 65,000 seats at the Superdome were filled that night. In perhaps what was the NWA's last-ditch effort to stay on par with WWF, Steamboat and Flair put on one hell of a classic match. The competition was great, but the pomp and circumstance of the WWF would ultimately win this professional wrestling war. Flair and Steamboat gave us that memorable last dance in a relationship destined to end. Showcasing grit, athleticism, and wrestling proficiency, Steamboat and Flair's trilogy of matches were the swan song that the territorial era deserved.

'THE HEARTBREAK KID' SHAWN MICHAELS V. 'THE BAD GUY' RAZOR RAMON (WWF INTERCONTINENTAL CHAMPION—DISPUTED)

THE MATCH DATA

EVENT: WrestleMania X

DATE: March 20, 1994

VENUE:
Madison Square Garden, New York City, NY, USA

CROWD: 18,065

PROMOTION:
World Wrestling Federation (WWF)

PROMOTER: Vince McMahon Jr.

STAKES:
Undisputed Intercontinental Championship

CORNER PEOPLE:
Diesel (Michaels) / None (Ramon)

REFEREE: Earl Hebner

COMMENTARY TEAM:
Vince McMahon Jr. and Jerry 'The King' Lawler

RING ANNOUNCER: Bill Dunn

MATCH TIME: 18:47

THE BUILD

A take on the classic "who is the true champion" professional wrestling story line. Shawn Michaels was stripped of his intercontinental title for being, well . . . the pre-2000s prima donna that he was. Razor Ramon, whose gimmick had almost instantaneously caught fire, won the vacated belt. Michaels, claiming to be the true champion, would take issues with Razor holding himself out as the real intercontinental champion, and the feud was on.

THE MATCH

It was about two hours into the less than three-hour Wrestle-Mania X show. This was not the evenings main event. The camera focuses on the two intercontinental belts hanging above the ring, the music hits, and we are off and running.

The difference between the two men is stark. The flamboyant Michaels prances around the ring leaving the early '90s spectator questioning his sexuality, Razor swaggers down to the ring oozing machismo and invoking no such questions regarding his sexuality.

They lock up and Shawn instantly showcases his in-ring quickness and wrestling proficiency. Razor spills to the outside where his future tag team partner 'Big Daddy Cool' Diesel, aka Big Sexy, aka Kevin Nash, levels him. The ref senses the outside interference and ejects Diesel from the ringside area; now the two combatants can wrestle unencumbered. There will be a decisive winner in this one.

Razor fights his way back into the ring and delivers a series of power moves to Shawn. Shawn regains the advantage, back body dropping Razor outside of the ring onto the cold exposed concrete. The third participant in this battle, the ladder, enters the wild affair. Razor stumbles as he lifts the ladder onto the ringside apron. HBK delivers a swift baseball slide knocking it straight into the Bad Guy's chest. Michaels brings the ladder into the ring, he battering-rams it into Razor, then repeatedly and from various angles brutally tosses it onto Ramon. This ladder isn't like the ones we would later become accustomed to, it looks new, it looks solid, and it looks completely legit, the total opposite of a movie set prop that one might expect.

Shawn sets up the ladder and begins his climb for the belts. Razor grabs a handful of tights and pulls him down, exposing Shawn's bare ass to the crowd. Suddenly the arena sounds like a boy band concert and the female fans scream their appreciation for the Boy Toy. The camera zooms in on the Heartbreak Kid logo splattered across his ass, the mostly male audience is reminded of just why they should hate him.

Michaels sets up the ladder and positions Razor for a perfectly executed splash from the ladder. While Razor is dazed, Shawn steadies the ladder and climbs for the belts. Razor recovers rocks the ladder sending Shawn flying face first into the top rope. The two men gather themselves and collide into each other at full speed. They are stunned and worn down by the brutality.

Razor props the ladder up in the corner. He whips Shawn into the ladder, the powerful impact sends Shawn tumbling to the outside. The Bad Guy stalks Shawn with the ladder, violently slamming it into Shawn until he has him in position. Razor stands the ladder against the ring apron and catapults Shawn face first into the unforgiving steel. Gravity brings Shawn down to the ground, sandwiching him underneath the ladder. It's a scene reminiscent of another early '90s classic: *Home Alone*.

Razor rolls Shawn back into the ring and violently swings the ladder toward his head. He connects and the impact sends the Boy Toy flying out the other side of the ring. Razor positions the ladder and begins his first climb for the gold. Miraculously, HBK climbs up the ring and reaches the top corner turnbuckle, he launches himself toward Razor and the collision sends the three stars of the show sprawled out across the ring.

They regain their composure, Shawn and Razor each scale one side of the ladder. They reach the top, and Razor sort of scope slams Shawn from his side of the ladder down to the canvas. The momentum of the slam unsteadies the ladder causing the Bad Guy to lose balance and stumble down. Razor rises to his feet and once again begins the climb; this time Shawn hits the ladder with a dropkick and knocks Razor down.

Shawn whips Razor into the ropes and hits him with a crescent kick to the face. HBK follows it up with a piledriver. Michaels props the ladder up in a corner and rides it down onto Razor Ramon's limp body. HBK climbs for the gold once again. Razor rises and shoulder-butts the ladder, this time Shawn lands crotch first on the top rope. The fans cheer on as the Heartbreak Kid and his favorite toy are writhing in agony. Michaels ends up captive between the twisted ring ropes. Razor climbs the ladder, grabs ahold of both belts, and out of pure exhaustion drops down to the mat.

Razor Ramon climbs back up the ladder holding the belts up in the air in glorious victory, all while Shawn winches about on the canvas grabbing at his crotch.

THE LEGACY

Plenty of critics voiced their complaints about just how detrimental the Kliq was to the professional wrestling business. Amid this criticism these two men showed just what kind of positive impact the Kliq could have on the industry. Ladder matches may have existed before this one, but none before this match demonstrated just how entertaining this fan-favorite gimmick match could be. In his book *Hitman* Bret Hart wrote, "Not surprisingly, the ladder match between Shawn and Razor stole the show, and why wouldn't it." Despite of or maybe because of the fact that Bret called Shawn a thieving bastard for stealing his ladder match finish, the Hitman had to acknowledge the greatness of this encounter. This match was the start of HBK earning his 'Mr. WrestleMania' nickname. While HBK had wrestled at WrestleMania elfore, this match was the first of many of his to be considered the unquestionable match of the night.

The ladder match and its variants have evolved to become as prominent a gimmick match as the storied steel cage. All who have participated in any kind of gimmick match and stolen the show have these two men to thank for paving the way. Edge, the Hardyz, the Dudley Boyz, Mick Foley, and every other professional wrestler who has had a pay-per-view gimmick match that delivered a career defining performance, have these two men to tip their hats to.

'STONE COLD' STEVE AUSTIN V. BRET 'THE HITMAN' HART

THE MATCH DATA

EVENT: WrestleMania XIII

DATE: March 23, 1997

VENUE: Rosemont Horizon, Rosemont, IL, USA

CROWD: 18,197

PROMOTION:
World Wrestling Federation (WWF)

PROMOTER: Vince McMahon Jr.

STAKES: Pride/Submission Match

CORNER PEOPLE:
None (Austin) / None (Hart)

REFEREE: Ken Shamrock

COMMENTARY TEAM:
Vince McMahon Jr., Jim Ross,
and Jerry 'The King' Lawler

RING ANNOUNCER: Howard Finkel

MATCH TIME: 22:04

THE BUILD

On June 23, 1996, Steve Austin won the King of the Ring tournament and declared that "Austin 3:16 means I just whipped your ass." On that day 'Stone Cold' Steve Austin was born. The unleashed Texas Rattlesnake began insulting pure babyfaces of which Bret Hart, who was out with an injury, was the current torchbearer. When Hart returned to the WWF in the fall of 1996, he accepted Austin's challenge. The two wrestlers met at Survivor Series where Hart was narrowly victorious in a perfectly balanced match.

The following Royal Rumble, Austin and Hart were the two final participants in the match. During the match, Austin was tossed over the top rope by Hart with both feet hitting the floor but the referees, somehow, were distracted and the elimination was not official. You just have to accept these head scratching, bending of the rules, moments as a part of professional wrestling. Stone Cold dastardly snuck back into the ring and ran up behind the Hitman, he grabbed on to his tights and tossed him over the top rope and onto the floor. Bret was furious.

Austin continued tormenting Hart costing him an opportunity to win the WWF championship with a solid steel chair shot. There was only way to settle this dust up, a showdown at WrestleMania in an "I quit" match. It was a philosophical battle between a man holding on to that classic storybook ending of good always triumphing over evil and another man embracing the reality that this colorful world is full of a lot of gray. It was respect for the historic way of doing things versus a screw that let's do what it takes to put butts in seats attitude.

THE MATCH

The now iconic sound of glass shattering kicks off the brutality that lays ahead. Bret hits the ring to the usual welcoming ovation he had grown accustomed to. The bell tolls and Austin pounces on Bret with punches. The two exchange blows in a schoolyard role around until they spill outside of the ring. They take turns utilizing the environment to punish each other. The two fighters escort the mayhem around the stands, they offer the hype fans a closeup view of the action.

The gladiators return the fight to the ring. Bret, with his master level technical prowess, quickly gains control hitting Austin with a swinging neck breaker. The Excellence of Execution focuses in his attack on Steve's perpetually injured knee. Austin hits a stunner out of nowhere but it only buys him a few minutes of reprieve before Hart is back on his leg attack.

While the announcers heap praise on Austin's "never say die" resiliency, the Hitman heelishly scurries up weapons from around the ringside area. There is a certain artform to heelish use of weapons in a match. For a heel in this position, the weapon use needs to be cheap, not badass. Bret hesitates, and Austin quickly reminds us that while Bret is unaccustomed to such heinous acts, a rattlesnake has no problem striking first. Stone Cold takes control of the proverbial steel chair and batters Bret's body.

Austin throws down the chair and returns to a straightforward wrestling attack, and we can't forget the maneuvers that a man once called the Ringmaster is very capable of bringing inside the ring. The announcers debate Hart's cowardice as he rakes the eyes of Austin, escaping his hold and regaining control. Once again, the two men take the fight outside of the ring. Bret busts Austin's head open on the steel barricade. Hart continues to brutalize Austin and throws him into the ring, where he refocuses his attack on Austin's bad knees, this time, using the abandoned steel chair.

Bret's questionable tactics give him the edge over Austin. That is until Steve leaves no question about what tactics he is willing to employ and delivers a kick straight to Bret's groin. The Texas Rattlesnake starts stomping a mud-hole into Hart. Austin hangs Bret up with an electrical cord until, in an act of desperation, the Hitman grabs a nearby ring bell and smacks Austin in the head.

Bret ties Austin up in his signature sharpshooter leglock. Austin uses every ounce of rattlesnake vigor to try and escape the hold. Wearing a gushing crimson mask, Stone Cold withers in pain but his heart will not let the words "I quit" escape through his bloodstained teeth. The special guest referee Ken Shamrock, dressed in Heartbreak Kid style nut hugger shorts, declares Austin out and calls the match. A hateful Hart breaks the hold, declares victory and continues to kick Steve while he's down. Shamrock intervenes and tosses Hart away. Bret cowardly backs out of the ring and heads to the locker room. Hart shows his discontent for the fans, giving them several one finger salutes on his way past the curtain. Austin refuses any help and doggedly walks to the back on his on own. The flawlessly orchestrated double turn is complete, excellently executed indeed.

THE LEGACY

As much as André versus Hogan was the match that transitioned the professional wrestling world from the territory system to a few national professional wrestling promotions, this was the match that truly transitioned the golden era style of professional wrestling to the attitude era. The slow burn double turn was a masterclass demonstration of professional wrestling psychology at its finest. The revered wrestler fighting for professional wrestling's institutionalized systems squaring off against the rebellious heel who didn't (in character) give a damn about any of it.

It was a story ripped from reality. Bret, after decades of perseverance, ultimately thrived in the established system. While Austin rightfully felt the establishment held back his true potential and set out to burn it all down, Bret in his autobiography *Hitman* said it himself when speaking about the end of this match: "If I ever wanted my fans to remember a moment, just one picture of me, it would be that moment." It was a glorious moment for professional wrestling history. The attitude era had officially ushered in the reality-based mature product that the professional wrestling world was longing for.

REY MYSTERIO JR. V. EDDIE GUERRERO
(WCW CRUISERWEIGHT CHAMPION)

THE MATCH DATA

EVENT: Halloween Havoc

DATE: October 26, 1997

VENUE:
MGM Grand Garden Arena, Las Vegas, NV, USA

CROWD: 12,457

PROMOTION:
World Championship Wrestling (WCW)

PROMOTER: Ted Turner

STAKES:
Luchas de Apuestas; Title v.
Mask for the WCW Cruiserweight Championship

CORNER PEOPLE:
None (Mysterio) / None (Guerrero)

REFEREE: Scott Dickinson

COMMENTARY TEAM:
Tony Schiavone, Mike Tenay, Dusty Rhodes,
and Bobby 'The Brain' Heenan

RING ANNOUNCER: None

MATCH TIME: 13:51

THE BUILD

Three weeks before Halloween Havoc, WCW produced a series of educational documentary style vignettes showcasing the history of lucha libre in Mexico. Eddie Guerrero the newly crowned WCW cruiserweight champion was the current torch bearer for lucha libre style wrestling in the Atlanta based southern rasslin' promotion. The history of the masks in lucha libre and Mexican culture was emphasized when Rey spoke about the personal importance of never losing his mask. Rey's uncle was a luchador (Rey Mysterio Sr.), and Junior had spent years wrestling in Mexico. The man who started his training at eight years old was all too aware of the mask's importance for his career. Rey may have been one of the shortest competitors on the roster, but with his mask on he was larger than life.

The final educational segment on WCW's *Monday Night Nitro* go-home show simply hyped up Mysterio. Eddie would heelishly run in to the ring and interfere with Rey's match, yet more attention was paid to Jacqueline coming to the ring to attack Rey's opponent Disco Inferno. The build was the exact opposite of celebrated soap-opera-inspired child custody papers ladder match storyline that these two luchadors would later engage in during their respective WWE runs. Not much attention was put into the match beforehand, but due to the exceptional in-ring performances that would all change.

THE MATCH

About thirty minutes into WCW's Halloween Havoc not a single word mentioning the luchador showdown came out of the broadcast booth. That effort went to hype up a match between two past-their-prime household names firmly grasping on to that dwindling limelight. Being the third match on a nine-match card can be an undesirable place. A spot usually reserved for filler and forgettable matches.

Rey hits the ring in an apropos to the holiday Spiderman-esque purple ring attire. Rey's mask was attached to his costume, adding an extra layer of protection should anyone attempt to pull it off. Eddie slowly struts to the ring with all the mannerisms of a Chicano homie. It's in his music, the font showing his name, and even in his glare. The two men allow each other the momentary dignity of warming up the crowd before they quickly engage in battle.

Rey leads the dance and the two men fly around the ring until the squared circle proves incapable of containing the action. Guerrero slides Mysterio into the steel steps and rolls him back in the ring. Eddie hammers on Mysterio delivering a combo of punch-kicks, fast paced slams, and technical holds all while using his heelish mannerisms to antagonize the crowd.

Rey escapes the menace, bouncing off the top rope and hitting a springboard backflip DDT spiking Eddie's head off the mat. A high degree of difficulty maneuver, flawlessly executed. The dance moves around the ringside apron and back into the ring. For every offensive move that Mysterio delivers Eddie has three more. Guerrero slams and stretches the smaller man while ripping away at Mysterio's, practically sacred to the luchador culture, mask.

Mysterio withstands the assault and narrowly ducks out of the way of a sliding dropkick. Eddie slides groin first into the steel ring post. His treachery against la cultura has not gone unpunished. Mysterio flies after him, the fast-paced action takes the two warriors flipping in and out of the ring. The highflyers display the grace of and agility that would rival any Cirque du Soleil performers or Olympic gymnasts.

A series of near falls builds the anticipation. The crowd gets louder in their jeers toward Guerrero. Eddie's ego will not let it go unnoticed; he has to play to them. The showmanship costs him as Mysterio turns the tables and hits a series of eye-catching offensive moves. Eddie quickly regains control with a mid-air reversal into a backbreaker. He hits the top rope looking for his signature frog splash. Guerrero soars and misses. The two luchadores battle into a position where Guerrero is attempting to hit Rey with a razor's edge off the second rope. Rey rolls through and reverses it into a hurricanrana pinning combination. One, two, three, a new champion is crowned.

THE LEGACY

Professional wrestlers from Mexico and of Mexican descent tearing down the house in major league matches across the United States was still relatively new at this point. While many high-flying matches had come before it none produced the fast-paced innovative offense of the match that occurred at this Halloween themed event. It's a match that can't be replicated. Not only did the match exemplify just how entertaining the luchador style could be, it also highlighted how two highly skilled smaller scale wrestlers can outwork the older and larger established names on any professional wrestling card.

Many have said that WCW's cruiserweight division was one of the now defunct promotion's highlights. Paramount in that division was the stellar work of the luchadors. Throughout the match, the broadcast team discusses the rich history of the lucha libre and the two men representing it. This history lesson serves as the backdrop for the revolutionary in-ring action. Like the Mexican-American culture, the match took from the best of both worlds, it was a perfect blend of Mexican luchador high spots and American ring psychology. It's a nod to professional wrestling's past and a glimpse of its future. There is a special brilliance in all the dualities present in this one.

MICK 'CACTUS JACK' FOLEY
V. TRIPLE H (WWF CHAMPION)

THE MATCH DATA

EVENT: Royal Rumble

DATE: January 23, 2000

VENUE:
Madison Square Garden, New York City, NY, USA

CROWD: 19,231

PROMOTION:
World Wrestling Federation (WWF)

PROMOTER: Vince McMahon Jr.

STAKES: WWF Championship/Street Fight

CORNER PEOPLE:
None (Foley) / None (Accompanied to the ring
by Stephanie McMahon-Helmsley) (Triple H)

REFEREE: Earl Hebner

COMMENTARY TEAM:
Jim Ross and Jerry 'The King' Lawler

RING ANNOUNCER: Howard Finkel

MATCH TIME: 26:48

THE BUILD

In a prophetic storyline, Triple H married Stephanie McMahon and quickly began flexing his, inherited by marriage, professional wrestling management authority. It didn't take long before Triple H began, as heel authority figures are inclined to do, abusing his power. Foely, playing the unlikely hero, stood up to the McMahon-Helmsley era causing the Game to set his sights on the Rock 'n' Sock connection.

Triple H forced the Rock and Mankind into a "Pink slip" on a pole match, which the Mickster ultimately lost. A couple of weeks later the Rock brought out the entire locker room and demanded Mick Foley's reinstatement. Threatened by a total superstar walk out, Triple H was forced to acquiesce. A Royal Rumble match between Mankind and Triple H was quickly made. Mick Foley stated that Mankind may not be ready to face the Game at the Royal Rumble but, while revealing his signature black and yellow wanted dead T-shirt, Cactus Jack was. The hardcore bout was on.

THE MATCH

Mrs. Foley's baby boy and the Game standoff face to face, we anticipate what brutality the billed "Street Fight" will deliver. The punches start flying. Cactus Jack, still being called Mankind by the announcing team, gains control and takes the action outside of the ring. Mick hits Trips with a swinging neck breaker. Triple H tries to take the fight into the somewhat controlled parameters of the squared circle, but Cactus hits him with a leg drop and Triple H retreats again. Jack pursues him on the outside slamming Hunter's face into the steel ring steps.

Triple H fights back grabbing the ring bell and smacking Jack right between the eyes. Hunter grabs the most trusted weapon in professional wrestling, yes, it's the steel chair! Hunter goads Jack to run at him. Undeterred, Cactus charges ahead. Hunter swings wildly and directly connects with a thunderous chair shot to Cactus's skull.

That would be lights out for a mortal man but Cactus pops up and brawls at his foe leaving the Game laying down flat on the mat. The Hardcore Legend lays the steel chair down over Hunter's head and charges at him dropping a devastating leg drop. Foley hits Hunter with a punch/kick offensive barrage until the two spill out of the ring and over the guardrail.

The men battle through the mass of humanity that is the WWF universe, until they hit the entrance way. Cactus slams Trips into some shiny trash cans and suplexes him onto a pair of stacked wooden pallets. The mayhem continues and Cactus bounces the trashcan off his opponent's skull, then slams Triple H's face against a wall.

Cactus walks Triple H back to the ring as the crowd chants for Foley. The announcing team is quick to point it out, lest anyone thought a boring chant had broken out. They stammer to the ring, Triple H hits Foley with a side suplex onto a trash can. Cactus quickly recovers and delivers more punishment to the Game. Hunter's weary body rests against the steel steps and Cactus charges at him with a running knee. It connects and the crowd hears the roaring crash of flesh and steel.

Cactus rolls Triple H into the ring, he searches underneath and pulls out a sadistic looking two by four wrapped in barbed wire. Cactus enters the ring, but Triple H hits a low blow and gains control of the medieval looking primitive weapon. Trips hits Jack's torso and groin with the twisted wood, its wires get tangled up in Cactus's iconic dead or alive T-shirt. Never deterred by a few barbed wire shots, Cactus regains control of the board and retaliates with his own nut shot to Hunter. Jack follows it up with his signature double arm DDT.

The two men rise and Triple H charges and inadvertently knocks out the ref. Professional wrestling's referee core really need to spend more time training on how not to get knocked out during a match. Cactus, who now has what looks to be a second two by four wrapped in barbed wire, runs forward and bounces his instrument of destruction off of Triple H's head. As Triple H lies on the mat Cactus rushes at him dropping a flying barbed wire laced board squarely on the Game's head. Mick goes for the cover.

Triple H survives the near pinfall and rises to his feet. The bloodied Game is once again rammed with the barbed wire. Cactus cheese graders Hunter's one regal face and the two roll outside the ring. They end up at the top of the announce table. Cactus goes for a piledriver, but the Game manages to reverse it, sending Jack onto the table with a back body drop. Good God the announcers are just trying to do their jobs and call the action!

The two men crawl back into the ring. Triple H hits Cactus with heavy punches and goes for the pedigree. Jack reverses with a catapult and then bulldog's the Game face first onto the barbed wire bat. Another cover. Another near fall.

Cactus hits a running clothesline knocking them both back to the ringside area. Foley feels at home until Triple H reverses his fortune, executing a hip toss that sends his opponents legs smattering against the steel steps. No one's body should contort about the way Mick's does during a match. Hunter picks Mick up and throws him into the steps once more. This time Jack's knee hits and he goes tumbling toward what's left of the announcer tables. The Cerebral Assassin focuses in, hitting a series of chop blocks on Jack's knee, he strikes at the knee with the barbed wire bat and grabs a pair of handcuffs from the ring side area.

Jack fights back; he grabs control of the cuffs and brass knuckles the Game with them. Triple H kicks his knee and slaps the cuffs on the Mickster. The crowd collectively winches, they all remember the brutality of the eleven unprotected steel chair shots the Rock viciously hammered onto Foley's skull about a year ago. Triple H brings the steel steps into the ring. He rushes at Cactus, but Cactus ducks and hits a drop toehold sending Hunter's face colliding with the steps.

Like a hungry lion Foley gnaws at his prey biting at Hunter's ear. The Game fights back and hits Foley's back with a pair of booming chair shots. The impact is so hard that parts of the chair are literally sent sailing toward the crowd. Foley's still handcuffed body collapses and falls outside of the ring. Triple H follows and smacks Jack with an unprotected chair shot to the head. The deranged Jack begs for more.

Out of nowhere the Rock runs in and hits Trips with a chair shot of his own. Jack is uncuffed and the People's Champ leaves the two men to finish the fight among themselves. Fight they do, brawling back and forth to the habitually demolished Spanish announce table. Cactus hits a piledriver spiking Triple H's skull off the table top. For what may be the first time in professional wrestling history, the Spanish announce table holds and survives the action.

Cactus rolls Triple H back into the ring. He reaches underneath and grabs a bag, the crowd wails when they see the bag of tacks poured onto the mat and ready to enter the fray. Stephanie

McMahon runs to ringside pleading for the brutality to end. Foley pays little attention to her and brawls at Hunter. Triple H reverses and hits a back body drop sending Jack back first on to the tacks. "He's a human pin cushion!" screams Good Ol JR.

Triple H hits a pedigree and goes for the cover. Cactus kicks out, the crowd rallies behind him. Hunter hits a second pedigree, this one landing Foley's face squarely on the pile of tacks. One, two, three, the Game retains the belt. Hunter is put on a stretcher and Cactus Jack chases after him. Mick grabs a hold of the stretcher and wheels him back to the ring area. Cactus rolls him back into the ring and hits Trips with one more barbed wire bat shot for the road. The brutal majesty of this hardcore bout has finally ended.

THE LEGACY

Love it or hate it, being hardcore is an essential part of modern professional wrestling. It's a style routinely called upon to elevate matches, extend feuds, and build entire pay-per-views or premium live events around. Paul Heyman may be credited with bringing hardcore wrestling to the mainstream American audience, but no other professional wrestler has done more for the subgenre than Mick Foley.

Mrs. Foley's baby boy is perhaps the most unique and unlikely legend there is. Not many professional wrestlers, let alone Hall-of-Fame legends, share his physique and even fewer share his death-defying approach to the professional wrestling business. The *New York Times* best-selling author rewrote the book when it came to defining what a mainstream professional wrestler should look like.

On the other hand, Triple H is a very different kind of legend. He looks exactly like how an average fan thinks a WWF champion should look. His post in-ring career and WWF back office prominent position only adds to this match's legacy. If only one match can symbolize that old reliable storyline of the unlikely hero facing off against the professional wrestling promotion's chosen golden boy, this brutal hardcore battle is the one. It's the Beast versus Gaston inside of one of professional wrestling's most storied arena. The Royal Rumble is one of the most beloved gimmick matches of all time, and when you put on a match that out shines the rumble match itself, well, that's hardcore.

'MR. WRESTLEMANIA' SHAWN MICHAELS V. THE UNDERTAKER

THE MATCH DATA

EVENT: WrestleMania XXV

DATE: April 5, 2009

VENUE:
Reliant Stadium, Houston, TX, USA

CROWD: 72,744

PROMOTION:
World Wrestling Entertainment (WWE)

PROMOTER: Vince McMahon Jr.

STAKES: The Streak

CORNER PEOPLE:
None (Michaels) / None (Undertaker)

REFEREE: Marty Elias

COMMENTARY TEAM:
Jim Ross, Jerry 'The King' Lawler,
and Michael Cole

RING ANNOUNCER: Justin Roberts

MATCH TIME: 30:44

THE BUILD

For the twenty-fifth anniversary of WrestleMania, Vince McMahon had to deliver a show that was worthy of the groundbreaking pay-per-view's storied history. Pitting two of the all-time greatest professional wrestling performers against each other is pretty much as guaranteed an epic match as any promoter could hope for.

The Heartbreak Kid had to face two separate opponents to earn the privilege of facing the Deadman at WrestleMania. Yes, Shawn was already an all-time great and could still deliver in the ring, but, hey, there is a lot of weekly television time to fill. Michaels defeated each of his big man opponents, and the showdown was on.

THE MATCH

Shawn is dressed in all white and accompanied by angels hovering and singing in the air. Bright light is shining on him. Shawn's music hits, and with a stern look on his face the Heartbreak Kid makes his way to the ring. The bell tolls, the stadium lights dim, and fire flashes as the Deadman slowly paces toward the ring. The stark contrast between the two legends has never been so apparent. The highflyer versus the powerhouse, the silent monster versus the flamboyant talker, the demon versus the embodiment of love.

The bell rings, and the two icons start to brawl. Michaels' quickness gives him the upper hand but the Undertaker's power quickly evens things up. The crowd roars their support for both men. Taker twists up Michaels' wrist, climbs the ropes, and goes old school on Shawn. HBK's agility allows him to avoid Taker's follow up offense. Michaels relies on a time-tested strategy and focuses in on the big man's leg. The Heartbreak Kid channels Ric Flair and locks the big man into a figure-four leglock.

Taker punches his way out, but Shawn hits a quick dropkick to the Deadman's knees. Taker recovers and catches Shawn coming at him. The Undertaker slams him into the corner and unleashes an offensive barrage ending with snake eyes and his big boot across Michaels' pretty boy face. Taker covers Shawn, but it's only a two count. The Deadman signals for the choke slam. Shawn counters it into a cross-face, taking the big man down to the mat. Taker lifts Shawn up and side slams his way out of the submission hold. The two legends begin showing signs of fatigue. Everyone is aware that both men are past their prime, but on this night, they won't let anyone see it.

The two men battle back and forth until Shawn levels the big man with a flying elbow to the head. The Showstopper kips up and continues his attack. Shawn hammers on Taker and climbs to the top rope, Taker sits up and catches a diving Shawn by the throat. The two legends brawl down to the canvas. Michaels goes for the figure-four once again. Undertaker reverses it into hell's gate. Shawn scrambles toward the ropes forcing the break. Taker positions Shawn where half his torso is dangling off the ring apron. The Deadman goes for the running leg drop, but Shawn rolls back into the ring, avoiding the man in black's big leg.

Taker rises to enter the ring, but Shawn sweeps his feet out from under him with a baseball slide. Mr. WrestleMania climbs to the top rope and goes for a twisting moonsault. Taker swats him away, letting only the floor break his fall. The Deadman rolls back into the ring and sits up. He bounces off the ropes and flies over the top rope propelling himself at Shawn. Shawn pulls the camera man into harm's way. Taker barely makes contact with either of them and lands headfirst on the ground.

Shawn drags the referee back into the ring and the official starts the ten count. Taker rolls into the ring right at the count of nine as the crowd cheers on the action. Michaels stands in the corner tapping his foot in anticipation of the Undertaker's inevitable rise. Tuning up the band as they call it. Undertaker sidesteps the super kick and hits Shawn with a devastating choke slam. Taker goes for the cover . . . one, two—Shawn kicks out!

Undertaker grabs his resilient opponent and goes for another snake-eyes. Shawn counters, Taker counters the counter and grabs Shawn's throat for another chokeslam. Shawn smacks away the big man's grip and hits him with sweet chin music. Michaels covers, one, two—Undertaker kicks out!

Michaels kips up and hovers over Taker. Undertaker reaches up and grabs Shawn for a chokeslam. Taker turns it into the last ride but Shawn wiggles out and attempts a sunset flip. Taker reverses, pulling Shawn up headfirst and sending him crashing down with a towering last ride powerbomb. Taker goes for the cover . . . one, two—Shawn kicks out!

Taker climbs the ropes and attempts a flying elbow drop. Shawn rolls out of the way. The two Hall-of-Famers rise to their feet once again, the crowd roars with appreciation. Shawn rushes at Taker but the Deadman sidesteps and HBK goes flying over the top rope. Michaels skins the cat back into the ring. Shawn locks his ankles around Undertaker's massive neck. Undertaker pulls Shawn back into the ring and hits him with the devastating tombstone piledriver. Taker goes for the cover . . . one, two—Shawn kicks out!

Taker pulls down his singlet straps, lifts his fists and runs his thumb across his neck. Everyone watching knows the Deadman is signaling for the end of Michaels. Taker pulls Shawn up for a second tombstone but Shawn counters it into a DDT. Shawn follows it up with a smashing elbow drop off the top rope. Shawn retreats to the corner and slowly tunes up the band once more. Taker stumbles toward Shawn. Bam! Sweet chin music connects! Shawn goes for the cover . . . one, two—Taker kicks out!

The two weary competitors grab a hold of one another both in bewilderment of each other's resilience. The exhausted warriors balance on one another as they rise to their feet. They brawl back and forth exchanging exasperated blows. Taker flings Shawn into the corner turnbuckles. He charges in but Shawn lifts his leg catching the Deadman with his boot. Michaels climbs up the ropes and flies at Taker with a moonsault. Taker catches him and hits him with the tombstone piledriver. One, two, three! It's all over, the bell rings and the Undertaker is victorious. The streak lives on!

THE LEGACY

When professional wrestlers are asked who is the most respected wrestler of all time one name comes up more than any other: the Undertaker. When those same professional wrestlers are questioned about who their greatest match was against, one name comes up more than any other: Shawn Michaels. The Heartbreak Kid is a record setting eleven-time *Pro Wrestling Illustrated* match of the year award recipient. The Undertaker's 25-2 WrestleMania record is among the most revered accomplishments in professional wrestling history.

As WrestleMania celebrated a quarter of a century in existence, two of the all-time greats delivered a masterpiece. It was a match for the ages. One that showed just how damn good professional wrestling could be. In terms of professional wrestling matches, perhaps Jim Ross summed it up best when he said, "I feel like we've just seen heaven."

GLOSSARY

OF COMMON PROFESSIONAL
WRESTLING TERMS

ANGLE

A fictitious scripted storyline in the world of professional wrestling that can last minutes or years.

BABYFACE/FACE

A heroic professional wrestler whose gimmick is intended to be the good guy and a fan favorite.

BOOKING

The determination of the events of professional wrestling creative direction which includes deciding the schedule of events, ultimate outcome of matches, messaging conveyed during promos and other aspects of the creative direction of a show or promotion.

BUMP

To absorb physical contact or impact during the performance of professional wrestling.

CARD

The lineup of matches for any given professional wrestling event.

DARK MATCH

A match not televised on an otherwise televised card. Dark matches occurring before a card start are used to give wrestlers at the bottom of the card more exposure and to warm up the crowd. Dark matches occurring after the televised show ends are used to satisfy the live crowd and usually involve upper card talent.

DIRT SHEET

An "insider" professional wrestling publication that publishes rumors, backstage drama, or other news of interest to professional wrestling fans.

FACTION

A group of wrestlers bonded together for various reasons and who are at times integral to each other's matches and storylines.

FEUD

A scripted rivalry between wrestlers that drives storylines and is designed to increase interest in the involved wrestlers and wrestling matches.

GIMMICK

The basis of a professional wrestler's character.

GO HOME SHOW

The final televised show before an upcoming pay-per-view or premium live event.

GORILLA

Named after Gorilla Monsoon, the production area, usually sitting head creative directors, just behind the curtain where wrestlers come out to the ring.

HEAT

The negative reaction a professional wrestler receives, either from the fans, their colleagues, or a promotion's management.

HEEL

A villainous professional wrestler whose gimmick is intended to be the bad guy and elicit hatred from the fans.

JOBBER

A frequently losing wrestler who is used to build credibility for other wrestlers.

KAYFABE

The portrayal of professional wrestling events or characters as legitimate or real.

LOCK UP

The portion of a match when two wrestlers come together in a collar and elbow tie up. Also, the shorthand title of this publication.

MONEY IN THE BANK

A contact awarded by WWE to the winner of a multi-man ladder match that gives the holder the ability to challenge for any title they want at any time they choose. The term is used to describe the describe the match, premium live event, and contract.

OVER

A professional wrestler being embraced by the fans and receiving the desired reaction.

POP

An ovation received by a professional wrestler or on screen talent from a live audience.

POPCORN MATCH

A professional wrestling match that is designed to give fans in attendance a break from the action of the more prominent matches and allow for a concession stand break.

PROMO

An interview, monologue, or dialogue amongst wrestlers or on-screen talent used to build characters and further storylines.

PROMOTER

The organizer of a professional wrestling company or card who is often in charge of the creative direction and the booking of the events of the company or card they oversee.

PROMOTION

A professional wrestling organization that is the equivalent of a sports league with its own titles, traditions, and history.

REST HOLDS

A hold such as a headlock designed to give the wrestlers a breather without stopping the action.

RIBBING

A practical joke played on a wrestler or employee of a wrestling promotion.

RUB

An established star adding legitimacy or credibility to another talent.

SELL

To react to the ongoings of a professional wrestling performance in a believable manner.

SHOOT

Any unplanned sequence of events during a professional wrestling performance.

SPOT

A planned move designed to elicit a positive reaction from the crowd and have a huge effect on the match.

SQUARED CIRCLE

The professional wrestling ring.

SQUASH MATCH

A professional wrestling match where one competitor quickly dominates and defeats their opponent.

TURN

The transforming a professional wrestler from face to heel or vice versa.

TWEENER

A professional wrestler who is balancing the face/heel spectrum to make their alignment ambiguous.

WORK

Any planned sequence of events during a professional wrestling performance.

WORKED SHOOT

A planned professional wrestling segment intended to appear legitimate or real.

ABOUT THE AUTHOR

Ray Lopez is an avid, lifelong professional wrestling fan, author, and lawyer. He has a bachelor's of arts degree from Baylor University and a doctorate of jurisprudence from Texas Tech University School of Law. Ray is a proud brother of Omega Delta Phi service/social fraternity. He has been practicing law for fifteen years and resides in San Antonio, Texas, with his loving wife, son, and dogs.

After gaining a wealth of legal experience, Ray naturally expanded his career to include writing about professional wrestling. When Ray is not being consumed by the world of professional wrestling, he enjoys spending time with friends and family, traveling, and is an avid sports fan who can be spotted at many San Antonio Spurs games. *Lock Up: Professional Wrestling in Our World* is his first publication.

TWITTER: @LUCHALOCKUP
EMAIL: RAYLOPEZBU@GMAIL.COM
WWW.RAYLOPEZLAW.COM